Credible?

Mark Jackson PhD

Scripture quoted by permission. Quotations designated (NET) are from the NET Bible® copyright ©1996, 2019 by Biblical Studies Press, L.L.C. http://netbible.com All rights reserved.

Scripture quotations marked (NASB) taken from the (NASB®) New American Standard Bible®, Copyright © 1960, 1971, 1977, 1995, 2020 by The Lockman Foundation. Used by permission. All rights reserved. lockman.org

Scripture quotations taken from the Amplified® Bible (AMP), Copyright © 2015 by The Lockman Foundation. Used by permission. lockman.org

Scripture quotations marked (ESV) are from The ESV® Bible (The Holy Bible, English Standard Version®), © 2001 by Crossway, a publishing ministry of Good News Publishers. Used by permission. All rights reserved.

Scripture quotations not marked as above are either from the King James Version (KJV) or have been translated by the author.

PREFACE

Congratulations on purchasing this book!

You are about to begin a quest for the truth. Joining this quest took courage, but the potential rewards are worth it – more confidence in what to believe, what to disbelieve, and what to accept is unknown.

As you read, you will be watching over my shoulder as I assess the evidence behind doctrinal differences between and within Judaism, Christianity and Islam. We will examine scriptures and historical events surrounding the development of these three religions.

This book is packed with short historical anecdotes that provide relevant context. So, even though we will be traversing some serious evidence and concepts, I hope you will find these historical anecdotes educational and entertaining – I certainly learned a lot from compiling them.

I am no theologian or historian, so this quest will not involve a traditional theological approach. Rather, I am a criminologist and private investigator. On this quest I will be using the particular set of skills I possess, thinking about evidence in the way an investigator or intelligence analyst would assess the credibility of a new piece of 'intel'.

Fair warning: Expect to find some 'sacred cows' (excuse the pun) to be based on weak evidence. You will also discover how some beliefs are products of events occurring at the time and place they were created. However, others will be left standing as credible – even bolstered with insights created through corroborating evidence from different sources.

So, let's get stuck in. The sooner you begin this quest, the less of your life you need to spend wandering between doubts.

CONTENTS

1. HOW TO FIND THE TRUTH

"Who is this who obscures my purposes by words without knowledge?"

Job 38:2

1.1 THE PROBLEM OF IGNORANCE

Let's be honest with ourselves and admit there is much we do not know. In fact, the amount we don't know is many orders of magnitude greater than the amount we do. This level of ignorance is problematic because humans have an innate thirst for understanding and meaning in life. Our thirst can be hard to satisfy if our knowledge is limited. We are uncomfortable with uncertainty and therefore face a great temptation to create beliefs based on abstract slivers of evidence.

Philosophy, Science and Religion are three ways people seek to quench our thirst for knowledge and understanding. As a formal discipline, perhaps Science is the newest. Over the last few centuries in particular, Science has produced technologies and methods that help us attain knowledge by forming and testing hypotheses. Through these advances we have learned much and bettered our lives – at least materially, if not spiritually.

Before people established scientific method, we did not let this stop us from exploring ideas. We developed the discipline of Philosophy, which is the rational, abstract and methodical consideration of ideas. Whereas Science, in testing hypotheses, is often constrained by our ability to measure observations,

Philosophy is less constrained. It does, however, require disciplines of critical thinking and logic.

Religion requires no such disciplines or technologies whatsoever. In religious faith, you can simply choose to believe something you have heard, or practise some ritual required by the Religion that you choose (or are coerced) into following. Through Religion, people can seek to quench a thirst for understanding and meaning that we either cannot or choose not to satisfy through Science and Philosophy. However, in Religion, problems can occur when we fill in gaps in our knowledge with supposed facts we have come up with. Tensions, divisions, persecution and even wars arise when we impose those beliefs on others or reject others who do not share our beliefs.

This problem has plagued humanity throughout our history and is compounded by another problem at least as large – Confirmation Bias. Even when we discover some new truth, if this threatens our existing belief system, we find it hard to change our current beliefs in response to new evidence. We are conditioned to look for ways to preserve our existing belief system because if this is threatened, we risk losing the sense of meaning and identity we have developed. In turn, we risk losing our justification for the choices we make about how we are living our lives.

Cultural conditioning creates a strong barrier to innovation and learning. Modern Western society exacerbates this barrier by putting cultures on such a high pedestal that it has become socially and politically unacceptable to challenge a culture. This value holds even when the beliefs and practices within a culture are evidently flawed and harmful to people. Respect for a culture – particularly an ethnic or religious culture – is given precedence over the good of individual people. We may challenge a person but dare not challenge a person's culture.

1.2 OUR CHALLENGE

This book records a search for what is true[1], or perhaps more achievably, what is unlikely to be true, where the doctrines of Judaism, Christianity and Islam conflict. I cannot promise to reveal all knowledge. However, I do expect to serve up some insights that – if we are able to suppress our natural confirmation bias – may cause a shift away from some of the ideas we currently believe,

---

[1] "In accordance with fact or reality"; "accurate or exact". Google's dictionary, provided by Oxford Languages.

replacing them with other ideas for which the evidence is stronger. These changes in belief may cause us to change aspects of how we live our lives. I say this up front to help you process the potential impact of proceeding any further with what you may read, because without an openness to learn, grow and change, reading further will offer you little benefit.

At the outset, I will admit it would be either naïve or arrogant of me, or indeed anyone, to act as if we are certain about the things scientific evidence, philosophical reasoning and scriptural writings do not make certain. Even scripture has been written down by fallible humans and copied over time. As I will prove in Chapter 2, we now know from discoveries of ancient manuscripts, that parts of scripture previously accepted by many as authoritative, or even divine, were probably modified or added later than when the original document (known as the 'autograph') was written. In fact, many ancient manuscripts give conflicting versions of the same original source that has become lost to antiquity. In Judaism, Christianity and Islam, some of these manuscripts were chosen by early religious leaders to classify as divinely given scripture; others were not.

In exploring Religion, I will start from a Christian perspective because that is where I start in my own journey – I was raised in a Christian culture. However, I will refer extensively to the related religions of Judaism and Islam and will reveal some insights about their associated belief systems. Contrasting how different faiths deal with the same issue can help us to understand how the beliefs and practices associated with religious faith have been influenced by history and characteristics of humanity.

If previously trusted sources of 'truth' are revealed to be untrustworthy, an obvious question arises: How should we approach working out what is likely to be true? An inappropriate response would be to bury our heads in the sand, hiding from the truth because we want to believe that the version of scripture our ancestors believed without question is still true and divinely endorsed in its entirety, even though we now have compelling evidence that parts of it are not. Such an attitude would be a very unhealthy form of faith, rather than the faith the author of the Christian New Testament's 'epistle to the Hebrews' talked about: "*Faith is the substance of things hoped for, the evidence of things not seen*" (Hebrews 11:1). This verse is not advocating belief in things proven to be false.

I invite you to journey with me as I explore the evidence, accepting that this may cause us to change some things we believe. I invite you to join me in taking the risk of being willing to accept the truth, even where this might challenge one or more pillars of your current faith. This may be hard to do; maybe you like your life the way it is now and would struggle to let go of your comfort blanket – your cultural conditioning or current set of beliefs. Maybe you fear rejection by your family or the society in which you live if you reject their religious faith. I am well aware that some totalitarian faiths do not tolerate free thinking that might permit you to challenge or potentially abandon your faith. The cost of escaping such a religion can be unacceptably high for some. If a religion is one that does not tolerate free thought or apostasy based on genuine convictions, I see this as a red flag, alerting me that the basis for that religion is likely to be fragile.

For me, I cannot turn away from this journey. I know I am unlikely to find the truth if I am unwilling to change some things I currently like believing. I accept that others may see me as dangerously subversive if I come out with ideas that threaten their beliefs. In the society in which I live, some people may want to criticise or distance themselves from me if my views differ from theirs. However, I am grateful I do not live in a society where I am likely to be disinherited, imprisoned or put to death for my beliefs.

As I am writing this chapter, I have not yet undertaken this journey; I am just preparing myself – getting in the right mental state to be able to do a competent job and to be open to what I might learn. I am performing mental exercises to help my mind be agile and open. I encourage you to do the same.

To help you know what you might be in for, I am a criminologist by training and an investigator by profession. Taking a criminological perspective is an unconventional approach to apply in this context. However, I suspect it may provide a helpful contribution to the discussion. Criminologists study how offenders and victims of crime have conversations with themselves that reinforce beliefs and behaviours others may struggle to understand. Such insights into humanity are just as relevant when considering how humans develop beliefs and practices that are not necessarily criminalised in the society in which they live. Societies also change over time, as do their social norms and laws. Behaviour that was once treated as unacceptable or illegal may be accepted today, or vice versa. Similarly, behaviour deemed acceptable in one society may be punished in another.

By exploring these differences across time and cultures, we can broaden our understanding of humanity. Our resultant wider perspective will help prevent subjective bias based on our own conditioning and sense of morality. Such subjective bias, if allowed to flourish, can hinder learning. Criminologists are schooled in the risks of bias and threats to validity, as well as in mechanisms to defend against these challenges. We also study patterns in human behaviour to gain insights into humanity. We are trained to hypothesise and test such patterns. Therefore, we may be able to contribute a perspective that can help.

1.3 DIFFERENT NAMES FOR GOD

Things are going to get a bit confusing when I start to discuss God. So, before I do, it is worth developing a few linguistic concepts to help us navigate this problem.

Judaism, Christianity, and Islam each use different names and titles for the same persons in their scriptures. These different names arise from different languages: Primarily Hebrew for Judaism; Greek for Christianity; Arabic for Islam. Words don't always translate cleanly between these languages. For example, multiple different Hebrew names for divine beings are often mapped to the Greek θεός (theos - meaning god) and, as in English, theos can be used either as a title for the single supreme deity or just a word for any deity.

One of the Hebrew names frequently mapped to theos is אֱלֹהִים (elohim). Where the New Testament quotes a passage from the Tanakh/Old Testament containing the word elohim, this is typically translated theos. However, as pointed out by Maimonides, the most influential Torah scholar of the Middle Ages, *"I must premise that every Hebrew knows that the term Elohim is a homonym, and denotes God, angels, judges, and the rulers of countries ..."*[2]. We should not, therefore, assume when we read elohim (or theos translated from elohim) that this always means god. It could, for example, be referring to an angel or a divine being in general who may or may not be God.

Christianity has a more complex concept of God than do Judaism and Islam. Most Christians believe God is a Trinity consisting of three persons – the father, the son (Jesus of Nazareth) and the holy spirit. However, as we will see, Christian scriptures often refer to God and Jesus as distinct from each other, implying Jesus is distinct from God (as opposed to just being distinct from 'the father'). In this book, I will explore such passages to test whether we can reconcile the notion of the Trinity with the Christian scriptures.

Noting the limitations of language, I will adopt a convention of using the word 'god' (lower case) when I am referring to a deity in general; I will capitalise the name 'God' when using the word as a title for the supreme monotheistic deity. However, when quoting from scripture, I will endeavour to avoid capitalising in this way, because such capitalisation does not occur in the original manuscripts. To capitalise titles would assume a meaning that was not explicit in the original text.

---

[2] *Guide for the Perplexed*, by Moses Maimonides, Friedländer tr. [1904], at sacred-texts.com

I acknowledge that this approach may be confusing, particularly for Christians, who are not used it. Christians use the name God sometimes to refer to the father, sometimes to the Trinity and at other times where they do not specify precisely what they mean. Christians universally think of the father as the first person in the Trinity. When they want to specifically refer to the father, they typically say, 'god the father', or simply 'the father'. When praying, they may address the father as 'heavenly father''. When referring to the second person in the Trinity, the man Jesus (Yeshua – ישוע in Aramaic) of Nazareth, Christians typically say, 'god the son' or the 'son' rather than simply god. They also use other terms for the son, often being titles from their Old Testament, such as 'the Word' or 'Messiah', that they believe prophetically refer to Jesus. In the New Testament, we see the word 'Christ', derived from the Greek word Χριστός – 'Christos' which means Messiah. When referring to the third person in the Trinity, Christians typically say, 'god the holy spirit', 'holy ghost', 'holy spirit', or 'the spirit', rather than simply god. I will use such expressions where needed and will adopt a convention of not capitalising them.

Jews worship the same 'god the father' that Christians worship. When referring to this god in English, they typically use anglicised versions of Hebrew names for God. These anglicised names include Yashem, Hashem, YHVH or YHWH. They also use other titles that can mean God but can also mean lord, divine being, angel, or ruler. For example, such titles include Adonai and Elohim.

Judaism accepts that Jesus of Nazareth existed but holds that he was neither the Messiah nor divine. Given that Jesus was born and lived as a Jew, Jews prefer to refer to him with his Aramaic name, the anglicised version of which is Yeshua. The names Jesus and Yeshua are different versions of the same name. In the Koine Greek language commonly spoken in the time and place of Jesus' life on earth, Yeshua was translated to Ἰησοῦς (Iēsous), which sounds similar to Jesus. Unless discussing language, I will adopt a convention of using 'Jesus'.

Whereas Jewish and Islamic scriptures refer to the spirit of God, Jews and Muslims do not see this spirit as a distinct person in the way most Christians do. In Chapter 7, I will explore how each of these three religions understands the spirit of God.

Islam formed within Arabian culture. Islam holds that their most central scripture, known as the Qur'an, is a copy of an inscription made by the Islamic god before time began on a tablet that exists in heaven. The anglicised version of the Arabic name for this god is Allah, who was the chief god in the polytheistic Arabian culture into which Islam's prophet, Muhammad, was born.

Muslims believe this is the same god as the Christian 'god the father' and Jewish 'Hashem'. They also believe that Jesus was a prophet whom they call Isa, although they do not pay him much attention or behave in a way that demonstrates they revere him as much as they do Muhammad.

The Qur'an also makes numerous references to Abraham. However, Islam's beliefs about their god, Isa and Abraham differ markedly from how God is presented in the Jewish and Christian bibles. Accordingly, Muslims' beliefs about God, Jesus and Abraham, differ from those of Jews and Christians. Consequently, many Jews and Christians who have studied Islam or read the Qur'an, do not see Allah as the same god, but as an idea made up by Muhammad, the person who created Islam.

Muslims revere Muhammad as their preeminent prophet to whom God revealed the Qur'an through various revelations during the course of Muhammad's life. They also believe that Islam existed before Muhammad, even though the pillars of Islam were not yet 'revealed' by Muhammad. Islam claims as prophets of Islam, some of the Jewish patriarchs and prophets, including Moses. However, Islamic beliefs about these prophets are light on detail, and conflict with Jewish and Christian scriptures and beliefs. I will therefore examine evidence about these differences in beliefs.

1.4 HOW TO EVALUATE EVIDENCE

Before outlining the criteria that I use to evaluate evidence, I should acknowledge two points:

1. I am not a historian or a forensic expert in ancient religious manuscripts. So, for these areas of expertise, I have looked to the writings of relevant experts and sought to gauge the level of certainty and consensus amongst them on questions I am considering. Rather than a formal quantitative assessment, I use two qualitative approaches: (1) a meta-analysis approach, looking for commentaries by subject-matter experts that summarise the level and nature of consensus in their field and (2) Pawson's theory-driven approach[3], to test whether an idea is supported by evidence. In the latter, it is important I seek to understand the meanings and contexts writers give to their words.

---

[3] Pawson, R., (1996), *Theorizing the Interview*, The British Journal of Sociology, 47(2), pp295-314

2. I acknowledge that members of any religious group may simply exercise faith that their scriptures are 'God breathed' and that inclinations they may have to take a particular action are inspired or prompted by God. Some may look for and identify 'signs' confirming an idea they had. I am not trained to evaluate such things. So, I will limit myself to the more pedantic objective of investigating historical and physical evidence. I acknowledge that this may help some people but be of little interest to those driven more by faith than evidence.

In any investigation, the approach I take to evaluating evidence follows the way an intelligence analyst would assess the credibility of new information. A multi-dimensional assessment is required, including:

- Whether the account was given by a direct witness or is hearsay;

- The circumstances under which the information was obtained (e.g. Were duress or conflict of interest present? What state of mind was the witness in?);

- The strength of the source's bona fides and sensor capabilities;

- The time delay between an event occurring and the account being recorded;

- Whether forensic evidence exists (particularly if we would expect there to be forensic evidence) and, if so, its consistency with the account;

- Whether the account contains internal inconsistencies;

- Whether independent sources exist and, if so, how well these sources align in their evidence (i.e. corroboration);

- Past performance of the source – Is this source reliable in terms of credibility of evidence given at other times;

- Consistency and appropriateness of writing style in the account.

I will be applying such considerations to Jewish, Christian and Islamic scriptures to assess their credibility. As well as these objective criteria, we should also exercise judgement, but in doing so we need to be aware of the potential for our own fallibility and subjective bias. That said, we can take the following analytical approaches:

- We can use techniques from Philosophy to determine if an argument contains a logical flaw or fallacy;

- Using our knowledge of history and social anthropology, we may recognise part of an argument as an artefact of an ancient culture rather than being an eternal truth;

- Consistency with other scripture or evidence should affect credibility as well (e.g. If someone is quoted in one place as saying we are saved by grace alone and elsewhere by doing good works or by obeying all laws, at least one account must be wrong because these statements are mutually exclusive).

1.5 WHY NOT RELY ON WHAT CHURCH AUTHORITIES TELL YOU TO BELIEVE?

In this argument I will differentiate between the terms Christianity and Christendom. I use the term Christianity to mean the various collections of beliefs and customs of the followers of Jesus. Christianity today takes many forms with varying degrees of authority exercised by church leaders. I use the term Christendom to mean the dominant Christian church establishment whose leaders exert authoritative power over ordinary people.

From the time of the Council of Nicaea in 325 CE until the 16th century CE, the terms Christianity and Christendom were almost interchangeable, because Christianity was controlled by the church establishment in league with political government(s)[4]. In the East, Christendom was experienced as the Eastern Orthodox church; in the West, it was the Roman Catholic church. In the 16th century CE, attrition from the established church picked up as people began to gain access to a more extensive range of translations of original manuscripts than those previously used by the church establishment. To many, it became evident that Christendom had been teaching doctrines and practices that were not what the original scriptures taught, and that smacked of human corruption[5]. Consequent disillusionment with the established church caused schisms,

---

[4] Spencer, Sidney et al. (2025). *The history of church and state*. Encyclopaedia Britannica, https://www.britannica.com/topic/Christianity/The-history-of-church-and-state Accessed 16 July 2025

[5] The most well-known corruption was the selling of indulgences. For further information, see https://www.historyextra.com/period/medieval/indulgences-catholic-church-what-why-sold-absolution-sin-reformaton/ Accessed 3 September 2025

birthing more progressive denominations who, for guidance, looked more to scripture than to church authorities.

SUCCESSION OF SOVEREIGNTY

Some people may argue that an authoritative judgement by an appropriate human or committee of humans carries some sort of divine certification of authenticity. In Christendom, the Vulgate and King James Versions of the bible were endorsed in this way. The Masoretic Text of the Hebrew bible is still thought of as accurate by followers of Judaism. Similarly, the Qur'an is thought of as accurate by Muslims. However, as I will show in Chapter 2, we now know these texts contain errors, fabrications and/or extensions. Similarly, in Christendom, the Nicaean Creed and other creeds and canon that were developed over time by church leaders are still believed by many to be endorsed by God because of a supposed succession of human sovereignty from the first apostles over such things.

It is easy to see why some people would want the notion of succession of sovereignty to be true. It provides an easy way of obtaining answers to challenging questions for which the evidence is unclear or where evidence points to an unpalatable answer. However, the argument for accepting succession of sovereignty in preference to evidence and reason is weak. As I will show, considerable evidence exists of successive religious leaders becoming corrupt and making mistakes throughout history; even murdering others to reinforce their own power and influence.

To reinforce their legitimacy, some of the older branches of a faith claim succession of sovereignty for themselves – Jesus to his disciples, these disciples to their proteges or Muhammad to his proteges. Sometimes schisms occurred over which is the legitimate line of succession. For example, in Christendom, in 1054 such a division occurred between the Western (Roman Catholic popes and bishops) and Eastern (Orthodox patriarchs and bishops) branches for reasons I will discuss in the next section.

To enhance their legitimacy, followers of these branches of Christianity often seek stories of supposed miracles by selected pious deceased followers whom they refer to as 'saints'. Some even encourage prayer to deceased saints to intercede with God on behalf of the living. Jesus instead taught us to pray directly to God (Luke 11:1-4). Protestant denominations tend not to claim succession of sovereignty but are more inclined to rely solely on scriptures of the Old and New Testaments (an approach known as 'sola scriptura').

Although Islam holds that its Qur'an and laws supported by Hadiths are unchanging, schisms exist between sects that have differing interpretations about the meaning or implications of various passages. The most well-known and significant schism is between the Shi'ite and Sunni sects of Islam. These sects disagree which is the true line of succession that Muhammad and Allah would have endorsed to lead and interpret their faith. I will show how Islam became particularly intolerant of dissenting views. As a consequence, these major Islamic sects have a long and bloody history of waging bitter wars against each other with no hope of resolution other than the prospect of one wiping the other out.

Other than perhaps Protestant Christianity, of the three religions, Judaism includes the least claims of succession of sovereignty by its leadership. In fact, a healthy debate of truth is a defining characteristic of Judaism. However, Judaism arguably has the strongest sense of cultural identity, tradition and ritual rules its members must contend with that pose barriers to objective free thinking.

HUMAN REASONING

If one is not indoctrinated from childhood with beliefs and practices such as praying to saints or succession of sovereignty, such notions may seem far from credible. However, having studied the reasoning that criminal offenders sometimes give to explain their actions, such thinking is not actually at all inconsistent with how the human mind can work. As a person constructs a rationale for his or her beliefs or actions, corollary questions commonly arise that require an elaboration of the belief or story. We don't like our belief system to come tumbling down. So, when we encounter what appears to be a weakness in our reasoning, we tend to seek a way of preserving our argument by elaborating on our original simple rationale. Our argument can develop into an increasingly complicated and fragile house of cards that may not seem credible to another person encountering it for the first time.

Rather than relying on one's own, often uneducated, reasoning to find answers to the deep and challenging questions of life, when unable to immediately determine an answer ourselves, we might seek an authoritative interpretation. We might even seek such an authoritative interpretation before forming an opinion ourselves. Whenever a question does not have a straightforward answer in scripture, an easy solution is to resort to human authorities to tell us what is true, but where do these authorities get their answers from?

Throughout history, religious authorities tended to be more educated than the masses, which is a valid reason to consider their opinions as having potential merit. However, these opinions should still be subjected to logical analysis. I do not treat opinions by leaders or experts as facts, based on the education or leadership position of that person. Rather, I test all opinions using the same criteria.

At this point in my argument, a fundamental question of faith arises: Should we believe that religious authorities have greater access to divine revelation than do ordinary people? Many people like to believe this; perhaps for some, this is because it absolves them from taking responsibility. However, if you read both the Jewish and Christian scriptures, you will find a strong theme of God bypassing the powerful and the religious leaders to reach down to the lowly, uneducated and humble with his revelations. Looking at the life of Jesus from before his birth until his post-resurrection ascension, this message is clear, and the examples are numerous. Similarly, in Jewish scriptures, God selected the lowly, such as the boy Samuel to be a judge, David the shepherd to be a military champion and king, and many others of lowly positions to be his prophets. Therefore, I find the evidence in scriptures sufficient to put aside the notion that we should believe religious leaders have a monopoly on divine revelation. Even in Islam, Muhammad was supposedly an illiterate shepherd and caravan merchant who only married into wealth and power, and who subsequently grew his power and influence.

EVOLUTION OF DOCTRINE

As I will show in Chapter 2, religious leaders in all three faiths shaped and controlled the canon of their religions to reinforce their power, often making mistakes and even creating schisms from minor academic differences in beliefs that need not impact how followers live their lives. For example, within Christendom, the council of Nicaea in 325 CE discussed a difference of opinion between Alexandrian clerics Arius and Athanasius on whether Jesus was created by god the father. Athanasius won, and Arius was excommunicated with his belief designated 'anathema'. A century later, at the Council of Ephesus in 431 CE, another Bishop of Alexandria, Cyril, disagreed with Bishop Nestorius of Constantinople on whether Jesus' human and divine natures existed in a 'hypostatic union' or a 'prosopic union', and whether his mother, Mary, should be called the Christ-bearer or God-bearer. Cyril won and Nestorius was deposed as Bishop. He and others on his side of the argument split off from the church of the Byzantine empire but were accepted in Persia where they formed the Nestorian church.

Throughout his life, Cyril manoeuvred to increase his political power in Alexandria, culminating in his instigation of the brutal murder of the philosopher Hypatia, who was an advisor to the Roman governor, Orestes. Through this act Cyril demonstrated the power he had over his followers, and in doing so gained dominance over Orestes and Alexandria. After his death, the church honoured Cyril by designating him a saint and a 'Doctor of the Church'. In doing so, they effectively endorsed his terrible acts because of their contribution to strengthening the power of the church. Numerous such power-plays and excommunications of those who were defeated in these confrontations occurred throughout subsequent centuries.

By examining such acts, it is obvious that by the 4th century CE, the church had become corrupted by power, leveraging arguments over dogma to effect power plays. They had departed from the simple faith advocated by Jesus. Soon after this period of history, Muhammad encountered Christianity in Arabia. As I will show, this encounter fundamentally shaped his attitudes, beliefs, and actions.

Twenty years after the Council of Ephesus, another schism occurred over a disagreement about the nature of Christ. At the Council of Chalcedon in 451, some bishops proposed Christ only had one nature (a view known as miaphysitism). Unfortunately for them, the council affirmed Cyril's position from 20 years earlier. Those who lost the dispute split to form the Coptic church, the Syriac church and later the Ethiopian church.

Much later, in the 16th century CE, when people began to be able to read the original scriptures in their own language, they discovered how the church had deceived them about many doctrines and practices. This development triggered what I will refer to as schisms of enlightenment, rather than the schisms of power plays that occurred within the church leadership. As a result, today the world 'enjoys' a wide diaspora of Christian denominations and some groups who consider themselves the true Catholics but reject the pope, claiming that the office of the Pope (known as the Holy See) is vacant. Although less numerous, different sects exist within Judaism and Islam as well.

Christendom developed its canon and doctrines through successive popes and bishops. Similarly, Rabbinic Judaism has its Talmud, and Islam its Hadiths, which have become part of their respective canons. Islam's Hadiths became necessary because the Qur'an lacks sufficient information to adequately define a religion and associated expectations of its followers.

CONTRADICTIONS IN SCRIPTURE

The Qur'an is the collection of supposed 'revelations' from God received by Muhammad throughout his lifetime – or at least a collection of many of them collated from various sources decades after his death. As we will see in Chapter

2, unfortunately for Islam, some of Muhammad's revelations conflicted with others. As a result, the Qur'an is full of contradictions and leaves most questions of life unanswered. So, after Muhammad's death, his followers over succeeding generations created other writings, known as Hadiths. These attempt to sort through these problems and provide additional answers. Hadiths include accounts of things that happened in Muhammad's life. Muslims believe Muhammad is the best example of how a human should live. By reading about his life as recorded in Hadiths, Muslims gain additional insight into how they should live, beyond what the Qur'an can provide.

Also, because the Qur'an *(supposedly inscribed by God on a tablet in heaven, unchanged for all time)* contains numerous internal contradictions, Islam created the rule of abrogation that defines which verse is correct when two verses contradict each other. This rule is that whenever Muhammad produced a new revelation that contradicted an earlier one, his new one supersedes the old one[6]. From an evidential perspective, particularly given that no corroboration exists for Muhammad's testimony, this rule could be seen as, *'Whenever Muhammad changed his mind, we are supposed to disregard what he originally said and believe the new version instead'*. No sound modern justice system would disregard earlier evidence in this way. In fact, such contradictions would seriously harm the credibility of the witness. Should Muhammad therefore be viewed as an unreliable, and possibly dishonest, witness? Before drawing such a conclusion which would have profound implications for the credibility of Islam in its entirety, I will, in this quest, look at aspects of Muhammad's life and teachings to understand his motivations and character.

Like Muslims, some Christians also believe their scriptures are inerrant. They base this belief on an interpretation of 2 Timothy 3:16a, which says *"All scripture is God-breathed"*, interpreting this expression to mean that the actual words were conveyed to the authors by God. This belief is based on weak evidence because the quality of writing varies between authors and contradictions exist. For example:

- We read in 2 Kings 8:26 that King Ahaziah commenced his reign at 22 years of age, but in 2 Chronicles 22:2 we read he was 42. In the same chapter, Ahaziah is found hiding in Samaria before being brought to Jehu, whereupon Jehu killed and buried him (2 Chronicles 22:9). However, the account back in 2 Kings records Ahaziah being shot

---

[6] Tangelder, Johan D. (2007). *The Islamic doctrine of abrogation*. Christian Library. https://www.christianstudylibrary.org/article/islamic-doctrine-abrogation Accessed 16 July 2025

whilst ascending Gur in Ibleam, dying in Megiddo, then his body being brought back to Jerusalem by his servants (2 Kings 9:27-28).

- The genealogy of Jesus given in Matthew's gospel contradicts that given in Luke's gospel.

- Similarly, Acts 1:18-19 and Matthew 27:3-8 give conflicting accounts of the death of Judas, at least one of which must be poetic or legend that evolved over time; they both can't be literally correct.

- Also, the prophets in the Tanakh often spoke against laws in the Torah. For example, we read that in Leviticus 16, not long after God led the Hebrews out of slavery in Egypt, God commands the Hebrews to make burnt offerings and sacrifices. However, in Jeremiah 7:22 we read, *"For in the day that I brought them out of the land of Egypt, I did not speak to your fathers or command them concerning burnt offerings and sacrifices."*

These examples reveal that, if God is real and perfect, a belief in the perfection of every word we find in scripture is not supported by the scriptures themselves.

Genesis 2:7 provides a possible alternate interpretation of the idea of *"god-breathed"*; it says, *"And the Lord God (YHWH) formed man of the dust of the ground and breathed into his nostrils the breath of life, and man became a living soul."* This verse contains the idea of God breathing life into a man. Following this idea, 2 Timothy 3:16 may be intended to contain the idea of God breathing life into scriptures. This idea fits the narrative of the verse, which goes on to say, *"and is profitable for teaching, reproof, correction, and for training in righteousness"*. Accordingly, the alternate understanding many Christians have about this verse is that God inspired the authors to write the scriptures; they are therefore useful (*"profitable"*) rather than needing to be literally perfect.

With this latter understanding, the Jewish and Christian scriptures become less vulnerable to being deemed invalid due to internal contradictions, as long as one accepts that they consist of a series of accounts written by different human authors over hundreds of years. Unlike Islam, most Christians and Jews do not claim their scriptures (with the possible exception of the 10 commandments) are inscribed on a tablet by God (Exodus 31:18).

As I will show, Judaism and Christianity have their weaknesses. A core message throughout the teachings of Jesus was how the Jewish religious leaders fundamentally missed the point about the law, which was intended to serve man rather than man serving the law. Jesus frequently pointed out the hypocrisy, arrogance and lack of compassion of many Jewish religious leaders of his time. This criticism infuriated them, causing them to want his death.

Later, during the 'Dark Ages', when Christendom arguably reached its nadir[7], Muhammad birthed Islam. As I will show, it is clear from the Qur'an that he did this, at least in part, as a response to the diversity of Christian doctrine that he was exposed to. He would have encountered Christian 'heretics' (excommunicated followers of Jesus) travelling East to propagate their message after Christendom's leadership had agreed on creeds that contradicted what some followers of Jesus believed. Also, Arab Christian monks in Muhammad's time were participating in debates across Christendom about what to believe (such as the Immaculate Conception of Mary, which I will discuss later). As will become evident, such differences in beliefs between Christians are likely to have influenced Muhammad to create an ideology that is, at its core, intolerant of such contradictions, and violently suppresses diversity and freedom of belief. Muhammad did not want the weakness that caused division in Christendom to repeat itself in the part of the world under his influence.

Soon after Christianity began, we see in Paul's writings that he was critical of numerous other early Christian teachers, even the apostles Barnabus and Peter (Galatians 2:11). The Pauline school of thought succeeded in exerting the most significant influence on early Christian doctrine[8]. However, this success does not mean Paul was right; neither does the fact that church leadership (over time) decided to include most of his writings and reject most contemporary writings by others. Such church authorities are fallible. For example, consider the division in the Church of England in the 21st century CE after its leaders changed their stance on issues related to gender. Was their previous stance right or is their new stance right? Similarly in Roman Catholicism, many Catholics rejected as heretical the Vatican 2 council decisions or the decisions by, or behaviour of, earlier popes or councils. Again, who was right and how can we make such a determination?

It may be comfortable for Christians to choose to accept the Nicaean Creed and the latest decisions of the current leaders of their particular denomination. However, in undertaking a credibility assessment, we would be foolish to 'take

---

[7] https://en.wikipedia.org/wiki/Christianity_in_the_7th_century Accessed 27 July 2025

[8] Novenson, Matthew V., and R. Barry Matlock (eds) (2022). *The Oxford Handbook of Pauline Studies.* https://doi.org/10.1093/oxfordhb/9780199600489.001.0001, Accessed 16 July 2025

as gospel' such decisions. A belief which we refuse to expose to critical examination has no more value than a child's comfort blanket.

1.6 THE THREE MAIN BRANCHES OF CHRISTIANITY

I have identified similarities between Roman Catholicism and Eastern Orthodoxy. Both emphasise succession of sovereignty, church tradition and praying to saints. However, they also have important differences. Before concluding this chapter, it may be helpful to take a brief aside to introduce some key doctrinal differences between the three main branches of Christianity: Roman Catholicism, Eastern Orthodoxy and Protestantism. Be warned, some of these beliefs may seem strange and complicated. Don't worry if you find them confusing; I will address this later. For now, this aside merely serves to illustrate the nature of these differences.

First, a little history: Christianity has always been characterised by concern about variations in doctrinal teaching. Biblical accounts of the early church report such differences along with concerns about 'false teachers'. After the Roman Emperor, Constantine, embraced Christianity, he sought to stamp out such disagreements, which he saw as divisive and a threat to his empire. Through the Council of Nicaea in 325 CE and subsequent church councils, the evolving church dealt with such disagreements about doctrine and church practices, often causing schisms between different factions.

One of these schisms occurred in 1054 where, following a series of disputes, the Western church authorities in Rome asserted that their leader (whom they designated 'Pope') had supreme authority over all of Christendom. They also asserted a range of doctrinal claims that the Eastern church did not support, such as whether the holy spirit proceeded from the father or from the father and the son, and whether leavened or unleavened bread should be used in the Eucharist sacrament (which I will discuss later). In short, a series of events resulted in a schism between the Eastern and Western churches.

Later, during the European enlightenment of the early 16th Century CE, various members of the Western church came to believe that the church (now known as Roman Catholic) had departed so far from its origin and what it should be, that they rejected the authority of the Roman Catholic church and began what is known as the Protestant Reformation. This event was so concerning for the Roman Catholic church, that it underwent its own internal reformation. Some aspects of this Roman Catholic Reformation tidied up some of its more problematic doctrines and practices. However, with others, the church doubled-down, seeking to challenge and differentiate themselves from the Protestant reformers.

The Protestant reformers struggled to grapple with the challenge of no longer having an authoritative institution to tell them what to do and believe. They spent the next 400 years stumbling over questions of doctrine, splitting into different branches of Protestantism, known as denominations.

In general, the older churches rely more on their church traditions influencing their beliefs in comparison with Protestants, who give more weight to scripture. However, although Protestantism sprung from Roman Catholicism, its beliefs often align more with Eastern Orthodox beliefs than Roman Catholic ones, leaving Roman Catholicism to hold to its more extreme dogmas alone. Roman Catholics tend to believe that it is Protestants who have innovated new doctrines. However, the beliefs that Protestants share with the Eastern Orthodox church, reveal it may be Roman Catholicism that has created the most significant innovations, whilst Protestants and Eastern Orthodox Christians seek to retain the earliest beliefs of Christianity.

For example, Roman Catholic dogmas rejected by both the Eastern Orthodox and Protestant branches of Christianity include:

- **Papal Supremacy** – best articulated at the First Vatican Council on 18 July 1870: *"We promulgate anew the definition … which must be believed by all faithful Christians, namely that the apostolic see and the Roman pontiff hold a world-wide primacy, and that the Roman pontiff is the successor of our blessed Peter, the prince of the apostles, true vicar of Christ, head of the whole church and father and teacher of all Christian people."*

  Instead, both the Eastern Orthodox and Protestant branches of Christianity hold that the head of the church is Christ alone. Both hold that papal supremacy is an innovation by Roman Catholicism that lacks a biblical or historical basis.

- **Immaculate Conception** – that Mary, the mother of Jesus, was conceived without 'original sin'; that is, she *"was preserved from the common defect of estrangement from God, which humanity in general inherits through the sin of Adam. Her freedom from sin was an unmerited gift from God or special grace, an exception to the law, or privilege, which no other created person has received."*[9]

---

[9] Fr. John Hardon, Modern Catholic Dictionary

In 1895, the Eastern Orthodox Ecumenical Patriarch, Anthimus VII of Constantinople, in a response to Pope Leo XII's appeal for reunion, rejected the dogma of the Immaculate Conception as a theological innovation foreign to the early church.

- **Withholding the chalice**. Laity are denied the wine component of the Eucharist (Holy Communion) and only offered the bread component[10].

This departure from the practice of the early church and Jesus' example and instruction at the Last Supper, arose from a practical concern that spilling the wine would be seen as gravely profane. This is because Roman Catholicism holds that the wine becomes the actual blood of Christ through a 'miracle of transubstantiation'.

- **Purgatory** – *"The place or condition in which the souls of the just are purified after death and before they can enter heaven … The sufferings in purgatory are not the same for all, but proportioned to each person's degree of sinfulness. Moreover, these sufferings can be lessened in duration and intensity through the prayers and good works of the faithful on earth."*[11]

Neither the Eastern Orthodox church nor Protestants believe in purgatorial punishment after death, which they see as doubting the atoning power of Jesus' crucifixion. They hold that such practices are an innovation not witnessed in the bible. *"The Orthodox church does not believe in purgatory … We object to the Catholic satisfaction model, which states that God requires payment even after he forgives our sins. Within the Orthodox theological paradigm, there is either forgiveness or punishment, not both."*[12]

- **Indulgences** – *"An indulgence is a remission before God of the temporal punishment due to sins whose guilt has already been forgiven … It removes either part or all of the temporal punishment due to sin."*[13]

For the same reason (denying the atoning power of Jesus' crucifixion), Eastern Orthodox and Protestant Christians do not believe in 'indulgences' as remissions from purgatorial punishments. In fact, the Protestant Reformation was, in part, triggered by the selling of indulgences by Roman Catholic church leaders who were enriching

---

[10] Code of canon law, Canon 925 (Vatican.va)
[11] Fr. John Hardon, Modern Catholic Dictionary
[12] Saint John the Evangelist Church. https://www.Saintjohnchurch.org/differences-between-orthodox-and-catholic/ Accessed 12 June 2025
[13] Catechism of the Catholic Church, 1471

themselves by exploiting the fear they were fuelling amongst their congregations.

As stated by the Eastern Orthodox church: *"The Orthodox Church does not believe in indulgences as remissions from purgatorial punishment. Both purgatory and indulgences are inter-correlated theories, unwitnessed in the bible or in the Ancient Church, and when they were enforced and applied, they brought about evil practices at the expense of the prevailing Truths of the Church."*[14]

1.7 SO, HOW TO START?

The beliefs of Judaism, Christianity and Islam conflict in significant ways. As I have outlined, variations also exist within each of these three religions. Clearly not all these religions, along with their various branches, denominations and sects, can have it right because they conflict on numerous points. I aim to consider such points of contention, identify which of them are likely to be false, then see what remains standing. Also, although personally I have separately explored and rejected atheism and antitheism, I do not intend to address these perspectives herein. Neither do I address Eastern religions. Instead, my focus is on resolving concerns about aspects of mainstream Christian doctrine. Therefore, if you are Atheist, Hindu, Buddhist or Daoist, this book should provide little threat to your current set of beliefs; you can probably relax your defences. If you are Jewish, Christian or Muslim, you may find relaxing your defences a little harder as you read. However, I encourage you to try because I am not an apologist trying to defend a particular set of beliefs; rather, I am an investigator searching for the truth.

By applying principles used to assess the credibility of information, and by exercising judgement in sound ways, I anticipate some beliefs will emerge as being more credible than others. From the resultant discussion, I hope to assist in addressing any confusion you may be experiencing in your own faith. If my efforts help advance your understanding of what you should believe, how you should live and why, this will have been a worthwhile effort. However, please don't blindly believe what I say; think about it and check the relevant sources.

At the core of Christianity are the person, teachings and life of Jesus of Nazareth, whom Christians believe is the Christ, or long-awaited Messiah – the saviour prophesied in the Jewish scriptures, perhaps most famously by the

---

[14] *Death, the Threshold to Eternal Life* (3 Sept 1990). https://www.goarch.org/-/death-the-threshold-to-eternal-life Accessed 12 June 2025

prophet Isaiah (Isaiah 53) and in various psalms of King David. Differences in positions taken regarding Jesus, mark important distinctions between Judaism, Christianity and Islam. Examining the credibility of these different beliefs about Jesus should therefore form a core part of my assessment.

The existence of Jesus is not in doubt; historical evidence is strong. The most detailed documented accounts that still exist of his life and teachings are contained in the four gospels – Matthew, Mark, Luke and John. The fact that the authors of these gospels were probably his followers creates an obvious conflict of interest and therefore source of potential bias. Fortunately, credible non-Christian Jewish and Roman historical records remain, including accounts by the Jewish priest and historian Flavius Josephus, and Roman senator and historian Tacitus. Numerous other historic records also appear to be referring to Jesus, including references by Roman historian Suetonius, a letter from Stoic philosopher Marea bar Serapion to his son; even the Jewish Talmud mentions Yeshua (although these latter sources do not provide sufficient details to be certain). Collectively, all these non-Christian records corroborate some important portions of the accounts given in the Gospels.

When examining scriptures that describe the life of Jesus, we should therefore start with a premise that they may be plausible, and examine factors such as internal consistency, contemporaneity, credibility of the authors and the writing style of the text. I will consider such factors where relevant when discussing scriptural evidence.

CREDIBLE?

2. SCRIPTURES

"How can you say, 'We are wise, and the law of the lord is with us?' But behold, the lying pen of the scribes turned it into a lie."

Jeremiah 8:8

2.1 WHAT TO LOOK FOR

Jews, Christians and Muslims hold conflicting beliefs about God, Jesus and prophecies. Arguably, the most significant source of their beliefs is the scriptures they use. We should therefore consider the credibility of these scriptures. To competently assess the credibility of any version of scripture we use today, we must consider the credibility of the source manuscripts from which our version was constructed. Factors contributing to credibility include historical evidence about the period in which the scripture was written, internal consistency and verifiability of content.

One threat to credibility is inadvertent errors that may have crept in across time because of successive copying and/or translation of earlier manuscripts; another is intentional modifications. As I will show, modifications to scriptural texts have occurred that reinforce particular doctrines. These edits often suspiciously support the doctrine advocated by the author (or copyist) and conflict with competing doctrines that might threaten their set of beliefs. Where conflicts occur, I aim to find which version is most credible.

2.2 JEWISH SCRIPTURES

ORAL LAW

Before discussing the Jewish bible, known as the Tanakh, it is important to understand that, as with Islam and both the Eastern Orthodox and Roman Catholic forms of Christianity, modern Jews have created additional canonical teachings or interpretations beyond the literal statements in their bible. For them, the Tanakh does not constitute all divine writings or religious law. Their religious leaders (Rabbis) have been permitted to create new doctrines and specific interpretations of general statements in scriptures.

Rabbinic Judaism is the predominant form of Judaism still in existence today. It evolved from the Pharisaic sect of Second Temple Judaism which existed when Jesus walked the earth. Jesus often spoke to and about the Pharisees. On these occasions, he was usually critical of their pride and the onerous legalistic burdens they placed on ordinary Jewish people. He taught that they had missed the point about what God really wants from us; he showed people another way.

Rabbinic Judaism formed in the 6th century CE with the codification of the Babylonian Talmud. The Talmud contains oral Torah (law) incorporating the teachings and opinions of thousands of rabbis from the period between the destruction of the second temple in 70 CE and the Arab conquest in the early 7th century. At its core, is the Mishna, the first written collection of Oral Law. Also contained within the Talmud, the Gemara provides subsequent commentary on the Mishna. This commentary in the Gemara and other broader Rabbinic literature often includes a Rabbinic interpretation technique known as Midrash.

The Talmud and Midrash contain some passages which weaken Rabbinic Judaism's credibility due to instructions that conflict with the Tanakh:

- In Sanhedrin 59a of the Talmud, *"Rabbi Yohanan says: A gentile* [non-Jew] *who engages in Torah* [biblical law] *study is liable to receive the death penalty; as it is stated: 'Moses commanded us a law [Torah], an inheritance of the congregation of Jacob' (Deuteronomy 33:4), indicating it is an inheritance for us, and not for them."* However, the Torah itself says to Abraham, *"Through you all nations of the earth will be blessed."* (Genesis 12:3) And the Jewish prophet Isaiah, records God telling him, *"It is too small a thing that you should be my servant to raise up the tribes of Jacob and to restore the protected ones of Israel; I will also make you a light to the nations so my salvation may reach to the end of the earth."* (Isaiah 49:6). However, the belief encouraged in the

Talmud persists within Rabbinic Judaism to this day that God is for the Jews and that gentiles are excluded or, at best, confined to some lesser status (such as Noahides).

- Sifrei Devarim 154 of the Midrash commands Jewish elders to obey their religious leaders even if they tell you right is left, and left is right. However, in Isaiah 8:20 we read, *"To the law and to the testimony! If they do not speak in accordance with this word, it is because they have no light in them."*

Other branches of Judaism such as the Sadducees, Samaritans and Karaite Jews, do not recognise oral Torah as divine authority. Similarly, Protestant Christian denominations do not recognise biblical canon created by Roman Catholic popes or Eastern Orthodox patriarchs as part of their denomination's canon. In Rabbinic Judaism, the written Torah (first five books of the Tanakh) and oral Torah together are referred to as Halakha. In modern times, many Rabbinic Jews are reinterpreting and relaxing interpretations of how binding Halakha should be.

TANAKH MANUSCRIPTS

The Tanakh was written mainly in Hebrew, with portions in Aramaic[15]. Manuscripts of the Tanakh that have survived time are copies of copies of copies; some are translations from the original language. Through these processes, manuscripts most likely underwent changes. In some places this looks to have been deliberate, as I will illustrate in the examples below. In other places, with so much copying and translation, it is understandable that changes would have crept in by mistake. This point is illustrated through the Dead Sea Scrolls. The discovery of the Dead Sea Scrolls in Qumran caves during the mid-20th century revealed earlier manuscripts than any other in existence today. These manuscripts contain differences from the Christian Old Testament, the Masoretic Text version of the Tanakh used by Rabbinic Jews, and the version used by the Ethiopian Jews who diverged prior to the Masoretic Text branching off.

The oldest complete manuscript of the Masoretic Text of the Tanakh is known as the Leningrad Codex. This codex was produced in Cairo, Egypt, in the year 1008 CE, and is the version of the Tanakh that Rabbinic Judaism relies on. Scholars have debated whether a more accurate bible might include corrections from other, probably more reliable, sources such as the earlier (920 CE) Aleppo Codex or even the much earlier Septuagint (250-130 BCE). Scholars tend to

---

[15] The Aramaic portions are: Daniel 2:4b-7:28, Ezra 4:8-6:18, Ezra 7:12-26, Jeremiah 10:11, and two words in Genesis 31:47

believe the Aleppo Codex is slightly more accurate than the Leningrad Codex, but it is missing large sections; the Septuagint is a Greek translation of the Hebrew bible.

From a credibility perspective, Masoretic text codices (such as Aleppo and Leningrad) have the advantage of being in Hebrew, therefore retaining more of the nuance of the Hebrew language that might get lost in translation. The Septuagint has the advantage of extant manuscripts that are over 1,000 years older than the Masoretic Codices, even pre-dating Christianity.

The Septuagint is likely to have been the most used version of the bible during the second temple period when Jesus gave his teachings. Greek was the predominant international language in use at the time and some scriptures quoted by early Jewish writers of the Christian New Testament are more consistent with the Septuagint than the much later Masoretic Text, thereby reinforcing the credibility of the Septuagint.

The Jewish Tanakh and Christian Old Testament contain very similar content and the same 39 books. The most obvious difference is the order of the books. The Tanakh orders books into the Law (Torah), Prophets (Nevi'im) and Writings (Ketuvim), whereas the Old Testament orders books into the Law, History, Wisdom, Major Prophets and Minor Prophets. However, a more important difference is that most versions of the Old Testament are translations, many of which are informed by other early translations such as the Septuagint (Greek translation from the 3rd – 2nd centuries BCE), Peshitta (Syriac translation from the 2nd century CE) or Vulgate (Latin translation from the fourth to 6th century CE). This variation in sources is one reason why different versions of the bible exist in the English language.

TANAKH VARIANTS

Scholars use the term 'variants' to refer to differences in content between early manuscript copies. These variants exist across different versions of the Jewish scriptures. Rabbinic Judaism holds to the Masoretic Text. However, the much earlier Septuagint and Dead Sea Scrolls conflict with the Masoretic Text in passages. For example, One variance across all three is found in Deuteronomy 32:8. Here we find the Masoretic Text saying, *"When the most high gave nations their inheritance and separated the sons of mankind, he established the boundaries of the peoples according to the number of the sons of Israel"*. In this passage, where the Masoretic Text says, *"sons of Israel"*, the Septuagint says, *"angels of God"* and the Dead Sea Scrolls (4QDeutj) say, *"sons of God"*.

The notion of setting boundaries for all of mankind based on the number of sons of Israel, seems unintuitive – Why would Israeli tribal divisions be relevant to other nations? The angels in the Septuagint and sons of God in the Dead Sea Scrolls seem more fitting and are similar to each other in that they both refer to heavenly beings. However, the existence of this variance may suggest a possible lack of clarity about the difference in identity between angels and sons of God. For example, in Genesis 32, is the person whom Jacob wrestles with throughout the night a man, an angel or God?

In Exodus 20:12, the Masoretic Text translates to:

> *"Honour your father and your mother so that your days be lengthened in the land that the Lord your God is giving you."*

Translating the Septuagint for the same passage produces a longer version:

> *"Honour your father and mother so **that it may go well with you and** that you may live long in the good land that the Lord your God is giving you."*

The Nash Papyrus dates from a similar period to the Septuagint but is in the original Hebrew language. It aligns more closely with the Septuagint for this passage, including *"that it may go well with you"*. In the Christian New Testament (Ephesians 6:2-3), this version of this verse is also quoted. So, we have three aligned sources that predate the Masoretic Text by around 1,000 years. Therefore, it is likely the Masoretic Text does not accurately preserve the original version of this passage.

Similarly, in Isaiah 40:5, the Masoretic Text translates to:

> *"And the glory of the Lord will be revealed, and all flesh together will see that the mouth of the Lord has spoken."*

However, translating the Septuagint for the same passage again produces a longer version:

> *"And the glory of the Lord will appear, and all flesh will see **the salvation of God** because the Lord has spoken it."*

Again, the New Testament quotes from Isaiah 40:3-5, including the words *"and all flesh shall see the salvation of God"* (Luke 3:6), as written in the Septuagint.

In 1 Samuel 17:4, Goliath's height is recorded in the Masoretic Text as being 6 cubits and a span. However, the Septuagint, Dead Sea Scroll and Josephus record Goliath's height as being only 4 cubits and a span.

These variants may have little doctrinal significance. Their significance is that they demonstrate that the Masoretic Text on the which the modern Jewish Tanakh is based has undergone changes since the Hellenistic period. It therefore cannot be relied on as completely preserving the original scriptures.

A SOURCE OF DOCTRINAL CONFLICTS

Significantly, and suspiciously, the Masoretic Text conflicts with the Septuagint and other earlier translations in some passages where the Septuagint appears to be prophesying events that correspond to the life of Jesus. The evidence supporting a motive to intentionally make such modifications is provided in the Christian New Testament. Jesus' ministry was popular with ordinary Jewish people. He was critical of the Jewish religious leaders and teachers, who saw him as a threat.

The Jewish religious leadership, including Annas, Caiaphas and the Sanhedrin (the Jewish judicial body), were the actors who sought to trap Jesus throughout his life. They eventually succeeded in persuading the Roman Governor, Pontius Pilot, to have him crucified. They would have hoped Jesus' crucifixion would end the movement that had formed around him, but it did not. The movement grew, both in numbers and geographical reach, thereby growing its threat to Judaism's leadership and tradition.

Jesus and his followers frequently quoted the Jewish scriptures, pointing out passages in the Tanakh that prophesied Jesus' coming, his life and his death. The existence of these prophecies was clearly a significant factor in legitimising a claim that Jesus was the long-awaited Messiah, causing many Jews to believe. Such prophecies being preached by a zealous and growing group of believers posed an existential threat to the form of religion that constituted the power base of the Jewish religious leadership at the time. As evidenced in the Acts of the Apostles (Acts) and various letters (known as 'epistles') contained within the Christian New Testament, Jesus' crucifixion itself was a factor in strengthening the claim that he was the Messiah. The Jewish leadership therefore had a strong motive to modify the parts of the Tanakh that most strongly appeared to point to Jesus as being the Messiah.

Until the middle of the 1st century CE, there is no evidence of Jewish dissatisfaction with the Septuagint. However, within a few decades after the crucifixion of Jesus, some Jews began reacting against the use of the Septuagint, partly because of Christian apologetics based on the Septuagint and partly to better align with what their Rabbis were teaching (which also would have been influenced by Jesus' life, teachings, and impact on many Jews). For example, around 130 CE, a leading Jew and pioneer of Halakha, Rabbi Akivi ben Joseph, hired a convert to Judaism, Aquila of Sinope, to produce a new Greek version of the Tanakh to replace the Septuagint. The Christians criticized Aquila's translation, alleging it translated passages about the Messiah incorrectly[16]. At that time, Akivi believed that Simon bar Kokhba, the leader of a rebellion against the Romans, was the Messiah. Therefore, Akivi had a motive to eliminate prophecies pointing to Jesus, rather than Simon, being the Messiah. Unfortunately, only fragments of Aquila's translation remain. However, from what we know, it seems likely that Aquila's version of the Tanakh would have been more palatable to Judaism's religious leaders than was the Septuagint, if for no other reason than that it challenged the Christian narrative. The extant fragments of Aquila's translation show that it was an excessively literal (word for word) translation, lacking context awareness, so would have failed to translate the original author's meaning to the extent that a 'Functional Equivalence' translation could achieve.

The Hellenistic Jewish scholar, Theodotion, is another translator who, in around 150 CE, attempted to produce a revised Greek language Tanakh. Like Aquila, Theodotion's translation took a very literal approach. His book of Daniel (which was originally written partly in Hebrew and partly in Aramaic) virtually superseded the Septuagint's Daniel within much of the early Christian church.

Around 180 CE, a Samaritan convert to Judaism, Symmachus, attempted a more elegant Greek version than the excessively literal versions of Aquila and Theodotion. Symmachus sought to make his version read better in Greek and better preserve the intended meaning of the original. 4th century Christian translator Jerome appreciated Symmachus' work but criticised his substituting the Greek word νεανίς (young woman) for παρθένος (virgin) in Isaiah 7:14 and Genesis 24:43[17].

Such versions produced by Jewish translators after the rise of Christianity are more likely to have been used within the Jewish tradition. In the earliest extant complete Hebrew bible manuscript – the Masoretic Text of 1008 CE – we find numerous conflicts with the Septuagint, some of which align with Jesus' claimed status as the Messiah. For example:

---

[16] Labendz, J. R. (2009). *Aquila's Bible Translation in Late Antiquity: Jewish and Christian Perspectives*. Harvard Theological Review 102:3. https://doi.org/10.1017/S0017816009000832
[17] https://en.wikipedia.org/wiki/Symmachus_(translator)#cite_ref-15 Accessed 25 July 2025

- Christians believe Psalm 22:17[18] refers to Jesus being pierced on the cross. However, in the Masoretic Text, the word *"pierced/dug"* (in the Septuagint, Syriac and Dead Sea Scrolls) has been replaced with *"like a lion"*. Also, the grammar in the Masoretic Text for this verse is not correct; it means *"like a lion my hands and feet"*, so Jewish interpretations are forced to assume the intended meaning and interpolate a modification.

The verse in Hebrew may be an intentional modification in the Masoretic Text. However, I have also considered the possibility the difference was accidental. The Hebrew in the Masoretic Text translates as *"like a lion"* is כארי (ka-a-ri). However, if the yod (י) at the end of this word was lengthened slightly, it would become a vav (ו), the Hebrew would instead be כארו (ka-a-ru), which means *"they dug/pierced"*. Not only would this align better with the Septuagint, it would also make the sentence more grammatically correct. It is possible that, sometime between 250 BCE and 1008 CE, a small variation in the length of a scribe's stroke may have changed the meaning of this verse.

The balance of evidence suggests the Masoretic text in this passage includes a modification from the original version. This change could have been accidental but may have been intentional; we will never know which.

- Isaiah 7:14 in the Septuagint says a *"virgin"* will give birth. However, the Masoretic Text replaces *"virgin"* with *"young woman"* (עלמה). Again, this change may have been intentional but could also have been accidental. The Hebrew word in the Tanakh in Isaiah's time and at the time the Septuagint was written may have been a word that 'literally' could mean young woman, but was used euphemistically for 'virgin', much like the historic use of the term 'know' (e.g. to 'know' a woman instead of saying to 'have sexual intercourse' with a woman). A well-known example of this is the word ἐγίνωσκεν found in Matthew 1:25, which speaks of Joseph not having sexual intercourse with Mary until after Jesus, the firstborn of her sons, was born (καὶ οὐκ ἐγίνωσκεν

---

[18] Note: Verse numbering differs between the Christian Old Testament, Masoretic Text and Septuagint. For example, Psalm 22:17 in the Masoretic Text and Septuagint is Psalm 22:16 in the Christian Old Testament.

αὐτὴν ἕως οὗ ἔτεκεν τὸν υἱὸν αὐτῆς τὸν πρωτότοκον· καὶ ἐκάλεσεν
τὸ ὄνομα αὐτοῦ Ἰησοῦν)[19].

If such euphemistic use faded over time, translators may be aware of
this and would translate the word originally understood to mean
'virgin' more literally as 'young woman'. What we find in the Peshitta
supports this hypothesis. The Peshitta is the standard version of the
Christian bible translated (probably in the 2nd century CE) into Syriac
from biblical Hebrew. Here, what could have been the Hebrew word
עלמה is translated as ܒܬܘܠܬܐ which means 'chaste maiden'; i.e. a young
woman who is a virgin.

- Isaiah 61:1 in the Masoretic Text omits *"recovery of sight to the blind"*,
  which is something the Christian gospels record Jesus doing. The
  gospels also record Jesus quoting this verse including *"recovery of sight to
  the blind"* (Luke 4:18), so it must have been in the version of the Tanakh
  in use at that time. Again, this looks likely to be an omission in the
  Masoretic Text.

All these passages in the Septuagint align with important details of the Christian
account of Jesus but are recorded in documents dating from over a century
before his birth, therefore could not have been fabricated by Christians.
Because Jews by the Middle Ages had an obvious motive to discredit the notion
that Jesus was prophesied in the Tanakh, the modifications in the Masoretic
Text seem suspicious. However, I have shown it is possible that the
understanding we have of how Hebrew words were used over 2,000 years ago
may have dissipated, leaving us with only the literal meaning of words rather
than the meaning intended by the original author. I have also shown how
inadvertent calligraphic variation could have materially changed the meaning of
a sentence. Therefore, it is possible that variances we find in the modern
Hebrew bible are not necessarily intentional modifications of what the Tanakh's
original authors intended to say.

CAN JESUS BE GOD IF HE IS ALSO HUMAN?

One argument used by both Jews and Muslims for Jesus not being God is that
he was human, and God cannot be human. I find this argument coming from
Judaism to be weak because the Tanakh makes numerous references to God
taking physical form:

---

[19] RP Byzantine Majority Text 2005, which is identical to Stephanus Textus Receptus
1550.

- In Genesis 3:8 God walks in the garden of Eden in the cool of the day.

- In Genesis 18:1-33 God appears to Abraham by his tent

- In Genesis 32:24-32 Jacob wrestles with God.

- In Exodus 3:4 God speaks to Moses from a burning bush.

- In Daniel 3:25 the son of God (or the gods) appears in the furnace with Shadrach, Meshach and Abednego.

These examples show that in Jewish tradition God can appear as a human and in other physical forms. A key difference between such instances and Jesus, is that these are fleeting events, whereas Jesus lived a human life from birth until he was over 30 years old. This difference raises other questions which I will discuss later. For the purposes of this chapter, Jewish scriptures provide evidence that God can take on human form, so Jesus having human form does not preclude the possibility of his divinity.

CONCLUSION AND IMPLICATIONS

On the balance of probability, it seems likely that what is recorded in the Masoretic Text (and modern Jewish bible) was altered by followers of Judaism, possibly to weaken passages that appeared to prophesy Jesus. Key factors in forming this conclusion include:

- The Septuagint was probably the predominant version of the Tanakh in use within mainstream Judaism between 250 BCE and 130 CE.

- Because the version we have today of the Septuagint was written before the birth of Jesus, it could not have been edited by Christians to support their claims.

- The Septuagint supports the claim that Jesus was the Messiah more strongly than does the Masoretic Text.

- Jewish religious leaders in the early centuries CE had a strong motive to destroy Christianity and its claim that Jesus was the Messiah.

- Evidence exists of at least one prominent 2nd century rabbi commissioning a new translation of the Tanakh whose accuracy Christians at the time disputed.

- The earliest remaining manuscript of the Masoretic Text post-dates the birth of Christianity and resultant animosity between Christendom and Judaism.

Jewish scribes therefore had the motive, the means, and the opportunity to edit their bible to reduce its support for Jesus being the Messiah, and evidence exists of such editing occurring. However, even with this conclusion, most of the modern Hebrew and Christian bibles are almost identical. So, although we should not accept that the entire Hebrew bible is authentic to the original meaning, it may well be mostly authentic.

The most obvious issue to explore because of these insights about the Jewish scriptures is the evidence on whether Jesus is the Messiah prophesied in the unedited Jewish scriptures. This will require we consider both Rabbinic Judaism's Tanakh and the Septuagint in relation to historical events described predominantly in the Christian gospels. I will do this in Chapter 5.

2.3 CHRISTIAN SCRIPTURES

As with Jewish scriptures, textual variants exist between different manuscripts from which Christian scriptures are sourced. So, let's start by exploring different types of manuscripts. We can then consider variances, both between different translations and between their source manuscripts. The nature of these variances and the history that led to them provide context to help compare the reliability of competing versions of scripture.

Some manuscripts were discovered after early translations of the bible were published. We now have over 5,800 extant New Testament source manuscripts. However, some have subsequently been found to be portions of others and most only contain part of the New Testament. There are around 5,500 distinct extant manuscripts in the original Koine Greek. Each is written on papyrus, parchment, or paper, and has been classified as Alexandrian, Western or Byzantine text-type[20].

Before discussing the credibility of each of these text-types, it is helpful to understand why they exist. Unlike Jewish scriptures, where professional scribes were responsible for preservation of the Tanakh, in early Christianity, particularly before the gospels and epistles were collated into the New Testament, copies were likely made by the individuals who wanted to retain a

---

[20] Some scholars also identify a Caesarean text-type. However, others identify this as a blend of Western and Alexandrian.

copy of a gospel or an epistle they had received. After copying, they would then send the original on to others to read. These Christians were not necessarily professional scribes; they were copying a document for their own use and the use of people they knew, rather than as a formal historical record. So, it is understandable that often they would paraphrase or be less careful than professional scribes would be.

The earliest documents were hand-written on papyrus which is not as durable as parchment or paper. To preserve the information, copies needed to be made from time to time, introducing the potential for variation and errors. Approximately 125 distinct papyrus manuscripts dating from the second and third centuries CE remain, many of which are in poor condition and are only sections of the original manuscript. These are all likely to be copies of the original sources written during the latter half of the 1st century CE.

Although not as early as the earliest papyrus manuscripts, parchment (vellum) manuscripts are more numerous. Parchment is more durable than papyrus; accordingly, extant parchment manuscripts tend to be in better condition and more complete.

ALEXANDRIAN MANUSCRIPTS

Most modern textual critics consider the parchment codices Sinaiticus and Vaticanus to be the two most important extant early manuscripts. Both date from the 4th century CE. They are often used by scholars in conjunction with the 5th century manuscript Codex Alexandrinus and various papyrus fragments for two reasons: (i) each misses some content, but collectively they cover the complete New Testament, and (ii) if at least two independent manuscripts contain the same content, that content is more likely to be consistent with an earlier (and hopefully the original) source. Most modern translations of the bible draw predominantly on these three codices and numerous papyrus fragments, which are written in what is known as the Alexandrian text-type (although the gospels in Codex Alexandrinus bear more resemblance to Byzantine text-type).

Alexandrian text-type manuscripts tend to be more succinct, with fewer extensions than other text-types. Scholars who favour their use suspect that the extensions in the newer Western and Byzantine text types are likely to be 'glosses' added to enhance their literary style, provide clarity, or support a particular doctrine. The more succinct content of Alexandrian manuscripts, coupled with their earlier publication dates, lends them credibility in comparison with more recent manuscripts which are therefore assumed to be the products of more copying.

WESTERN MANUSCRIPTS

The form of New Testament text seen in Old Latin and Syriac translations from Greek is known as Western text-type. The writings of 2nd and 3rd century Christians such as Irenaeus, Tertullian and Cyprian include quotations from such manuscripts which are characterised by loose paraphrasing and elaboration. This paraphrasing includes omission, insertion and modification of passages, apparently to enhance their emphasis or clarity. The result is more verbose than Alexandrian and Byzantine text types.

Significant Western manuscripts include the 5th century Codex Bezae, which contains all four gospels and the book of Acts. The 6th century Codex Claromontanus contains Paul's epistles. Various Old Syriac translations and some papyrus fragments from Egypt also contain Western text.

BYZANTINE MANUSCRIPTS

Some scholars prefer more recent Byzantine sources, most of which date from the 5th to the 12th century CE. At the beginning of the 4th century CE, Roman emperor Diocletian undertook the final and most severe persecution of Christians by the Roman Empire. His purge destroyed many Christian manuscripts. Diocletian was succeeded by Constantine, who not only decriminalised Christianity, but embraced it and exerted significant influence over its bishops to help ensure the stability of his empire.

Because of Diocletian's destruction of manuscripts, many needed to be replaced. Lucian of Antioch led a recension of various Western manuscripts of both the New Testament and the Septuagint. Through this process, opportunity was taken to polish grammar and include additions to address inconsistencies and theological issues. As a consequence of this project, the writing in the resultant Byzantine text-type tends to be more polished than in earlier manuscripts and these constitute the majority of extant manuscripts of the Greek New Testament. Accordingly, scholars today often refer to Byzantine text-type as the 'Majority Text'.

The fact that manuscripts of Byzantine text-type make up the majority of manuscripts lends them credibility in comparison with Alexandrian and Western text-types. However, Lucian's project offers a possible explanation for both the proliferation of and alignment between these manuscripts. So, constituting the majority should not necessarily be construed as implying this text-type is most authentic to the original.

PRIORITISING MANUSCRIPTS

Many Christians like to preserve the continuity of scripture over time by using bible translations such as the King James Version (KJV), whose New Testament is based on the 16th century 'Textus Receptus' of Erasmus (see below). However, most scholars take advantage of a wider range of manuscripts. Although almost all manuscripts are broadly in agreement, some differences exist, as I will shortly illustrate.

Being copies of copies, it is understandable that errors would have crept into most, if not all, extant manuscripts. Scholars have identified passages where the differences appear to be due to extensions having been made to a verse within a phrase. Numerous potential extensions and modifications have been identified in Western and (to a lesser extent) Byzantine Text manuscripts, and many of the Byzantine texts have very few differences between them. Extensions thought to have been added to manuscripts are sometimes referred to as 'interpolations'.

No high quality complete early manuscripts of the New Testament exist. So, to work out what the original autograph is likely to have said, it is necessary to construct the New Testament from different codices and fragments. Criteria known as 'apparatus' are applied to ensure some sort of logical consistency exists when deciding which passages to include from which manuscripts. Where different manuscripts vary in their content, some scholars give more weight to whatever text is contained in the **majority** of manuscripts, whereas most modern scholars give more weight to whatever text is contained in the **earliest** manuscripts. Few modern scholars tend to prioritise Western text-type, which is universally recognised as containing extensive paraphrasing and extensions. That said, there are exceptions. For example, as I will show below, some scholars point out that in Luke Chapters 22 and 24, the Western Codex Bezae contains fewer interpolations even than Codex Vaticanus, Codex Sinaiticus and Codex Alexandrinus. So, Codex Bezae should not be dismissed altogether.

In reading debates between scholars about the relative accuracy of various Greek manuscripts and translations, I noted a theme where some participants give weight to the version they see as being most prolific and influential over a long period, rather than favour evidence about the credibility of the source or content of such versions. A common reason given for holding such a belief is that the proliferation and impact of the person's preferred version is evidence of God's divine preservation of his word in that version. Such a 'religious', rather than 'evidential', belief is beyond the scope of what I am equipped to test. It therefore has little influence on my conclusions but is nevertheless important to note because of the insight it gives into the thinking of many Christians.

THE JOHANNINE COMMA

Copyists of manuscripts may have made edits for different reasons. In some instances, the copyist may have believed additional context would be helpful to the reader; elsewhere, he may have wanted to use the original verse to support a particular doctrine. One of the more well-known interpolations is found in 1 John 5:7-8. In the King James Version (KJV) we read: *"⁷For there are three that bear record in heaven, the father, the word, and the holy ghost: and these three are one. ⁸And there are three that bear witness in earth, the spirit, and the water, and the blood: and these three agree in one."* (1 John 5:7-8).

About 500 Greek New Testament manuscripts contain 1 John 5:7-8, but only five of these have this long version of the verse in the original text:

- Miniscule 629 written 1300-1399 (a Latin-Greek diglot)

- Miniscule 61 written 1500-1521

- Miniscule 918 written 1550-1599

- Miniscule 2473 written 1634

- Miniscule 2318 written 1700-1799

You may notice that oldest of these contains both the Latin and Greek manuscript and two of the others post-date the KJV English translation. Scholars note that the Greek has been revised to fit the Latin Vulgate[21] [22], so should not be trusted.

Fortunately, we have other manuscripts going back to the 4th and 5th Centuries CE, none of which contain what we see in these few late manuscripts. Earlier manuscripts (including both the Critical Text and Majority Text) simply state, *"⁷For there are three that testify, ⁸the spirit, the water and the blood, and these three are in agreement."*

This difference is significant, both doctrinally and for our confidence in the credibility of the manuscripts behind the KJV. It shows that this verse in the

---

[21] Gregory, Caspar René (1900). *Textkritik des Neuen Testaments.* Vol. 1. Leipzig: J.C. Hinrichs'sche Buchhandlung. pp277–278.
[22] Metzger, Bruce M. and Ehrman, Bart D. (2002). *The Text of the New Testament: Its Transmission, Corruption and Restoration.* Oxford University Press, p147.

original epistle of 1 John was later extended. This extension is one of the strongest passages in the bible supporting the doctrine of the Trinity. Differences in beliefs surrounding the notion that God is a Trinity consisting of three distinct persons have caused more contention and division than any other doctrine in Christianity. So, I give considerable focus to this doctrine.

The shorter version of this passage makes more sense in the context of the verse that preceded it: *"This is he that came by water and blood, even Jesus Christ; not by water only, but by water and blood. And it is the spirit that beareth witness, because the spirit is truth."* (1 John 5:6). Verses 7 and 8 in the shorter version naturally follow on from this passage, referring to the same three things: water, blood and spirit. However, the extended version talks about heaven and lists three different things it claims are located there: father, the word and the holy spirit. This clause seems somewhat out of context with verse 6. The KJV clearly contains an interpolation in this passage; the shorter version is more credible. This particular plank in the basis for the doctrine of the Trinity should therefore be removed. This has a material impact on the strength of evidence for the Trinity because it is the only verse in the bible that explicitly refers to the three persons of the Trinity[23]being in heaven.

Where verse 6 says that Jesus came by water and blood, some scholars interpret the reference to water as meaning water baptism, and blood to meaning Jesus's blood sacrifice on the cross. However, the verse is not explicit, and Jesus is quoted in John 3 discussing being born of water in response to a question about how a grown man can re-enter his mother's womb to be born again. So, a likely alternative meaning of Jesus coming by water may be his coming in the flesh through normal human childbirth. An important part of the Christian narrative is that the Messiah came as fully human in a humble way through normal childbirth, rather than directly from heaven in a powerful way.

TEXTUS RECEPTUS

The manuscripts listed above containing the longer version of 1 John 5:7 (the Johannine Comma) are part of a subset of Byzantine manuscripts known as Textus Receptus. This small subset of all the manuscripts available to modern scholars had a profound influence on Christian belief.

---

[23] Note: the father, son and holy ghost are listed together in 'the Great Commission' at the end of Matthew's and Mark's gospels but, unlike the Johannine Comma, nothing is said about them in those passages. Also, those passages are suspicious too, which I discuss below.

The work of translator Erasmus in the 16th century contributed to the subsequent popularity of scriptures based on Byzantine manuscripts. Erasmus had access to only 8 predominantly Byzantine manuscripts to construct what he hoped would be an accurate version of a complete New Testament. He called his first (1516) edition of the Greek New Testament 'Novum Instrumentum omne' (NIO)[24]. In this, Erasmus did not have a complete Greek manuscript for the last book in the bible (Revelation), so he translated some verses of the Latin Vulgate back into Greek instead. Approximately 2,000 passages in NIO differ from what is found in the Majority Text.

NIO was so popular that it was reprinted in 1519 with numerous typographical errors corrected. This edition too was popular, so Erasmus produced a third edition in 1522, this time with some modifications, including the insertion of the Johannine Comma, after he was accused of reviving Arianism (the belief that Jesus was a created being, as Paul may be intimating in Colossians 1:15). However, Erasmus himself remained convinced it was not part of the original 1 John epistle.

Erasmus went on to publish two more editions, then other editors such as Colinaeus, Beza, and the House of Elzevir, took up the task of continuing to revise NIO. During this period, it became known as 'Textus Receptus' (Latin for 'received text'). Textus Receptus influenced subsequent translations into other languages, including the original Luther bible in German, then Tyndale's original English translation, the Geneva Bible and the King James Version.

ENGLISH LANGUAGE TRANSLATIONS

Evolving from Textus Receptus, the Geneva Bible was an English language bible first published in 1557 and still in use when James 1st succeeded Elizabeth 1st as the British monarch in 1603. Soon after his coronation, James was persuaded by a council of church leaders to make some changes to the Geneva Bible because it contained passages and commentary that could be interpreted as encouraging (a) morals they did not approve of and (b) rejection of corrupt rulership. James enthusiastically took charge of the project and established a group of 47 scholars to make amendments which he subsequently 'authorised'. This is how the English language version of 1611 became known as the 'King James Version' (KJV) or alternatively the 'Authorised' version.

---

[24] Combs, William W. (Spring 1996). *Erasmus and the Textus Receptus*. Detroit Baptist Theological Seminary Journal. v1 pp35–53 https://www.illuminati-bg.bg/holy_bible/Textus-and-Chronology/Erasmus-and-the-Textus-Receptus-1996--William-Combs.pdf Accessed 26 July 2025

The KJV was subsequently altered sporadically until 1769. This 1769 version remained the most popular English translation of the bible until 2021, when the New International Version (NIV) eclipsed KJV sales. The next year, KJV slipped to fourth place after being overtaken by the New Living Translation (NLT) and the English Standard Version (ESV). In contrast to the KJV, which draws on part of the Majority Text, these more modern translations all draw on an apparatus known as 'Critical Text', which usually gives priority to earlier manuscripts such as those of the Alexandrian text type. This difference in sources and translations is currently stimulating a form of schism in the 21st century. In this schism, some supporters of the King James Version and Textus Receptus accuse others of intentionally corrupting the word of God.

In observing the debates surrounding this schism, I note a strong confirmation bias, particularly from a faction known as 'the King James Only movement' (KJO), who are amongst those who say they favour the Textus Receptus, within the Majority Text (Byzantine) set of manuscripts. Interestingly, when errors in translation from the Textus Receptus or Majority Text to the KJV are pointed out, I have seen some KJO apologists make it evident they believe KJV must be the inspired word of God because it has been preserved unchanged for centuries. When they are shown the translation error from the Greek source that they claim is original, this does not seem to register or factor into their logic, even though they had claimed this source as the justification for their choice of bible. Such apologists therefore take a hit to their credibility. Their behaviour seems more like religious fundamentalism than logical scholarship.

One small but doctrinally significant mistranslation in the KJV is found in James 2:14, which reads "*What doth it profit, my brethren, though a man say he hath faith, and have not works? Can faith save him?*" That second question is rhetorical, suggesting that faith cannot save someone. However, KJO apologists often argue that people are saved by faith alone[25].

More modern translations correctly translate the Greek by inserting the word 'that', such as in the following translation: "*What use is it, my brothers, if someone says he has faith but does not have works? Can **that** faith save him?*". The Critical Text and Majority Text are identical for this passage. Although separate clauses, in Greek these two questions are actually part of the same sentence[26]. What the translators of the KJV did not understand is that when the Greek word ἡ precedes the second use of a noun (in this case 'faith'), it is referencing the prior

---

[25] See some examples on https://www.kingjamesbibleonline.org/Bible-Verses-About-Justification-By-Faith-Alone/
[26] Note though, that the earliest Greek manuscripts did not include punctuation marks.

noun; in other words, **'that'** faith that was talked about earlier. Accordingly, more accurate translations imply that a type of faith not producing good works will not get someone saved. As we will see in the next chapter, this translation aligns better with the teaching of Jesus.

As discussed in Chapter 1, Religion does not require the disciplines needed in Science and Philosophy, such as valid logic. In religious faith one can simply choose what to believe, even if it fails credibility tests. The example I just gave appears to be an instance of such religious faith. For the purposes of my assessment, such a faith is not a credible position. It is, however, a very human position. It reflects the mentality behind the stories that repeat-offenders and repeat-victims tell themselves when they have acted in a way they have acted before or put themselves in a risky situation they have been in before.

CRITICAL TEXT

Critical Text is a response to variants between Greek source manuscripts. It involves reconstructing a version of the Greek New Testament based on careful comparison of numerous sources to determine the most likely original version.

Although Erasmus produced a kind of critical text by morphing a version of the Greek New Testament from 8 manuscripts with variants between them[27], Textus Receptus is thought of by some as being revealed by God (hence its name) rather than cobbled together by a man. Subsequently, when many more manuscripts were collated, not only did more variances appear, but so did patterns in those variances. With advances in knowledge about Koine Greek and the history of the extant manuscripts, coupled with analysis of language and writing, scholars began to gain insight into what the original version of each document was likely to have been. Today, panels of Koine Greek language experts work together to reconstruct what they believe is a version of the New Testament that is truer to the original than individual manuscripts or Textus Receptus. Prominent such panels include Nestle-Aland, United Bible Society and Tyndale House. Of necessity, these panels must exercise judgement in contexts where uncertainty exists so, understandably, don't necessarily always agree.

---

[27] 11th Century CE Codex Basilensis A. N. III. 11 (Pauline Epistles); 12th Century CE Codex Basilensis A. N. IV. 1 (Gospels); 12th Century CE Codex Basilensis A. N. IV. 2 (Gospels, Acts, Epistles); 12th Century CE Codex Basilensis A. N. IV. 4 (Acts, Epistles); 12th Century Augsburg I.1.4º 1 (Revelation); 13th Century CE Codex Regius 84 Miniscule 4 (Gospels); 15th Century CE Codex Basilensis A. N. IV. 5 (Acts, Epistles); 15th Century CE Codex Basilensis A. N. III. 15 (Gospels).

You might wonder why I am getting into this level of detail about Critical Text and textual variants within Christian scriptures. It is because some variants have profound doctrinal implications within Christendom. I gave the example of the Johannine Comma earlier. Another example is found in John 1:18 which in the King James Version reads, *"No man hath seen God at any time; the only begotten son, which is in the bosom of the father, he hath declared him."* The reference to "the *only begotten son"* (ὁ μονογενὴς υἱός) exists in some important manuscripts, including Codex Alexandrinus and numerous other manuscripts (particularly Byzantine ones). Accordingly, the Tyndale House Greek New Testament (THGNT) retains this reference to God's son, accepting the distinction between God and the son (universally taken to be Jesus). However, other manuscripts, including Codex Sinaiticus and Papyrus 75 instead say *"only begotten God"* (μονογενὴς θεὸς). Accordingly, the Nestle-Aland Greek New Testament retains this reference to an only begotten God. If taken to be referring to Jesus, as most scholars accept, this might imply John 1:18 claims Jesus is God. However, this variant raises other problematic questions: The verse starts by saying no one has ever seen God at any time, but Jesus was seen, therefore he can't be God because, if so, the verse would contain a logical contradiction. Also, how can God be begotten (μονογενὴς)? Would this mean one third of the Trinitarian godhead is a created being?

Whether or not Jesus is God is a key defining doctrine that differentiates Trinitarian Christianity from Judaism, Islam and other branches of Christianity such as various Unitarian denominations. Also, deciding whether or not Jesus is a created being (an idea known as Arianism) is arguably the most divisive problem within the history of Christianity. It influenced development of the creeds of the church and the nature of the church's authoritarian control of dogma.

INTERPOLATIONS AND EXTENSIONS

Key figures in stimulating the Critical Text approach were the late 19th century biblical Greek scholars, Westcott and Hort. In a quest to determine what the original Greek would have said, they compared differences between a wider range of early manuscripts than Erasmus used in 1516. In addition to Byzantine texts, Westcott and Hort could access Alexandrian texts such as Codex Vaticanus, Codex Sinaiticus, Codex Alexandrinus, and Western texts such as Codex Bezae.

In their seminal work 'The New Testament in the Original Greek' (1896), Westcott and Hort identified numerous passages they believed are interpolations. Some of these are found towards the end of Luke's gospel. Here,

Dr James Tabor observes[28] that scholars generally agree Codex Bezae is heavily interpolated, containing loose paraphrasing and considerable traditional and even apocryphal material. However, towards the end of Luke's gospel, as well as in a few other places, the Western text (Codex Bezae) is strangely shorter than the most neutral Alexandrian text (Codex Alexandrinus). Some surprising omissions, Westcott and Hort judged to be closer to the original. They referred to these shorter versions as *"Western non-interpolations"* because, rather than add extra content (interpolate) as Codex Bezae more commonly does, in these passages it is more succinct, omitting phrases that seem intuitively unlikely. Westcott and Hort therefore concluded that Codex Bezae in these sections was probably closer to the original Greek.

I present below, relevant passages from the NET bible translation of the final chapter of Luke's gospel. The "interpolations" are the phrases shown **(parenthesised in bold)**:

- Luke 24:1 "But on the first day of the week, at early dawn, the women went to the tomb, taking the aromatic spices they had prepared. [2] They found the stone had been rolled away from the tomb, [3] but when they went in, they did not find the body **(of the Lord Jesus)**. [4] While they were perplexed about this, suddenly two men stood by them in dazzling attire. [5] The women were terribly frightened and bowed their faces to the ground, but the men said to them, 'Why do you seek the living among the dead?' [6] **(He is not here but has been raised!)** Remember how he told you, while he was still in Galilee, [7] that the son of man must be delivered into the hands of sinful men and be crucified, and on the third day rise again.[8] Then the women remembered his words, [9] and when they returned from the tomb they told all these things to the eleven and to all the rest. [10] Now it was Mary Magdalene, Joanna, Mary the mother of James and the other women with them who told these things to the apostles. [11] But these words seemed like pure nonsense to them, and they did not believe them. [12] **(But Peter got up and ran to the tomb. He bent down and saw only the strips of linen cloth; then he went home wondering what had happened.)**"

---

[28] Tabor, James D. (2009); Older is Not Always Better: Remembering Wescott and Hort; The Bible and Interpretation, eds. Mark Elliott, Robert Rezetko, Martin Ehrensvard; The University of Arizona https://bibleinterp.arizona.edu/opeds/tabor_357913 Accessed 28 September 2025

- Luke 24:36 "While they were saying these things, Jesus himself stood among them, **(and said to them, 'Peace be with you.')** [37] But they were startled and terrified, thinking they saw a ghost. [38] Then he said to them, 'Why are you frightened, and why do doubts arise in your hearts? [39] Look at my hands and feet; it is me! Touch me and see; a ghost does not have flesh and bones like you see I have.' [40] **(And when he had said this, he showed them his hands and his feet.)** [41] And while they still could not believe it (because of their joy) and were amazed, he said to them, 'Do you have anything here to eat?' [42] So they gave him a piece of broiled fish, [43] and he took it and ate it in front of them."

- Luke 24:50 "And Jesus led them out as far as Bethany, and lifting up his hands, he blessed them. [51] Now during the blessing he departed **(and was taken up into heaven)**. [52] So they **(worshipped him and)** returned to Jerusalem with great joy, [53] and were continually in the temple courts blessing God."

Although we cannot be certain of exactly what the original author wrote, I find Westcott and Hort's conclusion credible for three reasons:

- The passage reads at least as well without the 'interpolations'.

- I can think of no reason why the author of Codex Bezae would have chosen to delete these if they were in the original.

- I can see a reason why an author of Gospel manuscripts might have chosen to add them: The 'interpolations' support a narrative that seeks to deify Jesus.

I find the history of the Revised Standard Version (RSV) interesting regarding these 'interpolations'. The RSV New Testament first came out in 1946, aiming to make the bible more readable and accurate than the American Standard Version (ASV) and King James Version (KJV). Its authors adopted Westcott and Hort's conclusions by omitting the above interpolations from the main text. Instead, the RSV referred in the footnotes to the fact that some manuscripts have them. Under popular pressure, in a later (1989) revision of the RSV called the New Revised Standard Version (NRSV), the interpolations were reinserted into the body. Readers liked to have them in there for consistency with other versions of the bible, despite concerns about whether they were in the original Greek.

It is likely Mark 16:9-20 was not part of the original gospel but was added later with the purpose of promoting faith in a particular doctrinal school of thinking developing within Christendom at the time it was added[29] [30] [31]. Its writing style is markedly different from the rest of the gospel and the earliest source manuscripts don't even contain these verses. This 'added' passage is dense with doctrinal points and contains a similar 'great commission' to Matthew 28:19, but with an extension promising that miraculous signs and wonders *"will accompany those who believe"*. Suspiciously, it contains a doctrine that runs counter to Jesus' ministry: *"He that believeth and is baptized shall be saved; but he that believeth not shall be damned"* (Mark 16:16). This doctrine of salvation through what you believe – your opinion – and undergoing the baptism ritual, rather than the spiritual transformation affecting one's behaviour that Jesus spoke of elsewhere (Matthew 7:16-21; John 3:5-6), came to become a defining requirement for membership in Christendom. Still today, many Christians refer to themselves as 'Believers'. However, not all continue the practice of baptism; amongst those who do, details about how and when baptism should occur vary dramatically.

Another passage where different source manuscripts vary is found in Matthew 18:11, *"For the son of man is come to save that which was lost"*. This line does not appear in any manuscripts before the 5th century CE. Consequently, although some older versions of the bible, including the KJV, still contain it, newer versions that have access to earlier manuscripts do not contain this verse. Scholars tend to believe it is likely this verse was copied into later manuscripts from Luke's gospel, not necessarily with the intent of perverting the truth, but because the authors believed the original manuscript inadvertently missed this information.

Although some passages in scriptures may have intentionally been changed to support a given doctrinal perspective, other changes have no doctrinal implications and may simply be an inadvertent consequence of being copied so many times. For example, Romans 8:1 in the KJV reads *"There is therefore now no condemnation to them which are in Christ Jesus, who walk not after the flesh, but after the spirit"*, but more recent translations that draw from earlier manuscripts omit the last part of this verse. Romans 8:1 in the New American Standard Version (NASB2020) simply reads *"Therefore there is now no condemnation at all for those who are in Christ Jesus."* Yet, shortly after, Verse 4 of the same chapter reads *"so that*

---

[29] Williams, Joel F. (1999). *Literary Approaches to the End of Mark's Gospel.* Biblical and Theological Studies Faculty Publications. 69.
[30] Stein, Robert H (2008). *The Ending of Mark. Bulletin for Biblical Research.* v18 (1) pp79–98. https://doi.org/10.2307/26423729
[31] Lombardo, D. J., & Reid, D. (2024). *Did Mark Write the Ending of His Gospel? Examining Mark 16: 9-20.*

the requirement of the law might be fulfilled in us who do not walk according to the flesh but according to the spirit". So, the author of the extension appearing in the KJV is not challenging that there is a distinction between people who walk in the flesh and people who walk in the spirit. The addition of the second half of Verse 1 in newer Greek manuscripts on which the KJV is based in no way alters the message of the chapter. Similarly, other passages, such as Mark 7:16, "If any man has ears to hear, let him hear" found in the KJV, also do not appear in more recent translations that draw on earlier, and possibly more reliable sources.

Armed with more data and new skills, numerous other verses traditionally included in older translations have now been rejected by most scholars as interpolations or copying errors. Although many modern translations of the bible delete some of these probable errors, they are judicious in doing so. Christian bible buyers don't like passages of their bible to be taken away. Publishers must listen to their customers more than scholars if they want to sell their bibles. So, passages like Mark 16:9-20 remain in virtually all bibles, but footnotes are usually included that subtly suggest they don't exist in the earliest manuscripts.

The examples I give from both Old and New Testament sources provide strong evidence that the copied documents used to inform our scriptures have changed from what the original authors wrote. If we have strong evidence of some parts of scriptures changing, it is reasonable to assume some other parts will have changed over time as well. The implication is that we will have to consider other factors in assessing the credibility of any given statement within the scriptures. Let us start by taking a big picture perspective.

NEW TESTAMENT CONTENT

If you consider yourself Christian, have you ever stepped back from the creed and traditions of the denomination you are a member of, to marvel at how little overlap there is between the teachings of Jesus as recorded in the gospels – particularly the synoptic gospels (Matthew, Mark and Luke) – and the teachings of the church since the late 1st century? If you do this, you may be amazed by how much foundational doctrine was introduced by Paul and subsequent leaders within Christendom, rather than by Jesus.

The Christian scriptures known as the New Testament commence with the gospels of Matthew, Mark, Luke, and John, which are accounts of the life of Jesus. These are followed by the 'Acts of the Apostles' (Acts), which gives an account of the early years of the first generation of Jesus' followers. Most of the remainder of the New Testament consists of epistles (letters) from various early church leaders, the bulk of which are traditionally attributed to Paul (formerly

Saul) of Tarsus. I will use the term Pauline doctrines to refer to teachings put forward in Paul's epistles that are not teachings of Jesus recorded in the gospels. I will use the term Johannine doctrines to refer to teachings recorded in John's gospel but none of the synoptic gospels or epistles.

The epistles within the New Testament do not contain much information about the life of Jesus. Rather, they contain opinions, interpretations and advice to Christians, as well as some accounts of the preaching and travel experiences of the epistles' authors. So, although the epistles do not contribute greatly in an evidential sense to our quest for the truth about Jesus, they do contribute to understanding some of the thinking within the early church, as well as some of the issues, challenges, and events that shaped the subsequent evolution of Christendom. It is helpful to take this thinking into account when seeking to understand what we see in the gospels.

Acts is primarily a historical account of the experiences of the apostles, who were the evangelical leaders and teachers of Christianity in the early decades after Jesus' departure. Of particular interest in developing doctrine is that Chapter 2 of Acts describes the coming of the holy spirit on the day of Pentecost in the Jewish calendar (Pesach). In this chapter, the author gives an account of Jesus' disciple (now re-designated 'apostle') Peter explaining to observers of this event that what they were witnessing was the fulfilment of a prophesy by the Jewish prophet Joel. Peter goes on to talk about the miracles Jesus performed, linking things that occurred in Jesus' life to other prophecies. Subsequent chapters in Acts detail numerous miracles performed by the apostles, accompanied by bold preaching on the significance and implications of Jesus' teaching, person, life, and actions.

Acts is believed to have been written by the same author as Luke's gospel. It has a similar writing style and is a natural continuation. It talks about the events that happened immediately following the conclusion of the account in Luke's gospel. Both books are addressed to Theophilus. Unlike the gospels, there are not four accounts of the Acts of the Apostles, although some of the epistles in the New Testament mention some events from it. Given this limited corroboration and that Acts does not give an account of the life of Jesus himself, I will focus more on the four gospels.

The Synoptic Gospels

For maximum credibility, it would be best if the gospels had been written by witnesses of the events they write about and written whilst Jesus was still alive on earth, or at least within a few years of his death. This isn't quite the case.

Scholars have conflicting opinions on when the synoptic gospels were written. Some believe Matthew could have been written as early as 41 CE and that Mark could not have been written until after 70 CE because in Chapter 13 it mentions the destruction of Jerusalem that occurred in that year. However, as I will show, a textual analysis reveals it is more likely Matthew drew on Mark as a source, and Mark 13 can easily be interpreted as a prophesy.

Many scholars believe Mark's gospel was written by John Mark, a travelling companion of Paul and Barnabas (Acts 12:12; Acts 12:25; Acts 13:5; Acts 15:37-39; Colossians 4:10). Also, early church fathers write of Mark being a companion of Peter[32], Peter's disciple and interpreter[33], Peter's scribe[34], and Peter being a contributor to Mark's gospel[35]. Peter himself signs a greeting from Mark (1 Peter 5:13) in a way that suggests Mark was with him and a protégé of his. So, if Mark was acting as Peter's scribe, then it is possible that Mark's gospel is Peter's eyewitness statement about Jesus. Additionally, this would place the date of the gospel before Peter's death, which traditional accounts say occurred between 64 and 68 CE. I therefore find it credible (a) that Mark's gospel was written first and (b) it was written before Peter's death.

Delay in writing about Jesus' life and teachings is not suspicious. It is evident that many of Jesus' followers believed that he would return during their lifetime. However, at the conclusion of John's gospel, we can see that by that time, Jesus' lack of reappearance was concerning some. This may be the reason the gospels were only written years after Jesus' life on earth. If his followers thought he would return in their lifetimes, there would be little need to create a written record of what he said and did. However, after eyewitnesses began dying out, it would have become evident that Jesus may not be returning soon. Concern would have developed that these things should be recorded for future generations. Also, as prophesied by Jesus (Luke 21:20-24), in 70 CE the Romans surrounded and destroyed Jerusalem and thousands of its inhabitants[36]. Many of the written records contained in the city would have been destroyed, so it is unsurprising that contemporary first-hand accounts of the life of Jesus do not exist today, with the possible exception of the gospel of Mark.

Some scholars consider it possible that the author of Matthew's gospel was the Matthew (also possibly known as Levi) within Jesus' inner circle of twelve

---

[32] Expositions of the sayings of the lord; Papias
[33] Adverses Haereses (Against Heresies), Book 3, Chapter 1; Irenaeus
[34] Hypotyposeus, Ecclesiastical History Book 2, Chapter 15; Clement of Alexandria
[35] Prescription Against Heretics; Tertullian
[36] Josephus, Flavius; The Jewish War, Parts 6 & 7

disciples. However, because this gospel appears to draw on other sources, it is more likely a different Matthew.

The author of Luke's gospel is likely to have been a gentile (non-Jewish) physician who was also a travelling companion of Paul (Colossians 4:14; Philemon 1:24). The opening words of Luke's gospel imply his account, and accounts by others, record events that were handed down rather than witnessed by the author. Luke makes it clear that his efforts are the result of research, rather than first-hand observation: *"Since many have undertaken to compile an account of the things accomplished among us, just as they were handed down to us by those who from the beginning were eye witnesses and servants of the word, it seemed fitting to me as well, having investigated everything carefully from the beginning, to write it out for you in an orderly sequence."* (Luke 1:1-3)

By analysing the content of these gospels directly, we observe features that reveal they are not independent witness accounts, but that they draw on each other. There is significant overlap and consistency between them – too much for them to be independent accounts.

Matthew contains 1068 verses, Luke contains 1149 verses, but Mark only contains 676 verses. All but 31 of Mark's verses appear in Matthew and/or Luke as well. 80% of Mark's verses appear in Matthew and 65% of Mark's verses appear in Luke. Approximately 230 verses appear in both Matthew and Luke, but not in Mark.

This overlap is what we would expect to see if Matthew and Luke had drawn on Mark as a source and added other material from one or more other sources. Such other sources may have been oral history or written sources lost to antiquity. Scholars refer to one of the possible missing written sources as Q. Some of the common verses in Matthew and Luke but not in Mark are repeated almost verbatim. This insight supports the notion that they draw on material from a common written source (Q) other than Mark, rather than just an oral history. Whereas Mark deals mainly with the events in Jesus' life, drawing from Q contributes more of Jesus' sayings.

By examining the sequence of events in the synoptic gospels, we observe that when one of Matthew or Luke diverges from the order in Mark, the other gospel does not. This suggests that Matthew and Luke are more likely to have drawn on Mark than the other way around. Matthew and Luke are written in better Greek than Mark too, which is also consistent with their having drawn on and improved on Mark.

Even though Matthew and Luke appear to draw on Mark and at least one other common unidentified source (Q), they do not align on all points, suggesting they each also draw on different sources from each other as well. Areas of difference include the genealogy, birth, infancy, and resurrection of Jesus.

The overlap in content between the three synoptic gospels has a significant implication for assessing their credibility: We should not treat them as three distinct independent accounts, but as three attempts at collating what was known by Jesus' followers at the time they were written. The fact that we still have three such collations suggests their content represents widely held beliefs, rather than just the narrative of a single author. I conclude, therefore, that they are three widely supported variants of one pieced-together narrative about the life and teachings of Jesus.

John's Gospel

John's gospel is very different in both style and content to the synoptic gospels. Significantly, it contains numerous stories and arguments that are not present in the earlier gospels. These differences demonstrate it is not merely a fourth attempt at collating stories circulating across Christendom, but a distinct narrative originating from a different author.

There is no consensus on who this author was[37] [38] [39]. The gospel does not name its author, but states he is *"the disciple whom Jesus loved"* (John 21:20-24). It is traditionally attributed to the John, son of Zebedee, who was one of Jesus' inner circle of 12 disciples, in part because Irenaeus wrote of John as being *"the disciple of the lord who had also leaned upon his breast"*[40]. However, some scholars have questioned this conclusion, suggesting other contenders, such as a later John, James the brother of Jesus[41] or an unknown later author writing pseudo-epigraphically

In Verse 26 of Chapter 19, the author records Jesus speaking about him from the cross: *"When Jesus saw his mother and the disciple whom he loved standing nearby, he said to his mother, 'Woman, behold your son!'"* In the culture of the time, responsibility for looking after a widowed mother rested with the eldest son and would pass in line of succession to the next eldest (in this case James), in

[37] Matkin, J. Michael (2005). *The Complete Idiot's Guide to the Gnostic Gospels.* Penguin
[38] Lindars, Barnabas; Edwards, Ruth; Court, John M. (2000). *The Johannine Literature.* A&C Black
[39] Kelly, Joseph F. (2012). *History and Heresy: How Historical Forces Can Create Doctrinal Conflicts.* Liturgical Press
[40] *Adverses Haereses (Against Heresies).* Book II, Chapter 22. Irenaeus
[41] Roman Catholicism holds that James was not the brother of Jesus

the event of his death. So, the original author of this gospel could have been Jesus' brother James. Of note, John's gospel places this group of Jesus' associates adjacent to the cross (John 19:25) – so close that he is able to speak to them in his dying breaths. However, the synoptic gospels all say the group was watching from "a distance"/"far off" (Matthew 27:55; Mark 15:40; Luke 23:49). If the synoptic gospels are to be believed, the account in John's gospel of Jesus speaking to people in this group would seem unlikely to be true.

Scholarly consensus is that John's gospel was written later than the synoptic gospels, not taking on its final form until between 90 CE and 110 CE. Some scholars have suggested it may have been written by a 'John the Elder' or may be the product of a community[42]. Even if the apostle John or James the brother of Jesus started this gospel, it seems likely to have been completed by someone else later.

By the time John's gospel was finalised, it looks to have taken a different, possibly updated, perspective, making it vastly different from the three earlier gospels. Unlike the synoptic gospels, which provide a record of things Jesus said and did, the author of John's gospel adds considerable personal interpretation of such things. It also records events omitted from the synoptic gospels and addresses points of contention about the divinity of Jesus that were becoming prevalent across Christendom at the time it was finalised[43]. I therefore conclude that John's gospel was likely written for a different purpose from that of the synoptic gospels. Whereas the primary purpose of the synoptic gospels appears to have been to create a record of the life and teachings of Jesus whilst on earth, the contrast in publication dates and content of John's gospel suggests its primary purpose was to support a doctrinal narrative about aspects of Jesus' divinity that was battling with other schools of thought in Christendom at the time this gospel was written.

Of significant note, the synoptic gospels predominantly provide a historical account of Jesus' life and teachings about how we should live, how people should treat each other and how we should approach god the father. Jesus warns people to prepare for the kingdom of God. However, in stark contrast, John's gospel contains fewer historical events and instead consists more of arguments for the divinity of Jesus, including allegorical stories of who Jesus is, such as "*I am the good shepherd*", "*I am the bread of life*" and "*I am the way the truth and the life*" – all absent from the synoptic gospels. The complete absence of parables from John's gospel is another significant difference between it and the

---

[42] Hengle, Eusebius, Balcom, and even Pope Benedict in his book *'Jesus of Nazareth'*
[43] Lieu, J. et al.(1979). *Gnosticism and the Gospel of John*. The Expository Times. v90(8), pp233-237

3 synoptic gospels. The teachings in the parables focus on practical things we should do in this world.

The later publication date and contrast in style, content and purpose do not mean the doctrinal interpretations conveyed through John's gospel are incorrect. However, as a witness statement of Jesus' life and teachings, its reliability falls short of the 3 synoptic gospels. So, when exploring the life and teachings of Jesus, I will make distinctions between the synoptic gospels and John's gospel. Where I cite content from John's gospel that is absent from the synoptic gospels, I will make this clear.

Even with the synoptic gospels, it would be naïve to treat them as totally reliable witness statements. First, no witness statement is ever completely reliable. As any investigator will have experienced, human memory is fallible and the mind can conjure up all sorts of things it thinks its owner saw or heard. Timeliness of a witness account is an important factor in assessing the likely accuracy of that account. Witnesses interviewed immediately after an event tend to give more accurate accounts than those interviewed much later. In the case of the gospels, all were written many years after the events they describe. Also, they were written by followers of Jesus who believed they had a mission to promote his message. Furthermore, after Jesus' death and resurrection, the church developed beliefs beyond what Jesus taught, some of which conflicted with each other. Different schools of thought were emerging.

Were the gospels modified to support particular doctrines?

It is possible that each of the gospels may have been drafted to preserve and convey a historical account of Jesus' life but subsequently underwent some editorial modification to serve the purposes of those who redrafted it. For example, whereas overall Matthew's gospel firmly anchor's Jesus' life and teaching in Jewish tradition, law and prophesy, curiously, what it says right at the end appears markedly different from earlier passages. This juxtaposition creates suspicion that Matthew's gospel may have been extended later by someone other than the gospel's original author. Matthew 28:19 quotes Jesus as saying *"Go, therefore, and teach all the nations, baptising them in the name of the father, and of the son, and of the holy spirit."*

Not only does this verse command teaching peoples beyond just the Jews, its reference to what the church later identified as the Christian 'Trinity godhead' of the 'the father, the son and the holy spirit', seems out of place with all accounts of baptism occurring in Acts. Here the apostles never baptise in the name of 'the father, the son and the holy spirit'; not even just in the name of 'the son'. Rather, they baptise in *"the name of Jesus Christ"*[44]. The identity here is 'Jesus the Messiah and lord', rather than Jesus being 'god the son', which is a very different concept. In fact, although Jesus refers to himself as 'the son of man' and scripture frequently uses the terms 'son of god' and 'sons of god' to refer to Jesus and other heavenly beings, it never uses the term 'god the son'. This title is a later innovation by the church[45] that I will discuss later in Chapter 6.

Although all extant manuscripts containing Matthew 28:19 include in this passage reference to the three persons Trinitarians identify in their godhead, *"some scholars have denied that the trinitarian baptismal formula in the Great Commission was part of the autographical text of Matthew"*[46]. So, this passage should not necessarily be interpreted as suggesting God is a Trinity. Neither should we assume that the baptism referred to means water baptism. The New Testament also refers to 'baptism in the holy spirit' (Mark 1:8) and 'baptism in the name of Jesus' (Acts 19:5), neither of which seem to be associated with water. More generally, the word 'baptism' sometimes refers to going through a cleansing or regeneration process of some kind, such as expressed by the common phrase 'a baptism of fire'.

Also, the notion of baptising in the name of 'the father and the son and the holy spirit' conveys a fundamentally different significance from the baptism of John the Baptist that Jesus himself underwent. That baptism wasn't undertaken in the name of anyone except the individual being baptised, who was making a public declaration of their repentance and a desire to live a righteous life. It is likely to have been the form in its day of the ritual within Judaism known as Tevilah[47]. This is a practice involving full-body immersion under water for ritual purification or conversion.

In contrast, baptism in the name of 'the father, the son and the holy spirit' may signify an act performed by the baptiser acting in line with the purposes of Jesus, who taught about the father and the holy spirit, whom John's gospel tells us Jesus later described as the helper (John 14:16; 15:26; 16:7). Therefore, if the Christians who wrote verse 19 into this chapter of Matthew's gospel intended it to mean water baptism pronounced in the name of a Trinity god, they may

---

[44] Acts 2:38; 8:12-17; 10:48; 19:5
[45] Hick, John (1993). *The Metaphor of God Incarnate: Christology in a Pluralistic Age (2nd ed.)*. Westminster John Knox Press. *ISBN 0664230377*.
[46] NET Bible – Full Notes Edition (2019), Text-critical note p1852
[47] Adler, Yonatan, *On the Origins of Tevilah (Ritual Immersion)*. TheTorak.com. https://www.thetorah.com/article/on-the-origins-of-tevilah-ritual-immersion Accessed 27 July 2025

have been creating and inserting new dogma that had not originated with Jesus, but which had become part of early Christian practice, as evidenced in the Didache (see below).

The expression *"in the name of"* is used numerous times throughout the bible, often to mean to act in a way consistent with the purposes of the one whose name is referred to. For example, in John 14:13, Jesus is quoted as telling his disciple Philip, *"And whatever you ask in my name I will do, so that the father may be glorified in the son."* Here Jesus is signifying that his purpose is to glorify the father and if Philip asks Jesus for things with the purpose of glorifying the father, Jesus will grant him those things. Similarly, 1 John 5:13-14 promises that those who "believe **in the name of** the son of god" that if they *"ask anything **according to his will**, he hears it"*. So, if Matthew 28:19 is genuine, and not a later extension, it may mean something like: *'Go therefore, and make disciples of all people, transforming them in the ways the father showed throughout history, and by doing what I have taught you whilst I have been with you, and with the support of the helper, who will guide and empower you after I have gone.'*

Early Christian historian and Bishop Eusebius of Caesarea (265 – 339 CE), is regarded as one of the most learned Christians of his time. In his position he would have had access to contemporary manuscripts and the library in Caesarea. So, where he quotes Jesus, he will be quoting earlier manuscripts than we have available today. In his major work 'The Proof of the Gospel', he does not record Jesus commanding his disciples to make disciples of all nations in the name of the father, the son and the holy spirit. Rather, he repeatedly refers to Jesus telling his disciples to make disciples in his own name, as the following three examples illustrate:

- *"Hence of course, our lord and saviour, Jesus the son of god, said to his disciples after his resurrection: 'Go and make disciples of all the nations,' and added 'Teaching them to observe all things, whatsoever I have commanded you.'"* (Book I, Ch.3, 6a, p.20)

- *"With one word and voice He said to His disciples: 'Go, and make disciples of all the nations in my name, teaching them to observe all things whatsoever I have commanded you,'"* (Book III, Ch.6, 132a, p.152)

- *"And he bids his own disciples after their rejection, 'Go ye and make disciples of all the nations in my name.'"* (Book IX, Ch.11, 445c, p.175)

I find it interesting that Eusebius more than once quotes Jesus commanding his followers to making disciples in his own name, rather than the name of 'the father, the son and the holy spirit'. If Eusebius was reading from an earlier manuscript of Matthew 28:19 than we still have available, this would suggest Matthew 28:19 in extant manuscripts contains an interpolation, replacing '*my name*' with "*the name of the father, and of the son, and of the holy spirit*".

Reinforcing this idea, in Acts 19:1-7, rather than refer to baptism being performed in the name of the father, the son and the holy spirit, we read of Paul differentiating between the water baptism of John and the baptism of Jesus. The latter involved Paul laying hands on those being baptised and resulted in the holy spirit coming upon them. Paul's act clearly demonstrates that this baptism involving the 'laying on of hands' and the 'holy spirit' is a different baptism from the water baptism ritual. Consistent with the writings of Eusebius, in Acts 19:5, Paul baptises people in the name of Jesus, not the father and the holy spirit as well.

Given the history of water baptism within Christianity, it is significant that the meaning and purpose of baptism underwent a change from the time of John the Baptist to its subsequent practice as a sacrament within Christendom. Originally, a person chose to undergo water baptism by emersion in flowing water as a publicly recognised symbolic purification act, announcing their decision to repent of their past sinful life and to live a righteous life instead. John the Baptist taught that the purpose of such repentance is for forgiveness of sins (Luke 3:3). Jesus himself, when challenged by John the Baptist about his need to be baptised, responded that it was right for him to be baptised "*to fulfil all righteousness*", suggesting Jesus' endorsement of the practice of making a public declaration of repentance for forgiveness of sins. Then in Acts we read of two distinct baptisms – the water baptism of John and the baptism in the holy spirit following 'laying on of hands' (Acts 8:17; 11:16; 19:4-6). However, as Christendom began to develop its own ritual practices, water baptism seems to have become part of the rite of passage for a new believer joining the Christian movement. In later centuries, the forms and requirements relating to water baptism continued to evolve and diverge between different branches, some creating rules for who could baptise a person, some permitting sprinkling with water rather than emersion, and some performing water baptism on infants too young to make their own choice.

One strongly corroborated account of water baptism across all three synoptic gospels is the baptism of Jesus by John the Baptist. These accounts read as follows:

- Matt 3:16-17 "*As soon as Jesus was baptised, he went up out of the water. At that moment heaven opened, and he saw the spirit of god descending like a dove and alighting on him. And a voice from heaven said, 'This is my son, whom I love; with him I am well pleased.'*"

55

- Mark 1:9-11: *"In those days Jesus came from Nazareth of Galilee and was baptised by John in the Jordan. And when he came up out of the water, immediately he saw the heavens being torn open and the spirit descending on him like a dove. And a voice came from heaven, 'You are my beloved son, with you I am well pleased.'"*

- Luke 3:21: *"Now when all the people were baptised, Jesus was also baptised, and while he was praying, heaven was opened, and the holy spirit descended on him in bodily form like a dove, and a voice came out of heaven, 'You are my beloved son, in you I am well pleased.'"*

On the surface, because these three accounts are extremely similar, this seems like strong corroboration. However, on closer consideration, the similarities are too close for independent witness statements, particularly if written years after the event. This extreme match is more consistent with what we would expect to see when witnesses collude, or their statements are subsequently modified by a common editor. As with Matthew 18:11, discussed earlier, some copying of this story from one of these gospels into the others almost certainly occurred.

The baptism of Jesus is an instance where John's gospel may help shed some light because it was likely written later and does not appear to draw on the same sources as the synoptic gospels. Most of the first chapter of John's gospel is taken up with a string of verses attesting to the divinity of Jesus. Much of this string is contained in a speech by John the Baptist to priests and Levites from Jerusalem sent to question him. This speech includes the following statements in verses 32-34: *"I saw the spirit descending from heaven like a dove, and it remained upon him. I did not recognise him, but he who sent me to baptise in water said to me 'The one upon whom you see the spirit descending and remaining on him, the same is he who baptises with the holy ghost'. And I saw, and bear record that this is the son of god."*

So, by the time John's gospel was finalised, the story had changed but retained the element of someone seeing a dove or something like a dove descending on Jesus. In John's account, rather than a voice from heaven saying that Jesus is his son in whom he is pleased, it is John the Baptist spotting the significance of a dove descending and claiming he was forewarned that when he saw such a sign this would indicate the person it landed on is the one who baptises in the holy spirit. In any event, this account contradicts the other accounts in detail, if not its overall message, and we don't know what really happened: Did a voice come from heaven at the point in time when Jesus rose up out of the water, or did John the Baptist recognise the sign of a spirit or a dove landing on Jesus as being something God had earlier revealed to him would happen? Both can't be true; at least one must contain an error.

It seems likely that, between the time Jesus walked the earth and the time John's gospel was finalised, the Christian movement had undergone significant change, with less emphasis on Jesus' teachings, and more on his divinity and on miraculous signs and wonders. One possible explanation for this is the coming of the holy spirit to Jesus' disciples, which is described in Acts 2 and which Jesus foretold (John 14:16-17; John 16:7; Luke 24:49).

Considering all this evidence together on the origin of 'baptism', I form two conclusions:

1. There are two distinct types of baptism in the New Testament:

    a. water baptism, which is the ritual baptism of repentance and purification, known in Judaism as Tevilah, and described in the Gospels and Acts as the baptism of John, and

    b. the baptism of the holy spirit which is the baptism of or in the name of Jesus that does not involve water but may involve the baptiser laying his hands on the person being baptised (Mark 1:8; Acts 19:2-6; 8:17).

2. The early church evolved the concept of baptism into a rite of passage of entry into membership of the church – eventually conflating the two distinct types of baptism taught in the Gospels and Acts into the Sacrament of Baptism (which I will discuss in Chapter 3).

This balance of evidence suggests that Jesus did not command his disciples to perform the water baptism ritual on people on behalf of a Trinity godhead consisting of 'the father, the son and the holy spirit'. However, early church history does reveal that changes in the ideas and practices associated with the term 'baptism' and beliefs about the identities of god the father, Jesus, and the holy spirit, occurred over the decades and indeed centuries after Jesus' time on earth. Therefore, as with 1 John 5:7 discussed above, I conclude that Matthew 28:19 is another plank in the basis for the doctrine of the Trinity that should be removed.

I find it intriguing that in the last chapter of all four gospels that have no sequel (as Luke's has), they switch what they were talking about and seem to round off their narrative with statements that tidy up various doctrinal points. Similarly, as discussed earlier, some scholars identify possible interpolations at the end of Luke's gospel that have the same effect. In Matthew the switch includes the great commission and the Trinity (possibly – if you believe the most common interpretation); in Mark (or at least the added portion) it is the great commission and foretelling miraculous signs and wonders; in Luke (if you believe Westcott and Hort's "*Western interpolations*" argument) it includes Jesus' ascension to heaven and being worshipped by his followers; in John it is concern about Christ not having returned.

I am left with the impression that the gospels contain accounts of many things Jesus said and did, but the final versions we have today are likely to have evolved from the original accounts through editing. Some of these edits were probably with good intentions to add in information a copyist thought the original author omitted, and some to reinforce doctrinal points concerning the church at the time they were written, some decades after Jesus' crucifixion.

Even if we accept the accuracy of the gospels beyond their obvious limitations, different interpretations on their meaning are possible. For example, in Matthew 18:19 we read *"If two or three of you agree on earth about anything that they may ask, it shall be done for them by my father who is in heaven"*. Many modern Christians believe such promises apply to them; however, this is evidently untrue. For example, Christians often pray together for healing of someone who is sick and often that person does not get healed. Consequently, many denominations believe that the age of miracles passed with the apostles (a belief known as Cessationism). Within the Eastern Orthodox church, there is a belief that such promises were given to Jesus' inner group of disciples at the time and pass on only to the unbroken succession of leaders (apostles or bishops) that today include their bishops but no other Christians. I have heard an argument in the Eastern Orthodox church that interprets the verse preceding Matthew 18:19 as justification for belief in the succession of authority to modern day Eastern Orthodox bishops, allowing them to extend canon: *"Truly I say to you, whatsoever you shall bind on earth shall have been bound in heaven; and whatever you shall loose on earth shall be loosed in heaven"* (Matthew 18:18).

Paul's Epistles

Most of the epistles in the New Testament have traditionally been attributed to Paul[48][49] (formerly Saul of Tarsus). Rather than document the life and teachings of Jesus, Paul's epistles provide encouragement, rebuke and teachings of his

---

[48] Strong consensus exists amongst scholars that Paul authored: Romans, 1&2 Corinthians, Galatians, 1 Thessalonians, Philippians and Philemon, Some scholars believe someone pretending to be Paul authored: 1&2 Timothy and Titus. Scholars are divided on whether Paul authored: Colossians, 2 Thessalonians and Ephesians. Also, although Paul may have written Hebrews, most scholars now think this unlikely.
[49] Savoy, Jacques (2019), *Authorship of Pauline epistles revisited,* Journal of the Association for Information Science and Technology. v70 pp1089-1097

own, which he wrote to different individuals and churches throughout the region that Christianity had spread to in his lifetime.

Doctrinal emphases in Paul's epistles include:

- **Departure from Judaism** by including gentiles (non-Jews) into God's covenant without requiring adherence to some of the Jewish laws (in particular, circumcision), but retention of others (such as abstaining from eating food offered to idols or meat from animals that were strangled) (Acts 15).

- **Salvation through faith and grace**. This is a departure from Judaism's requirement to adhere to its laws, substituting a belief that a person is saved from hell (and will therefore enter God's kingdom) by faith in Jesus alone who redeemed us by dying for us. As a result, we now need only rely on the grace of God's forgiveness, rather than sacrifices, human effort or good works (Ephesians 2:8).

- **The church is the body of Christ.** In his epistles Paul frequently encourages unity between different believers, particularly between Jewish and Gentile believers. He uses the metaphor of each person being a different part of the same body, all of whom have their particular role based on the "gifts" God has given them (1 Corinthians 12:12-27).

- **The importance of the relationship of the Jesus to God and to Christians**. Many scholars hold that Paul believed Jesus was God. However, part of their justification for this belief is that Paul writes of Jesus possessing attributes and power associated with God. Paul frequently writes of Jesus as distinct from God; not just distinct from the father (Philippians 2:6-11; 1 Corinthians 8:6; Romans 1:7). He does, however, write of God delegating authority and lordship to Jesus over all the earth (Ephesians 1:22), and he writes of Jesus as being the image of the invisible God (Colossians 1:15), thereby indicating we can get an understanding of what God is like from what we see in Jesus.

- **The importance of the entities that the church would later call the Trinity.** Although Paul does not articulate the doctrine of the Trinity as it was subsequently defined by the church, his epistles talk of the father, Christ and the holy spirit, attributing different roles to them, but sometimes blurring distinctions. In particular, he talks a lot about the role of the holy spirit, who had not appeared in an enduring way until after Jesus ascended to heaven following his resurrection. Luke's gospel records instances of the holy spirit 'coming upon' or 'filling' someone (John the Baptist in Luke 1:15; Elizabeth his mother in Luke 1:41; Zacharias his father in Luke 1:67; Simeon in Luke 2:25), but these seem to be transient events rather than an enduring infilling.

- **Predestination.** Paul's epistles talk of God having preselected who will be saved and who will not, regardless of an individual's choices or actions (Ephesians 1:4; Romans 8 & 9). Two passages in John's gospel (6:37; 10:26-30) could also be interpreted as supporting this doctrine, but the synoptic gospels do not provide similar evidence.

In numerous passages, Paul writes of God being distinct from Christ. In his letter to the Philippians, Paul elaborates on this idea, saying that the reason God exalted Christ with a name above every other name is because of his obedience to God, and especially his willingness to be crucified (Philippians 2:8-9). Although Jesus may be lord over those on earth and even in heaven, this is all to the glory of God (Philippians 2:10-11). So, Paul seems to contradict the intent of the author of John's gospel, which seems to be to deify Jesus.

One challenge faced by translators is that the earliest manuscripts did not contain punctuation, such as the commas we see in the English translations. Rather, the words are all capitalised and flow together. As a result, precise translation can be challenging. For example, some English language translations presume Paul writes in Romans 9:5 that Jesus is God:

- *"To them {the Jews} belong the patriarchs, and from their race, according to the flesh, is the Christ,* **who is God over all***, blessed forever. Amen."* (ESV)

- *"To them belong the patriarchs, and from them, by human descent, came the Christ,* **who is God over all***, blessed forever! Amen."* (NET)

However, *"who is God over all"* is a doubtful translation of the original Greek language which alters the case of nouns depending on their role in the sentence. If Paul had written that Jesus is God, he could have used the word θεόν (accusative case) for God, which indicates God is the object in the sentence. However, the word Paul actually uses for God in this verse is θεός (nominative case), which is used when the noun performs the role of a subject in a sentence. In other words, God is the actor doing some action. In this case, the action is extending blessing upon, or speaking well of someone or something, as indicated by the verb that immediately follows it (εὐλογητὸς – blessed). Accordingly, other translations align with this interpretation:

- *"Whose are the fathers, and of whom as concerning the flesh Christ came. Who is over all, **God blessed for ever**. Amen."* KJV

- *"whose are the fathers, and from whom is the Christ according to the flesh, who is over all, **God blessed forever**. Amen"* (NASB)

- *"To them belong the patriarchs, and from them, according to his natural descent, [came] the Christ (the Messiah, the Anointed), He who is exalted [and] supreme over all, **God blessed forever**. Amen."* (AMP)

Some scholars argue that Paul's epistles introduce doctrines that differ so markedly from what Jesus taught that he hijacked the interpretation of Judaism that Jesus gave with a new religion of his own. Others argue that he was merely adding further interpretation relevant in the time the young church was getting established. I observe that Paul's epistles concentrate more on Christology[50] than on the life and teachings of Jesus the man, who walked and talked around Galilee and the wider Judea and Samaria.

Both Acts and Paul's epistles include evidence that Paul had disagreements with other apostles, including Peter, who was one of Jesus' inner-circle of disciples in the gospels (Galatians 2:11-14; Acts 15:36-41). Peter himself has a less critical response in his epistles, simply saying that some of the things Paul teaches are hard to understand (2 Peter 3:15-16). Also, in Paul's epistles, he appears to express conflicting sentiments: In Galatians he rebukes followers of Jesus who were beginning to doubt some of the things Paul said, and he curses anyone who teaches something different from him, even if it is an angel from heaven (Galatians 1:6-9). However, in his letter to the Philippians he says he doesn't mind differences in motive so long as they preach Christ (Philippians 1:15-18).

Paul also appears to contradict John's gospel. He writes in some places that Christ lives in his followers, and elsewhere that the holy spirit lives in Christ's followers. However, in John 16:7 we read Jesus telling his disciples *"Nevertheless, I tell you the truth: it is better for that I go away, for if I do not, the Helper will not come to you. But if I go, I will send him to you."* In John 14:26, John quotes Jesus as clarifying that the Helper is the holy spirit. So, John 16:7 implies that Christ cannot live in us if the holy spirit does too because Jesus has gone away, thereby enabling the holy spirit to come. So, John and Paul cannot both be right; it seems that at least one must be wrong.

---

[50] *"Christology is the branch of Christian theology that focuses on the study of the person, nature, and work of Jesus Christ. It seeks to understand who Jesus is, both in His divinity and humanity, and His role in the salvation of humankind."* https://biblehub.com/topical/c/christology.htm Accessed 30 August 2025

Whereas many Christians may find Paul's epistles helpful, for the purpose of our quest, it is difficult to assign them much weight evidentially because they stand alone in many of their teachings and primarily offer opinions and advice, rather than accounts of events. Also, Paul's disagreements with other Christians, his lack of repetition of Jesus' teachings, and his significant shift in emphasis from Jesus' main messages all contribute to reducing their evidential credibility. That said, there is no doubt Paul's epistles strongly influenced church canon – arguably more so than the teachings of Jesus as recorded in the synoptic gospels. Much of the church over subsequent centuries moved from following Jesus' teachings to worshiping Jesus and his mother.

> *(Note: I am aware that Roman Catholics would argue they only 'revere' his mother. However, this reverence is so high that it appears to others almost indistinguishable from divinity and worship. Roman Catholic dogma puts Mary on a pedestal above all other people, even John the Baptist, who Jesus said was greater than all other humans (Matthew 11:11; Luke 7:28). For example, in the middle ages, after mistranslating Luke 1:28, the church decided Mary was sinless; in the 19th century they added the doctrine of 'The Immaculate Conception' to their dogma, meaning God gave her an exemption from being subject to 'original sin', which Augustine of Hippo in the 4th century CE described as the sinful nature inherited from Adam. Then in 1950 CE, Pope Pius XII added 'The Assumption of Mary' to Roman Catholic dogma, claiming Mary never died, but was raised alive into heaven in the same way that Luke records this happening to Jesus[51].*

> *I am making this point about the church apparently worshiping Jesus and his mother, because, as I will show, that is certainly what Muhammad thought, and **this mistaken belief played a significant part in the birth of Islam**.)*

The Catholic (or general) Epistles

Two epistles attributed to the apostle Peter were subsequently included in the New Testament. Some scholars have wondered whether the second of these was written by a different author pretending to be Peter after his death. This doubt is due primarily to its style being less restrained, containing numerous rare words not included in Peter's first epistle. Other scholars argue that the differences may be due to Peter employing a scribe to assist with his first epistle;

---

[51] As discussed Earlier, scholars Westcott and Hort argue that the verse stating Jesus ascended into heaven (Luke 24:50) is an interpolation that may not have been part of Luke's original autograph.

also, the two epistles may have been written years apart. Although not contradicting Paul's epistles, rather than introduce new doctrine, as Paul's epistles and John's gospel do, both of Peter's epistles focus more on reinforcing Jesus' teachings.

Similarly, James' epistle, which many scholars believe was written before those of Paul and well before John's gospel, also reflects Jesus' teachings and contains no Pauline or Johannine doctrines. Its overarching purpose is to encourage believers to persevere in the face of trials and temptations. Many scholars believe that the author of this letter may have been James the brother of Jesus, who became a leader in the early church and Bishop of Jerusalem.

Although the epistles of Peter and James are not witness statements of Jesus' life and teachings, both authors are likely to have lived with and known Jesus closely. The personal relationships the authors had with Jesus and the alignment of their epistles with his teachings lend these epistles credibility, possibly even greater credibility than any of the gospels, which show more signs of having been edited and which may not have been first-hand accounts.

There are also three short epistles in the New Testament by a John. Although scholars are not certain this John is the same author as that of John's gospel, the writing style and themes are similar, suggesting it may be. The predominant themes running throughout John's three epistles are that we should love one another and that what is good comes from God. Like Paul, John's epistle makes a distinction between Jesus and God, claiming Jesus is our *"advocate with the father"* (1 John 2:1) thereby suggesting the father is the real authority, and that *"No one has ever seen God"* (1 John 4:12).

The epistle of Jude is believed to have been written by another brother of Jesus and James (another son of Mary, but not of God). His short letter warns about false teachers within the church. This caution is a recurring theme throughout New Testament epistles, many of which warn their readers to watch out for false teachers who the authors claim are finding their way into the church and teaching false messages.

Conflicts in teaching have plagued Christendom throughout its life, driving councils of bishops to publish positions on myriad doctrinal questions. Selecting what to include in a religion's canon is one mechanism to help stabilise its doctrines. Although the gospels, Acts and Paul's epistles had informally become core canon by 200 CE, the final list of 27 books in the New Testament was not formally adopted until the Councils of Hippo and Carthage nearly 200 years later. As discussed in Chapter 1, subsequent councils, bishops and popes continued to rule on points of doctrine, often causing schisms as a result when the beliefs of some followers were rejected by those in authority.

Revelation

The final book in the New Testament, Revelation, is not considered an epistle. It records a vision believed to have been received by John the apostle, describing in colourful terms prophetic images of what will happen at the end of the world. The author would have had no understanding of modern technology. So, if he did see a vison of the end times, it is understandable that he would have had to describe what he saw in imagery based on things that existed in his time. As a result, Revelation is very colourful and cryptic. What it means has been the subject of much speculation by scholars.[52]

The Didache

The Didache is an early Christian writing that was not included in the New Testament, but which is recognised by scholars as an important historical document, providing insight into early Christian beliefs and practices. The Didache most likely dates from the late 1st century CE and is also known as '*The Lord's teaching through the twelve apostles to the nations (or Gentiles)*'. I mention it because it is the earliest extant example of church orders and the earliest extant written description of Christian sacraments, including Water Baptism and Eucharist. So, it gives useful insight into how Christian beliefs and practices evolved over time. I will draw on insights from the Didache when I discuss these beliefs and practices in subsequent chapters.

The Apocrypha or Deuterocanonical books

The Apocrypha is a term coined by the 16th century CE Protestant Reformation. It refers to various Jewish religious writings excluded from Jewish canon but preserved by Christendom. These were written between the end of the Old Testament and the start of the New Testament. The term 'Apocrypha' means "*Writings or statements of dubious authenticity*" (Merriam-Webster dictionary).

Different denominations vary in the status they attribute to books of the Apocrypha. Most Protestants are cautious of them, concerned that some writings in the Apocrypha conflict with teaching elsewhere in the bible, such as whether faith in Christ and his sacrifice is adequate to atone for sin. Parts of

---

[52] To get a flavour for some of the major schools of interpretation of Revelation, you can search the following terms in the same search string as the word 'Revelation': Preterism (both partial and full); Historicism; Futurism; Idealism; Premillennialism (both classical and pretribulational); Postmillennialism; Amillennialism.

the Apocrypha appear instead to support practices of praying for the dead and almsgiving for the atonement of sins.

Some of the older and more traditional Protestant denominations, such as Lutherans and Anglicans, include much of the Apocrypha in their bibles but attribute them less status than the rest of the bible and do not use them as the basis for doctrine. Eastern Orthodox churches also include the Apocrypha, but with varying degrees of authority.

Although the books of the Apocrypha were not originally part of church canon, the Council of Trent in 1546-1563 adopted them into Roman Catholic canon. The Roman Catholic church convened the Council of Trent in response to the threat of the rapid rise of Protestantism, which was gaining favour with European political rulers. By this time, Protestantism had rejected the Apocrypha. So, soon after the Council of Trent, Roman Catholic theologian, Sixtus of Siena, coined the term Deuterocanonical, which means 'secondary canon'. This reflects a theme running through the various declarations made by the Council of Trent to double-down on doctrines rejected by Protestantism and to differentiate Roman Catholicism from this new movement that sought to be true to what the bible teaches, dispensing with innovations subsequently introduced by the church. So, it is unsurprising that the books of the Apocrypha, which had been preserved by Christendom but not Judaism, were elevated at this time in history to Roman Catholic church canon.

Possible contradictions between teachings of the Apocrypha and other books of the bible pose less of a threat to Roman Catholicism than they do to Protestantism. This is because Roman Catholicism allows its leaders greater latitude in forming dogma in comparison with other denominations which give greater emphasis to what the bible teaches.

Denominations that include books from the Apocrypha in their bibles refer to them using Sixtus' term, 'Deuterocanonical'. Various early 'church fathers' make reference to them and clearly considered them 'recommended reading', if not canon.

2.4 ISLAMIC SCRIPTURES

Islam holds that the Qur'an was sent down from heaven to Muhammad in a piece-meal fashion over many years, recited to Muhammad by the angel Gabriel from a permanent inscription on a tablet in heaven next to God and that God's words cannot be changed (Surah 10:64; 6:34). This process began after

Muhammad reached 40 years of age and continued until the year of his death 22 years later in 632 CE. Muhammad was supposedly illiterate, so he did not write these revelations down, but instead conveyed them verbally to his followers.

Sunni Muslims believe that in 652 CE, the 3rd Sunni Caliph, Uthman, aware of existence of different versions of the Qur'an, decided that Abu Bakr's copy was to be the only version. The story goes that, until they were collated into the Qur'an, its various parts had existed in the memories of Muhammad's followers and in inscriptions on broad palm branches, the bleached scapulae of large animals and isolated parchment pieces. Supposedly, Uthman ordered a standardised version to be published, copies distributed, and all other versions to be burned. Contemporary corroborative evidence of this story is lacking. Also, despite supposedly being distributed to various Muslim provinces, no evidence exists of any mention of the Qur'an until the early 8th century CE. It would therefore be prudent to treat this account as a legend rather than a historical fact.[53]

Shi'ite Muslims hold that it was Mohammad himself who gathered and compiled the version of the Qur'an we have today. I find this Shi'ite belief even less credible. It is hard to imagine an author compiling the surahs in the order we find them. There is no 'flow' linking them; they are not sequenced by connected logical narrative or chronological order; neither are they grouped by topic. This structure and lack of flow of the Qur'an is more consistent with it being a collation of piece-meal passages from the memories of different people and various inscriptions. Whatever order the surahs had been placed in, there would still be no natural sequence or flow between them because the Qur'an is obviously a collection of different 'revelations' rather than a single coherent narrative. It seems more credible that a Muslim scribe, wanting to be careful to avoid presuming what his holy prophet would have wanted, decided to apply a simple principle of ordering surahs based on their size.

The Qur'an itself states it is the perfect word of God, sent down from heaven to Muhammad; no one can change it (Surah 6:115); it is protected by God (Surah 15:9). It is also supposedly complete, requiring no further revelation, and in fact no more revelation is permitted. Many Muslims hold that no variation of the Qur'an exists due to Allah's miraculous preservation of the original in

[53] Whelan, Esther (1998). *Forgotten Witness: Evidence for the codification of the Qur'an.* Journal of the American Oriental Society. v118, pp1-14
Shoemaker, S.J. (2022). *The traditional Narrative of the Qur'an's Origins: A Scholarly Sunnism.* In Creating the Qur'an: A Historical-Critical Study. 1st ed. University of California Press. pp17-42. ISBN 978–0–520–00000–0

perfect form. However, variants in the Qur'an do actually exist across the earliest manuscripts and codices. Some Muslim scholars, such as the influential 21st century scholar and jurist, Mufti Ebrahim Desai, acknowledged the evidence of these many variants, but claimed they were abrogated during Muhammad's lifetime. One of the most respected Hadiths (Sahih al-Bukhari, Volume 6) seeks to legitimise the existence of variations by stating that the Qur'an was revealed to be recited in seven different ways, so you can recite it in whichever way is easiest for you. However, despite the preponderance of evidence that the differences were material, some Muslim scholars hold that this statement simply refers merely to variations in Arabic dialect.

None of the six earliest remaining manuscripts of the Qur'an are complete or can be shown to be one of the original manuscripts produced under Uthman's reign. The 8th century CE Topkapi manuscript contains approximately 99 percent of the Qur'an, but the other five manuscripts only contain smaller portions. The earliest manuscript, (the Sana'a fragments) is thought to date from 50 to 70 years after Uthman's original copies. This manuscript is a parchment document that has been rubbed out and written over. Multispectral imaging technology has been used on this parchment, revealing an earlier and noticeably different version of the Qur'an that had been written over.[54] The implication of this finding is obvious, as Dr Mateen Elass concludes in Chapter 3 of his book Fairy-tale Islam, "*This indicates the Qur'an was not, as Islamic doctrine asserts, a text sent down from heaven complete and unaltered, recited by Muhammad and copied down and memorized verbatim by followers and scribes, but rather underwent a period of editing and change until a final standardized form was later imposed by Islamic leadership*".

I encouraged you in Chapter 1 to avoid blindly believing what I say, and instead to think about it and check the relevant sources. You should also be cautious when reading translations of sources. As explained by Dr Robert Spencer in his introduction to his English translation of the Qur'an[55], readers of English translations of the Qur'an face a challenge when reading translations by Muslim apologists who intentionally obscure the meaning of passages of the Qur'an, "*particularly its passages that are most problematic for non-Muslim readers: the exhortations to jihad warfare, the Sharia provisions that call for the denial of various rights to women, and the like*". Therefore, it is important to read translations by non-Muslim scholars of the Qur'an, and to investigate the reliability of different translations.

Such advice is particularly important for Muslims reading this book who genuinely wish to discover the truth. I frequently observe on Muslim chat

---

[54] https://bible-Qur'an.com/sana-Qur'an/ Accessed 24 February 2025;
https://www.historyofinformation.com/detail.php?id=180 Accessed 4 May 2025
[55] Spencer, Robert (2021). *The Critical Qur'an*. Post Hill Press, NY

forums, individuals who have come across evidence or arguments that run counter to the standard narrative they have been taught since childhood. When these individuals ask questions such as those raised in this book, by far the most common response is that such-and-such Muslim scholar has debunked the basis for the question, and this answer is usually accepted. Verifiable evidence and sound counter arguments are not usually given. It seems that the individuals using these forums tend to have been conditioned to accept the narrative of the recognised Muslim scholar, rather than trained to seek and analyse evidence for themselves that might challenge the tenets of Islam.

So, how should we assess the credibility of the Qur'an? Fortunately, the Qur'an itself gives us one possible test: Surah 4:82 reads "*Will they not ponder the Qur'an? If it had been from anyone other than Allah, they would have found much discrepancy in it*". This verse implies that it contains no discrepancies. So, let us use the Qur'an's own test to determine if it is likely to be from someone other than Allah.

INTERNAL CONSISTENCY OF THE QUR'AN

One consideration in assessing the credibility of a source is its internal consistency. Numerous passages in the Qur'an appear to show internal inconsistencies. For example, consider the following:

- Surah 19:67 says that man was created out of nothing, but Surah 15:26 says man is created from clay.

- Surah 6:12b says, "*Those who ruin their own souls will not believe*", implying individuals are accountable for their beliefs, however Surah 10:100 says that belief is determined solely by God's will.

- In Surah 2:256 we read, "*There is no compulsion in religion.*" However, Surah 9:5 instructs Muslims to kill others who worship idols. Surah 8:39 instructs Muslims to fight non-believers until they convert to Islam because "*Religion is only for Allah*". Surah 9:29 instruct Muslims to "*Fight against those who do not believe in Allah or the last day, and do not forbid what Allah and his messenger have forbidden, and do not follow the religion of truth, even if they are among the people of the book, until they pay the jizya with willing submission and feel themselves subdued.*"

- In Surah 6:14, 6:161-164 and 39:11-12, Muhammad appears to claim to be the first to become a Muslim. However, the Qur'an repeatedly talks about Abraham and Jesus also being Muslims, both of whom lived and died prior to Muhammad's birth.

The Qur'an contradicting itself in many places is an obvious weakness. This flaw is unsurprising, because the Qur'an is not just one book written at one point in time, but rather, numerous 'revelations' supposedly received by Muhammad across many years.

Although the Qur'an does not present surahs in chronological order, Scholars have formed a rough consensus about their chronological order. This is fortunate and necessary to navigate the Qur'an's internal contradictions because, for each contradiction, Muslims apply Islam's rule of abrogation, where the most recent revelation trumps the earlier revelation. To non-Muslim scholars, the 'abrogation' mechanism is an obvious weakness in Islam because it shows that either God changed his mind or makes mistakes (Surah 2:106; 16:101), which are things that Muslims don't believe are possible. Various arguments have been made by Muslim scholars to challenge such conclusions. All such arguments I have read contain flaws or weaknesses. These arguments therefore lack credibility to non-Muslim scholars. Perhaps the most eloquent of these arguments is as follows:

"The truth is that abrogation is further evidence of the divine origin of the Qur'an because it has delivered appropriate rules to be applied in different situations, reflecting the Wisdom of the Creator who intended Islam to be applicable to all times, places, and people. If the text had a rigid set of rules, it would have been too inflexible for modern people, let alone the early Muslims, to follow its guidance in their lives. Abrogation occurs by the Will and Wisdom of Allah, Who knows what teachings people need in the precise moment that they need it. It can occur between verses of different divine books or within the same divine book."[56]

However, this argument has numerous weaknesses. It is an overly glib response because some commands are clearly not contextual but directly oppose others. Also, why would an all-knowing God make his scriptures so confusing by revealing on one occasion a command that seems clear at the time, then later issue a different one that appears to contradict the first, requiring scholars to argue that the latter applies to a different, more nuanced, context when the verses themselves do not make this clear but rather, appear to contradict each other?

For many, this weakness in Islam's fragile 'house of cards' is sufficient to bring the whole house crashing down. So, one might ask how such a weak belief system can have survived so long? At least two fundamental attributes of Islam can explain this – intolerance and indoctrination. Islam is particularly intolerant of any criticism of the Qur'an or its source, Muhammad, and Islam has a history

---

[56] Published by the Yaqeen Institute's website on 27 December 2023 and attributed to an anonymous author

of violent suppression of dissent. Also, Islam requires submission to a regime of ritualistic indoctrination, partly through mandatory recitation of standard prayers reaffirming core beliefs that must be repeated at least five times per day. Indoctrination starts in early childhood. The lives of followers are guided by religious teachers called 'Imams', whose role has similarities with the political commissars of Communism. Imams are charged with keeping the masses on the straight and narrow path. Freedom is seen as evil; submission and fear of straying from the permitted path are seen as right. People are taught to believe what Imams say and to fear challenging them. Shia Islam, in particular, extrapolates Surah 2:124 to claim that its Imams are divinely appointed leaders and infallible. They are seen as spiritual successors to Muhammad, much as Roman Catholics see their popes as successors to Jesus.

AUTHORSHIP AND STYLISTIC INSIGHTS

I find it revealing that the Qur'an is not written in pure Arabic. 275 foreign words (*Aramaic, Coptic, Ethiopic, Greek, Hebrew, Nabatean, Persian, Sanskrit and Syriac*) occur repeatedly throughout the book. The integration of languages in use in the region at that point in history seems inconsistent with the claim that the Qur'an existed in heaven prior to the rise of the civilisations in which these languages developed. In his book, Fairytale Islam, Dr Mateen Elass explains "*The natural explanation is that Muhammad, as a man of his times, heard and learned words from other cultures, or utilized words that had come into contemporary Arabic from surrounding language groups and incorporated them into his message. Yet if this is the case, then the message of the Qur'an is not timeless, pure Arabic revealed by Allah, but the collection of human thoughts constructed from the building blocks of religious thinking that prevailed in the Arabian Peninsula during the seventh century AD.*" Supporting this idea, the Qur'an expresses many of the cultural prejudices of the time and place it was written, such as the misogynistic belief that the testimony of one man is equal to that of two women (Surah 2:282).

But was it Muhammad who wrote the Qur'an? Some of the Qur'an is written in the person of someone other than Allah talking to Allah. For example, Surah 1:2 reads "*Praise be to Allah, the Lord of the Worlds*". Then in verse 5 we read "*You do we worship; you do we ask for help*". The Qur'an is supposedly Allah speaking, but God would not be speaking of himself in this way. Clearly, the real author of the Qur'an is a human. Who have we received the Qur'an from? – Supposedly Muhammad, so he must be our initial suspect.

I have heard arguments from non-Muslim polemicists claiming that Muhammad is a fictional character, constructed prior to the reign of Uthman to help unite Arab peoples around a unifying religion. However, whereas I acknowledge we cannot be certain of the existence of Muhammad, I find it more credible that he did exist and that he was the original author of the surahs. This is because of the way the Qur'an constantly praises and affirms Muhammad, seeking to reinforce his legitimacy as the only person who can speak for God. He had the most to gain from his 'revelations' being accepted. If Muhammad was invented, the authors of the Qur'an would not have included such verses that undermine its credibility.

Although Muhammad may have 'revealed' the surahs, their disconnected content, coupled with the evidence suggesting the Qur'an was compiled decades after Muhammad's death, support the assertion that someone other than Muhammad collated them.

WHAT THE QUR'AN SAYS ABOUT THE TORAH AND THE CHRISTIAN GOSPEL

Because the Jewish and Christian scriptures contradict numerous statements in the Qur'an, many Muslims understandably believe that these scriptures must have been corrupted, and that only the Qur'an can be relied upon. So, let us examine what the Qur'an says about Jewish (Torah) and Christian (Gospel) scriptures.

Surah 3:3 says, "*He* [Allah] *has revealed to you* [Muhammad] *the book with the truth, confirming what was before it, even as he revealed the Torah and the Gospel.*" Respected 14th century CE Muslim scholar, Ibn Kathir, explains that "*these books* [the Torah and the Gospel] *testify to the truth of the Qur'an, and the Qur'an also testifies to the truth these books contained, including the news and glad tidings of Muhammad's prophethood and the revelation of the Glorious Qur'an.*"[57]

The Qur'an makes other statements affirming the Torah and the Gospel, indicating that Jews and Christians should follow what had been revealed in them. For example, referring to the Jews and Christians, the Qur'an in Surah 5:66 says, "*If they had observed the Torah and the Gospel and what was revealed to them from their Lord, they would surely have been nourished from above and from beneath their feet.*" Then in Surah 5:68, "*Say, O people of the book* [Jews and Christians], *you have nothing until you observe the Torah and the Gospel and what was revealed to you from your Lord.*" Similarly, Surah 5:47 commands, "*Let the people of the Gospel judge by what Allah has revealed in it. Whoever does not judge by what Allah has revealed, such are transgressors.*"

---

[57] Qur'an Tafsir Ibn Kathir English. Internet Archive. Identifier: 002BaqarahI

In Surah 6:115 we read, *"The word from your Lord is perfected in truth and justice. There is no one who can change his words. He is the hearer, the knower"*. Consistent with this verse, Surah 18:27 says *"And recite what has been revealed to you of the book of your Lord. There is no one who can change his words, and you will find no refuge besides him"*.

These verses seem to confirm that the Torah and the Gospel cannot be corrupted. However, the Qur'an appears to contradict itself in Surah 2:75, saying *"Have you any hope that they will be true to you when a party of them used to listen to the word of Allah, and then used to change it knowingly, after they understood it?"* This is where the abrogation rule comes in handy, allowing the apparent contradiction to be ignored within the Islamic belief system. However, even this verse does not explicitly say that the Torah or Gospel have been corrupted. So, although in my own examination I found evidence of some changes being made to original versions of parts of both the Tanakh and the Gospels, it is interesting that the Qur'an does not make such claims but seems to instruct Jews and Christians to follow their scriptures.

For completeness, the following list contains all 12 references in the Qur'an to the Gospel: Surah 3:3, Surah 3:48, Surah 3:65, Surah 5:46, Surah 5:47, Surah 5:66, Surah 5:68, Surah 5:110, Surah 7:157, Surah 9:111, Surah 48:29, Surah 57:27. None of these verses mentions the Torah or Gospel being corrupted. Paraphrasing what they say into a complete narrative:

> God sent down the Qur'an confirming the Torah and the Gospel were previously revealed before it as a guidance to mankind (3:3) and those who don't believe these signs of God [which would include Jesus' life, crucifixion and resurrection] shall have a severe punishment. An angel told Mary that God will reveal the Gospel to Jesus who is the Messiah (3:48). Neither the Torah nor the Gospel were revealed before Abraham lived (3:65). God sent Jesus who confirmed the Torah, and to him was revealed the Gospel (5:46). Christians must judge by what God had revealed to them in the Gospel, otherwise they are iniquitous (5:47). If Jews and Christians had observed the Torah and the Gospel they would have received nourishment from God, but many of them did not observe the Torah and the Gospel, and so behave in evil ways (5:66). Jews and Christians will have no real religion until they observe the Torah and the Gospel, and they shouldn't grieve for those who don't believe (5:68). God tells Jesus to remember (a) how he strengthened Jesus with the holy spirit, enabling him to speak to mankind from the cradle to adulthood, (b) how he taught Jesus the Torah, the Gospel and wisdom, (c) how with God's permission Jesus performed miracles including producing a live bird from clay, healing

sick people and raising the dead, and (d) how, when Jesus gave Jews clear proofs, they didn't believe him but accused him of sorcery, but God prevented them from harming him (5:110). Muhammad is described in the Torah and the Gospel. He will tell his followers what is right and wrong and will allow his followers to do anything that is good for them and prohibit them from doing anything filthy. He will relieve them of their burdens and chains, and if they honour him, he will make them successful (7:157). The Torah and the Gospel promise paradise to those who kill and are then killed for God (9:111). The Torah and the Gospel describe Muslims as a seed that grows strong and stands firm (48:29). God gave Jesus the Gospel and made Jesus' followers merciful and compassionate people. However, they built monasteries to please God, which God hadn't commanded them to do, so God is going to give their reward to others (57:29).

Note: The grammatical tense used in the Qur'an when referring to the Torah and Gospel implies the versions of the Torah and Gospel being referred to are the ones that were still presently available ('between his hands', meaning in his presence). In Surah 3:3 it can therefore be taken that the Qur'an is saying that the Torah and the Gospel were not corrupted at the time the Qur'an was written. Surah 5:46 also uses the term 'between his hands', meaning present in his time to indicate that the Gospel confirmed the Torah that was available at the time it was revealed.

FACTUAL FLAWS IN THE QUR'AN

Confusing Mary with Miriam

Through reading the Qur'an it is easy to see that Muhammad had a lot of contact with Christians, picking up elements of their beliefs about Jesus. Unfortunately, Muhammad did not go to sufficient effort to get his facts right, so made numerous mistakes. One such mistake is that he confused Mary the mother of Jesus with Miriam the sister of Aaron and Moses, who were the children of Amran. Confusing the names Mary and Miriam is not a credibility concern, because this is the same name in Arabic. However, Mary was not the sister of Moses and Aaron, nor the daughter of Amran (or Imran). These people lived and died over 1,000 years before Mary was born.

The Qur'an frequently refers to Jesus as the son of Mary. It has a lot to say about Mary and even has a surah named after her (Surah 19). This surah contains a version of the account found in the first chapter of Luke's gospel, where an angel announces to Mary that she, a virgin, will give birth to a son.

We read in Surah 19:27-28 *"Then she* [Mary] *brought him* [Jesus] *to her own people, carrying him. They said, O Mary, you have come with an amazing thing. O sister of Aaron, your father was not a wicked man, nor was your mother unchaste."* We read elsewhere in the Qur'an, Mary referred to as the daughter of Amran. The Tanakh records the father of Aaron, Moses and Miriam as being Amran (1 Chronicles 6:3). So, the Qur'an confuses the identity of these two different women.

Evidence exists that Christians in Muhammad's time pointed out this error to Muslims, who went to Muhammad to ask for an explanation. In the Hadith, Sahih Muslim 5326, we read *"Mughira ibn Shu'ba reported: When I came to Najran, they (the Christians in Najran) asked me: You read 'O sister of Huran (Aaron)' in the Qur'an, whereas Moses was born much before Jesus ..... When I came back to Allah's messenger (Muhammad) I asked him about that, whereupon he said: The (people of the old age) used to give names (to their persons) after the names of apostles and pious persons who had gone before them."*[58] Scholars take this to mean that Christians had a practice of referring to people with the name of someone who had gone before them. In this instance, this would have to mean the people in Mary's time referred, or would have referred, to her as Miriam the sister of Aaron' and/or 'Miriam the daughter of Amran'.

Not only does such a practice seem far-fetched, but no evidence exists in any Jewish or Christian records of such a practice existing in 1st century CE Israel. I therefore conclude that either Muhammad or the author of Sahih Muslim, made this story up. I find it most likely that Muhammad was in error, because we also read in Surah 3:35-36 *"Behold! When the wife of Imran said: O my Lord! I do dedicate unto thee what is in my womb for thy special service: So accept this of me: for thou hearest and knowest all things. When she was delivered, she said: O my Lord! Behold! I am delivered of a female child! – And Allah knew best what she brought forth – And no wise is the male like the female. I have named her Mary, and I commend her and thy offspring to the protection from the evil one, the rejected."* So, Muhammad clearly thought Mary the daughter of Amran was the same person as Mary the mother of Jesus.

In Ibn Kathir's commentary, Muhammad Ibn Sireen states he was told that Ka'b said the verse reads *'O sister of Harun* [Aaron]' does not refer to Aaron the brother of Moses. Aisha (one of Muhammad's wives) replied to Ka'b, *'You have lied.'* ..... to which Ka'b responded by saying *'O Mother of the believers. If the prophet, may Allah's prayers be upon him, has said it, and he is more knowledgeable, then this is what he related. Besides, I find the difference in time between them (Jesus and Moses) to be 600 years.'* He said that she (Aisha) then remained silent.

---

[58] Accessed from Hadithcollection.com on 18 June 2025

This commentary is telling because when someone tells Aisha that Mary isn't the sister of Aaron and Moses, Aisha calls him a liar. She would only have done this if she was convinced the Qur'an said there was a single Mary who was both the mother of Jesus and the sister of Aaron and Moses. When I consider this insight together with the above account of Muhammad (only after the error was pointed out to him) coming up with the uncorroborated story about Mary being named after Miriam, the truth is obvious: Muhammad knew he had been caught out with an error in the Qur'an, in which he confused the identities of Mary and Miriam.

Confusing who is in the Trinity

The Qur'an reveals its author was aware that Christians worship a triune god (Surah 4:171; 5:73). However, he mistakenly believed that this Trinity consists of God, Jesus and Mary the mother of Jesus (Surah 5:116), rather than the father, son (Jesus) and holy spirit. An omniscient God as author would not have made such mistakes, but a fallible human author like Muhammad could.

I do not blame Muhammad entirely for his confusion about Mary. Around that time in Christendom, debates were raging about Mary. These debates would have reached the Arab peninsula. For example, during the 6th and 7th century CE, an idea that Mary herself was conceived without sexual intercourse between her parents, was being debated. The 7th century CE Arab Christian monk John Damascene was an active participant in this debate, asserting that even the material of Mary's origin was pure and holy and suggested even Mary's parents were purified during Mary's generation. So, given the extent to which some within Christendom in Arabia around that time revered Mary, it is easy to see why the Qur'an's author may have picked up the ideas he included in the Qur'an.

Was Jesus crucified?

Surah 4:157 states that Jesus (son of Mary) was not actually crucified, but it was only made to seem so. Muhammad may have picked up his belief that Jesus was not crucified from Christian Gnostics, who abhorred the carnal nature of the physical word and, in keeping with this sentiment, did not believe that the Messiah could suffer on the cross and die. Instead, the Gnostics claimed that Jesus ascended to heaven before he could be crucified, and that someone else was substituted in his place. By Muhammad's time, Gnosticism had been labelled heretical by mainstream Christendom, so Gnostics were spreading eastward through the Arabian Peninsula and beyond to find new potential converts outside the reach of the established church.

Countering Muhammad's claim in Surah 4:157, in addition to the Christian gospels' records of Jesus' crucifixion, historical evidence from 1st century CE historians Flavius Josephus (in his Antiquities 18:3:3) and Tacitus (in his Annals) also state that Jesus was crucified. This evidence supports the most intuitive scenario – that Jesus was indeed crucified. It seems extremely unlikely that the Jewish leaders who had engineered Jesus' crucifixion, or the Roman authorities who needed to demonstrate their authority, would have allowed Jesus' followers to substitute someone else to be crucified instead. Faced with the evidence from such recognised historians without a religious conflict of interest on this question, I conclude that on the balance of probability, Jesus was crucified and the Qur'an's account in Surah 4:157 is false.

The setting place of the sun

Surah 18:85-86 says the setting place of the sun is a spring of muddy water. Now, informed by Science, we can see this claim as being a product of humanity's primitive knowledge of astronomy existing at the place and time the Qur'an was written.

Religion of peace

Frequently, the Qur'an claims God is merciful but only to Muslims and commands its adherents to hunt out and kill others. In contrast to Judaism and Christianity in which God acts with power, Islam's God does not seem to have this power that the God of Judaism and Christianity has, because he relies on his followers to adopt a strategy of violent aggression and intolerance of others. Muslims are only to show mercy to other Muslims, including people who convert to Islam when threatened; not to people who do not follow Islam, no matter how genuine or good such people may be. However, even Muslim women do not enjoy God's protection from violent husbands. Surah 4:34 allows Muslim men to hit their wives. Some Muslim scholars say this permission only extends to beating their wives 'lightly', but the Arabic does not say 'lightly'; rather, it says to beat or scourge. Similarly, Bukhari's Volume 4, Book 52, Hadith Number 260 records Muhammad saying, "*If somebody* [a Muslim] *discards his religion, kill him.*" So, rather than being a religion of peace, Islamic scriptures reveal it to be a religion of intolerance and violence against anyone outside Islam and against women within Islam. This is one reason why many Jews and Christians hold that the Muslim god is different from their god.

Jews and Christians believe that God is omnipotent. However, in Islam, the need for Muslims to spread their faith through violence and intolerance, rather than relying on God to do it himself, suggests the Muslim God is not omnipotent. Examples of Muhammed issuing such commands are found in

Surah 9:29 which says, "*Fight against those who do not believe in Allah or the last day*" and later in verse 130 "*O you who believe, fight those of the unbelievers who are near to you, and let them find harshness in you, and know that Allah is with those who keep their duty.*" Similarly, verse 5 of the same surah says "*Kill idolaters wherever you find them, and take them, and besiege them, and prepare for them every ambush. But if they repent and establish prayer and give alms, then leave their way free. Indeed, Allah is forgiving and merciful.*"

Note in this verse that Mohammad commands his followers to proactively set about to kill people who worship idols, but that if they convert to Islam, then spare them. This verse characterises a strong repeating theme throughout the Qur'an that Islam requires its followers to use violent aggression against others and that God's mercy is only to be shown to Muslims. The mercy that the Qur'an commands to be shown only to people who convert to Islam, reveal Islam to be more a strategy of converting the world to Islam, rather than a religious faith in God, as Judaism and Christianity are.

Do Jews claim Ezra is the son of God?

As an example of this intolerance, in verse 30 of the same surah, Mohammed prays for God to curse Jews and Christians because he thinks Jews say that Ezra is the son of god and Christians say the Messiah is the son of god. Whereas Muhammad was correct regarding this belief of Christians, he was mistaken in his claim that Jews believe Ezra is the son of god. Mainstream Jews have never believed this. Some historic Muslim sources suggest a small group of Jews might have held such beliefs, possibly around Yemen, at the time[59][60]. If true, this may be where Muhammad got this idea from. The author of the Qur'an clearly did not have a good understanding of mainstream Judaism or Christianity. An omniscient god would have known that mainstream Judaism did not hold that Ezra is the son of god; it certainly would not have cursed all Jews because a small group may have believed something different. This claim in the Qur'an therefore is sufficient evidence to conclude that the Qur'an cannot be relied on to perfectly convey the words of God. Islam's insistence on the Qur'an being the perfectly preserved word of God is therefore proven to be false.

---

[59] Lazarus Yafeh, H. (2012). *Uzayr*. In P. Bearman (ed.), *Encyclopaedia of Islam New Edition Online (EI-2 English)*. Brill. https://doi.org/10.1163/1573-3912_islam_SIM_7787
[60] Skolnik, Fred (2007). *Encyclopaedia Judaica. 2nd ed.* Thomson-Gale. v6, p653

Understanding Muhammad

If, as tradition says, Muhammad was illiterate, it is understandable that he only possessed a limited knowledge of Judaism and Christianity. The fact that we find errors in the Qur'an such as those given above (and many more) is therefore unsurprising. These factual errors that fundamentally shape the message of the Qur'an demonstrate that the Qur'an is not the accurate word of an omniscient god. A more credible explanation is that the Qur'an contains ideas that Muhammad constructed, then modified over time.

The examples provided above of Christian activity and interactions in the Arabian Peninsula around Muhammad's time help explain why he would have come up with some of the ideas he included in the Qur'an. So, due to its factual errors, internal contradictions, contextual factors, stylistic limitations and doubtful stories of how it came into being, when considered together, the evidence is compelling that the Qur'an could not have been the word of God. What we can conclude is that it is the product of one or more fallible humans, with the objective of establishing and promulgating the Islamic ideology. However, to put this conclusion beyond reasonable doubt, we should also establish a likely motive for constructing such a document and a likely process through which it came into being. I will do this in Chapter 8 by examining the life of Muhammad.

IS ALLAH THE SAME GOD THAT JEWS AND CHRISTIANS WORSHIP?

The descriptions of Allah in the Qur'an are incompatible with the God of Judaism and Christianity. We can therefore conclude that they are not the same god. Given that all three religions are monotheistic, both Allah and the god of the Tanakh cannot co-exist as the monotheistic supreme God. Given that the Qur'an is the most evidently flawed of these scriptures, its credibility is weaker than the credibility of the Tanakh (or Christian Old Testament). It follows that the existence of the Allah that Muhammad 'revealed' seems unlikely. So, where did the concept of Muhammad's Allah come from?

Although numerous scholars discuss Allah as a pre-Islamic deity, variation exists in their accounts about this deity. Some argue that the word Allah (a contraction of the Arabic term 'al-ilah' meaning 'the god') may have been used as a title rather than a name. Muhammad was born into the Quraysh tribe in Mecca. Some scholars argue that Allah was another name for the supreme god of the Quraysh people, Hubal, which is a name possibly derived from the Canaanite god Baal, referred to in the Tanakh.

According to some Islamic sources, the goddesses Al-lat, Al-Uzza and Manat (referred to in Surah 53:19-20) were the daughters of Allah[61]. Muhammad may have innovated the concept the Quraysh had to form his version of Allah, dispensing with all the other gods that formed part of the polytheistic belief system from which Allah came. Although definitive evidence on the precise origin of Allah is light, what is clear is that Muhammad reconceptualised the version of Allah that pre-existed Islam. Regarding the background to the appearance of these Quraysh goddesses in the Qur'an, Dr Robert Spencer in his commentary on the background to Surah 53:19-20 in "The Critical Qur'an" observes:

> *"According to Ibn Hisham, in a passage preserved by Tabari, the incident took place because of Muhammad's worrying over the Quraysh rejecting his message. 'The apostle was anxious for the welfare of his people, wishing to attract them as far as he could.' In fact, 'He longed for a way to attract them.' At that point, the leaders of the Quraysh came to him with an offer: 'You will worship our gods, al-Lat and al-Uzza, for a year, and we shall worship your god for a year.' According to the story, Muhammad was so intent on reconciling his people that he wanted to do this, but Allah twice told him not to do so. Then, however, according to the story, he received a revelation saying that it was legitimate for Muslims to pray to al-Lat, al-Uzza, and Manat, the three goddesses of Quraysh. This new message directly contradicted the substance of his preaching up to that point".*

An iconic site in Islam is the Kaaba – a cube-shaped building in Mecca that was used to hold approximately 360 idols of various gods, including Quraysh gods. Muhammad destroyed these idols and claimed the Kaaba as Islam's holiest site. Although Islam claims to oppose idolatry, it preserves the practice of making pilgrimages to the Kaaba and performing religious rituals there, similar to venerating an idol – a practice not wholly dissimilar to what occurred at that site in its pre-Islamic polytheist period.

The Kaaba has been rebuilt many times. The Qur'an in Surah 2 claims that Abraham and his son Ishmael rebuilt the Kaaba at one stage. However, it seems unlikely that Abraham would have rebuilt a storeroom for multiple polytheistic idols in the pre-Islamic period. Also, the Jewish and Christian scriptures give a detailed and credible account of Abraham's life and death, making no mention of Mecca. What is mentioned is that Abraham banished Ishmael and his mother

[61] For more details, see Al-Wahidi's Asbab al-Nuzul; Ibn Sa'ad's Kitab al Tabaqat al Kabir; Ibn Isaq's Sirat Rasullallah; Ibn Jarir al-Tabari's *History of the World*

after Abraham's second son Isaac was born (Genesis 21:14). So, this story of Abraham and Ishmael together rebuilding the Kaaba lacks credibility.

The preservation of one of the Quraysh gods and the Kaaba may have been an attempt by Muhammad to make his religion appeal to people living in the region at the time. Similarly, the mention of Abraham in the Qur'an may have been an attempt by Muhammad to make his religion appeal to Jews, and his recognising Jesus as a prophet and the Messiah a sop to Christians. Unfortunately for Muhammad, his strategy of seeking to appeal to people by borrowing from what they already believe then adding onto it was weakened by his failure to research others' beliefs properly. As a result, he frequently got facts wrong, causing those he was trying to persuade to reject his teaching. As will be seen in Chapter 8 when I discuss Muhammad's life, to promulgate his teaching, he then was forced to resort to violence and military power rather than evidence and reasoned argument.

THE ISLAMIC DILEMMA

The Qur'an affirms that the Torah and the Gospel are from God, yet the Torah and the Gospel contradict the Qur'an. However, the Qur'an states that God's words cannot be changed.

Surah 29:46 instructs Muslims to declare to Christians, '*We believe what has been revealed to us and revealed to you; our god and your god are one and to him we submit.*' However, as discussed earlier, Christian scriptures contradict the Qur'an.

In response to this problem, Muslims have been taught not to believe in Christian scriptures because they have been corrupted. For example, In Sahih al-Bukhari 7363 (Book 90, Hadith 90) we read:

> *Narrated Ubaidullah: Ibn Abbas said, "Why do you ask the people of the scripture about anything while your Book [Qur'an] which has been revealed to Allah's Messenger is newer and the latest? You read it pure, undistorted and unchanged, and Allah has told you that the people of the scripture [Jews and Christians] changed their scripture and distorted it, and wrote the scripture with their own hands and said, 'It is from Allah,' to sell it for a little gain. Does not the knowledge which has come to you prevent you from asking them about anything? No, by Allah, we have never seen any man from them asking you regarding what has been revealed to you!"*

As I showed earlier in the chapter, some editing of the scriptures of Judaism and Christianity has occurred. However, whereas I found variants between manuscripts, most of these are minor; certainly not sufficient to fundamentally distort the overall message of the Tanakh and New Testament. The vast majority of the text in both the Jewish and Christian scriptures is consistent, if not identical. Also, we have manuscripts of both Jewish and Christian scriptures dating from before Muhammad lived, so these could not have been corrupted in response to Islam.

Surah 3:3-4 says that God revealed the Torah and the Gospel before the Qur'an, as guidance to mankind. Surah 18:27 says "*And recite what has been revealed to you of the book of your Lord. There is no one who can change his words, and you will find no refuge besides him.*"

Some Muslims believe Surah 18:27 must refer only to the Qur'an. However, it does not specify this and Surah 3:3-4 clearly includes the Torah and Gospel as God's words. Islam accepts that no one can change God's words.

Surah 7:157 suggests the Torah and the Gospel had not been corrupted in Muhammad's time because it tells Muslims that they will find Muhammad described in them. Islamic scholar Ibn Kathir (IV, 178) confirms this interpretation, stating, "*This is the description of the prophet Muhammad in the books of the Prophets. They delivered the good news of his advent to their nations and commanded them to follow him. His descriptions were still apparent in their books, as their rabbis and priests well know.*" So, his position was that the Jews and Christians knew Muhammad was described in their scriptures and wilfully chose not to follow him.

We now have manuscripts from and prior to the time of Muhammad, so can check the credibility of Ibn Kathir's claim. Unlike evidence for Jesus, negligible evidence exists for Muhammad in the Jewish and Christian manuscripts dating from Muhammad's time and earlier, or even in manuscripts discovered in relatively recent times. The passages most strongly argued by those Muslims who identify specific passages they claim refer to Muhammad are the following:

- In Deuteronomy 18:15-18, Moses tells the Hebrew people that God will raise up a prophet like him from amongst their countrymen and he will speak the words God commands him.

  I find it unlikely that this verse is referring to Muhammad because there have been many Hebrew (Jewish) prophets, including Jesus, who fit this prophesy more closely than Muhammad. They were all Moses' countrymen (Jewish), but Muhammad was not.

- In John 14:26 Jesus says, "*But the helper, the holy spirit whom the father will send in my name, will teach you all things and remind you of everything I said to you*", and in John 16:13-14, Jesus says, "*When he, the spirit of truth, is come, he will guide you into all truth; for he shall not speak of himself, but whatsoever he shall hear, that shall he speak; and he will show you things to come. He shall glorify me: for he shall receive of mine, and shall show it unto."*

I find it unlikely these verses are referring to Muhammad because in both they are referring to a spirit rather than a prophet, and John 16:14 says this spirit will repeat what Jesus taught and will glorify Jesus. Although there is a small overlap between the teachings of Jesus and Muhammad, most messages taught by each of these men were not taught by the other.

Despite such an overwhelming volume of evidence about weaknesses in the Qur'an (or perhaps because of it), Surah 5:101-102 cautions Muslims against questioning what Muhammad had 'revealed'. It warns that *"A people before you asked, and then became unbelievers."* This surah evidences the awareness its author had that if people start asking questions about what Muhammad had 'revealed', they are likely to realise his revelations are false.

Having discussed Muhammad's teachings, particularly as revealed in his Qur'an, how do these compare with what Jesus taught?

3. WHAT DID JESUS TEACH?

"In a lawsuit the first to speak seems right, until someone comes forward and cross examines."

Proverbs 18:17

The historical accounts of Josephus and Tacitus provide credible evidence of Jesus' existence, crucifixion and public impact. However, they do not describe what he taught, although Tacitus alludes to his teaching at the Last Supper, thinking Jesus' followers performed cannibalistic practices (eating Christ's body). As discussed in the previous chapter, the synoptic gospels provide the most credible evidence of Jesus' teachings. So, before considering wider sources, I will commence by considering what our most credible sources say about his teachings.

3.1 HOW DID JESUS TEACH?

Jesus was a Jew and lived as a Jew, generally observing the requirements laid out in the Torah, but also stepping beyond the mere ritualistic or legalistic practice of the law. He repeated what the prophets before him had conveyed about what God really wants of people. He challenged people to genuinely seek God and to provide practical love to their fellow man. He talked of his actions as "fulfilling the scriptures" and "fulfilling righteousness".

Jesus taught people in a way that resonated with them. They would follow him into the countryside in large numbers to hear him teach. He often referred to the Tanakh in his teaching, sharing insightful interpretations in ways that religious leaders had failed to do. Jesus made clear the intent of the scriptures – God's desire for how we should live our lives, how we should treat each other, and how we should approach God, whom he usually referred to as 'the father' or 'my father'.

When asked what the greatest commandment is, he quoted from the Torah *"Hear, O Israel: The lord our god, the lord is one. You shall love the lord your god with all your heart and with all your soul and with all your strength."* (Mark 12:29; Deuteronomy 6:4-5). After saying this, he immediately went on to say the second greatest commandment is like it, quoting again from the Torah, *"You shall love your neighbour as you love yourself"* (Leviticus 19:18b). These two commandments constitute the overarching thrust of his message.

Many of Jesus' recorded teachings are contained in his 'Sermon on the Mount', the most comprehensive version of which is found in Matthew Chapters 5-7, and in his parables, which are spread across all three synoptic gospels.

PARABLES

One of Jesus' teaching styles was to use analogies which he communicated in parables – short fictitious narratives illustrating something that could actually occur in life. In general, each of these parables made a particular moral point with practical implication for how a person should live his/her life. In particular, the parables tend to focus on what an individual should do, rather than what society as a whole should do. Jesus spoke to the individual.

24 parables are recorded in the 3 synoptic gospels (12 in Matthew, 4 in Mark and 17 in Luke); 7 of these are contained in more than one of these gospels. Perhaps the most well-known of Jesus' parables is 'The Good Samaritan'. At that time, the Samaritan people were despised by Jews. In this parable, a man is mugged and left for dead. Pious religious leaders passing him crossed to the other side of the road without offering assistance, but a Samaritan passing by generously helps the mugging victim. Through this parable, Jesus is teaching people that our "neighbours" referred to in Leviticus 19:18 should be interpreted more widely than many Jews may have interpreted it. Jesus uses the parable to challenge people to see that a good person is one who cares selflessly for others, even natural enemies, and is not someone who needs to be Jewish or whom society sees as good and respectable due to his/her position.

This parable is consistent with themes that recur throughout Jesus' teachings, not only in parables, but in association with the miracles he performed and his preaching, most notably the Sermon on the Mount. The most extensive record of this sermon takes up 3 chapters of Matthew's gospel (Matthew 5-7).

THE SERMON ON THE MOUNT

According to the gospel of Matthew, the Sermon on the Mount commences with the beatitudes: *"Blessed are"* different types of people, and in what ways they are blessed. Next, he tells his listeners they are the salt of the earth and a light that must shine before men. He then claims he did not come to abolish the law but to fulfil it. Doctrinally, this is an important point of difference between Judaism, Christianity and Islam, and is at the core of the overarching themes woven into much of Jesus' teaching throughout his ministry. Given its significance, I will discuss this issue in more detail in the next chapter.

Jesus elaborates on what he means by 'fulfilling the law', which is that our heart must be right with God and toward people then, if it is, the behaviour and actions God wants from us will flow. He says the ancestors were told '*You shall not murder*'. However, Jesus teaches that such actions come from the heart, so if you are angry with someone or if someone is angry with you, make peace with them before it gets so bad someone goes to prison or gets murdered. Similarly, he then teaches that the law states '*You shall not commit adultery*', but Jesus says that if you look at a woman lustfully, you have already committed adultery in your heart. The implication of this teaching is that you fulfil the law by putting your heart in order, rather than by following laws literally.

Jesus then moves on to teaching how to put your heart in order. He starts by advising to remove temptation and opportunity. This aligns strongly with what we have learned in modern times from Crime Science, which identifies opportunity as the strongest precursor to offending. Temptation is associated with reward and risk of sanction. Again, Crime Science has shown that reducing the rewards and increasing both the barriers the certainty of sanction, all contribute to reducing offending. To emphasise his point, Jesus says it would be better to lose one of your body parts than let it cause you to sin.

He then returns to examples of what it means to fulfil other laws. The Jewish law allowed a man to divorce his wife, but Jesus teaches that if your heart is in the right place, it will usually be wrong for you to do so. He then addresses the law against making false vows, by telling people not to take any oath at all; just mean it every time you say yes or no; anything else is evil, he says. Next, he addresses the Jewish saying, '*An eye for an eye and a tooth for a tooth*', teaching instead that if someone slaps you on your right cheek, turn the other towards him also, and if someone forces you to go one mile, go two.

Some scholars suggest these passages arise from meanings relevant to the time[62]. Jesus may therefore have been teaching to avoid escalating an aggressive situation by passively inviting further offence, thereby shaming the offender. Alternatively, in Jesus' time, striking a person of lower class with the back of your right hand may have been a means of shaming or exerting authority; however, if the recipient turned their left cheek to you, this created a dilemma because the left hand was used for unclean purposes, so a backhanded slap on the left cheek would not be performed. Therefore, by turning the cheek the recipient was demanding equality. Similarly, a Roman soldier was permitted to force a Jewish subject to carry his pack for 1 mile[63], so if you offered to carry it for another mile, you would be demonstrating a free choice that couldn't be forced on you. This offer would create a dilemma for the soldier, who was not permitted to force someone to carry his pack further than one mile. So, if it was discovered that someone had carried a pack for two miles, it would look like the soldier had broken the law by forcing the person to carry it further. The soldier would then risk being at the mercy of what the carrier might say if questioned. Again, this strategy would be a passive demand for equality[64].

However, the truth may be simpler and less devious than such explanations because Jesus immediately went on to challenge his listeners with another Jewish saying: '*You shall love your neighbour and hate your enemy*'. Jesus instead said you should love your enemies and pray for those who persecute you. In later teachings, such as the Parable of the Good Samaritan outlined above, he taught we should think of everyone as our neighbour, even supposed enemies. Jesus teaches that God "*causes the sun to rise on the evil and the good, and sends rain on the righteous and the unrighteous*", so we should not treat some groups of people better than others.

The sermon then moves on to teaching humility and how to pray. Jesus teaches to pray to our heavenly father (rather than to himself or the holy spirit). He then cautions against prioritising earthly treasure; we need to see that what matters is serving God instead of seeking material goals in this world. He tells

---

[62] Cook, John Granger (2014). *Matthew 5.39 and 26.67: Slapping another's cheek in ancient Mediterranean culture.* Journal of Greco-Roman Christianity and Judaism. v10. pp68-89

[63] Horsley, G.H.R. (1981). *New Documents Illustrating Early Christianity: A Review of the Greek Inscriptions and Papyri published in 1976*, The Ancient History Documentary Research Centre Macquarie University

[64] Rev. Dr. Alison L. Boden (20 February 2011). *Going the Extra Mile*, Princeton University. https://chapel.princeton.edu/news/going-extra-mile

his listeners that God looks after the birds and the flowers, yet we are more important than them, so we should prioritise seeking God's kingdom and his righteousness, rather than being anxious about the future.

Next Jesus teaches we all have faults, so if we do not want to be judged ourselves, we should not condemn others. He encourages people to seek God, saying that God wants to support us just as a parent wants to support their child. He then teaches the golden rule: treat people the way you want them to treat you, explaining that the path that leads to life is narrow and few find it, and warning that there will be "false prophets" who will try to prevent you, but you can tell a false prophet because of the fruit they bear (how they behave and the consequences of their actions). Not everyone who thinks they will get into heaven will make it; you have to actually do the will of God.

So, in summary:

- It is what we do as an individual that counts.

- Our actions and our heart for God and all other people are more important than our station in life.

- We should not do good works to gain the admiration of others, but because we have prioritised God and his righteousness.

- Our actions will be good (lives bearing good fruit) if we are put right on the inside.

John's gospel omits many of the most significant teachings of Jesus as recorded throughout the synoptic gospels, but includes additional teachings which, if accepted, have profound implications regarding the identity of God, how humans can enter God's kingdom (heaven) and who humans actually are. So, how do we gain entry to the kingdom of God?

3.2 ENTRY TO GOD'S KINGDOM

Most Christians believe that after death – eventually if not immediately – people will end up living on eternally, either apart from God in distress (often said to be in hell) or in God's kingdom, a place of peace, joy, and love with God. To achieve entry to God's kingdom one must repent of one's sins and follow Jesus. Some denominations believe salvation from hell requires a more complex set of beliefs, such as belief that God is a Trinity and that one must follow certain practices or religious rituals including water baptism or confession of sins to a priest, followed by performing some act of penance. This is all part of being a member of the church (the legitimate body of believers approved by the religious leadership). However, the balance of evidence shows that Jesus did not teach such doctrines.

What do the synoptic gospels say about this?

In Mark 9:38-41 we read of one of Jesus' disciples asking him: "*Teacher, said John, we saw someone driving out demons in your name and we told him to stop, because he was not one of us. Do not stop him, Jesus said. For no one who does a miracle in my name can in the next moment say anything bad about me, for whoever is not against us is for us. Truly I tell you, anyone who gives you a cup of water in my name because you belong to the Messiah will certainly not lose their reward.*" Jesus did not elaborate on the nature of this reward, whether he means salvation, karma or something else. However, he was very clear that being a member of the body of believers (the church) is not necessary to do things in his name or to be rewarded by God.

Neither did Jesus teach that we need to believe and have an accurate understanding of the correct doctrines. Rather, he taught that unless we receive the kingdom of God like a child, we shall not enter it. (Mark 10:13-16; Luke 18:15-17; Matthew 19:13-15). An example of someone who did not know all the things early Christians thought important to know is the preacher Apollos. In Acts 18:24-28 we read that Apollos was effective in preaching about Jesus, even though his knowledge was limited and other believers (Priscilla and Aquila) needed to explain things more accurately to him.

It is worth noting that the Greek word used in the New Testament for believing in Jesus or believing in God is πιστεύω (pisteuō). A given word can vary in its precise meaning, depending on the context. Pisteuō can mean to have faith in a person or thing or to entrust (particularly one's spiritual well-being) to someone. So, we should not take it to only mean 'believe' in the sense of the most common meaning of this English word – to accept that something is true. In fact, the richer meaning better aligns with Jesus' teachings than this overly simple English definition does. Jesus taught that repentance from sin and belief in him is insufficient for salvation; self-sacrificial commitment was required (Mark 8:34). The evidence of where a person is truly at will then be seen through their words and actions (Matthew 7:17-20).

What new concept does John's gospel introduce about this?

John's gospel records Jesus teaching the requirement for an internal spiritual transformation. Chapter 3 of John's gospel records Jesus teaching that "*Unless someone is born again, he cannot see the kingdom of God*". Jesus described this rebirth as being "*born of a spirit*". He then provided insight into this statement by saying "*That which has been born of the flesh is flesh, and that which has been born of a spirit is spirit*" (John 3:6). Later, in his trial before the Roman governor, under questioning Jesus responds, "*My kingdom is not of this world*" (John 18:36a). So, many Christians take John's account of Jesus' teachings to mean that spiritual birth into a spiritual kingdom is required, but what is this spiritual kingdom like?

In John 14:20, 21&23, the author records Jesus as saying that in the future: "*You will know that I am in the father, you are in me and I am in you. He that has my commandments and keeps them, it is he who loves me; he shall be loved by my father, and I will love him and reveal myself to him ..... If anyone loves me, he will follow my words, and my father will love him, and we will come into him and make our dwelling with him.*" This declaration suggests the kingdom Jesus spoke about will involve some sort of mutual indwelling. In John 17, Jesus again speaks of the nature of his oneness with the father extending to his followers. This significant teaching of oneness and mutual indwelling running throughout John's gospel is absent from the synoptic gospels.

Historically, some Christians have linked this spiritual rebirth to their water baptism ritual. In the 2nd century CE, the influential Bishop of Lyon, Irenaeus, contributed to developing a doctrine of water baptism being necessary for salvation by mistranslating John 3:5. He said that Jesus declared: "*Unless a man be born again through water and the spirit, he shall not enter into the kingdom of heaven*" (Irenaeus Fragment 34b), interpreting Jesus' requirement to be born again as involving both being born of water and the spirit. I will explain below how Jesus' teaching on baptism differs from this. However, first, I should extend Irenaeus a little grace: His error may not have been intentional. He is known to have used a Codex Bezae manuscript, which modern scholars generally agree contains numerous 'interpolations' (extensions) and loose paraphrasing. Whether intentional or not, by subtly paraphrasing Jesus, Irenaeus contributed to creating a doctrine that became a pillar of Christendom.

In Acts 19:1-6 we read of Paul discovering that some new disciples had only been baptised with the baptism of John the Baptist, which Paul described as the baptism of repentance. He immediately expressed the need for them to be baptised in the name of Jesus, which he effected by laying his hands on them, after which "*the holy spirit came on them, and they began speaking with tongues and prophesying*", thus demonstrating that the baptism of Jesus is not water baptism, but a baptism of the spirit, causing transformation. This may have been an example of the spiritual birth Jesus taught Nicodemus about in John 3:3-8.

Throughout his epistles, Paul elaborates on the idea of Christianity involving a spiritual dimension. He spoke of this as Christ living in you and of "*the spirit of him who raised Jesus from the dead dwells in you*" (Romans 8:9; Corinthians 3:16, 2 Timothy 1:14, Ephesians 3:17, Colossians 1:27, John 14:23). In Romans 8, Paul teaches extensively on what it means to live in the spirit, as opposed to in the flesh. In Romans 12:1-2, Paul goes on to talk about a transformation of the mind occurring following offering one's body as a living sacrifice to God. This idea of presenting one's body as a living sacrifice perhaps refers to what Jesus was talking about in Luke 9:23, Mark 8:24 and Matthew 16:24-26, where he says anyone who would follow him [and have eternal life] must deny himself and take up his cross daily.

Some denominations – most notably Roman Catholicism and Eastern Orthodox (both of whom claim authority due to succession of sovereignty) – put a lot of emphasis on the importance of a set of ritual practices they call 'sacraments', which they claim Jesus commanded his followers to perform.

3.3 DID JESUS COMMAND THE SACRAMENTS?

A sacrament is a ritualistic church practice believed by some denominations to have been instigated by Jesus (Roman Catholicism) or his apostles (Orthodox church). Roman Catholicism has seven sacraments:

- **Water Baptism** – Admission to the faith, most commonly of infants and new converts. Believed to put to death the old sinful self, a new self emerges, filled with the holy spirit.

- **Confirmation** – Confirms a baptised person in their faith once they are a bit older, typically around 13 years of age. Signifies the inner presence of the holy spirit who will provide the strength to live out a life of faith.

- **Eucharist** (also known as Holy Communion) – A practice in response to blending Jesus' teachings given at the Last Supper and in his preaching on being the "bread of life" (see below for details).

- **Reconciliation** – Confession (of sins) and penance – a mechanism by which a member who sins is brought back into communion with God and the church.

- **Anointing of the sick** (previously known as Extreme Unction) – Comforts people who are ill.

- **Marriage** – Positions marriage as reflecting the union of Jesus with the church as a mystical body.

- **Ordination** – Confers authority to perform various rites on church leaders (deacons, priests and bishops).

The Eastern Orthodox church has the same seven sacraments, but with some differences in associated beliefs and practices. It considers various other blessings and special services to be sacramental as well.

The beliefs and practices of other denominations regarding sacraments vary. For example, the Anglican church (Church of England) is aware of the above seven sacraments but holds that only Water Baptism and Eucharist were ordained by Jesus and necessary to salvation (1662 Catechism). Even so, their belief about Eucharist differs significantly from that of the Roman Catholic and Eastern Orthodox denominations.

Some denominations believe the above three traditional denominations put too much weight on the importance of sacraments; they adjust their practices accordingly. Most do not practise infant water baptism or confirmation but do practise a form of adult water baptism more consistent with the baptism performed by John the Baptist which Jesus underwent. Some view sacraments such as Eucharist as simply a reminder of Jesus' sacrifice. Concerned that sacraments were diverting people from what God really wants, some have ceased practising sacraments altogether or substituted other symbolic practices.

BAPTISM

I will only discuss the two sacraments considered by many to be the most important – Baptism and Eucharist. In Chapter 2, I discussed how Baptism originated and signified repentance. I will now extend this discussion by considering what Jesus taught about water baptism.

Water baptism is a common, but not universal, religious practice about which beliefs vary. Baptism as practised by John the Baptist was a symbolic gesture in which a person chose to demonstrate their decision to turn from sin and live a righteous life. It may have been the Judaic practice of Tevilah (ritual practice used to signify purification or conversion) involving immersion under water. It would appear from all four gospels that Jesus thought it appropriate for him to be baptised in order to endorse this symbolism.

By the time the gospels were written, water baptism within Christendom may have evolved from a symbolic personal declaration by an individual into a required ritual when one is accepted into membership of Christendom. This would explain the apparent editing of the gospel accounts to give it added emphasis and a particular character. Still today, some Christians believe water baptism is necessary if one is to enter God's kingdom; others do not, instead seeing it as only a symbolic gesture.

The conversation between Jesus and Nicodemus recorded in Chapter 3 of John's gospel sheds some light on this question. Jesus tells Nicodemus that to see the kingdom of God he must be born again. Nicodemus finds this hard to understand, asking "*How can a man be born when he is old? He cannot enter his mother's womb a second time and be born, can he?*" Jesus responds, saying "*Unless one is born 'from/out of' (ἐξ) water and the spirit he cannot enter into the kingdom of God. That which is born of the flesh is flesh, and that which is born of the spirit is spirit.*" (John 3:5-6)

Some Christians believe Jesus' reference in Verse 5 to being born of water refers to water baptism. They argue that Jesus is teaching in this passage that water baptism is necessary for one to enter the kingdom of God. However, Jesus' response continues into Verse 6 where he clarifies that being born of water means to being born of "the flesh", a term Jesus uses elsewhere to refer to the normal biological human condition with all its weaknesses and passions (Matthew 26:41; Luke 3:6; Luke 24:39; John 1:13; John 6:63; John 8:15). Yet, to be distracted by this distinction would miss the main point Jesus was making to Nicodemus, which is that it is necessary to be born of the spirit to enter the kingdom of God. Christians who have experienced this spiritual birth (as opposed to merely a ritual) refer to it as being 'born again'.

A repeating theme in the gospels and in Acts is that the route to heaven requires an internal spiritual transformation or rebirth, rather than following mere rituals or practices. Within the Christian Trinity concept, the role of Jesus when on earth was to teach and to enable people to enter the kingdom of God, and the role of the holy spirit is to pick up after Jesus left earth, impacting in many ways those who have been born of the spirit. I will explore more what the Christian scriptures say about the holy spirit in Chapter 7.

Given Jesus' teaching recorded in John 3, along with my suspicions about likely editing of the final chapters of Matthew's and Mark's Gospels, I find it unlikely that Jesus taught his followers to baptise people in the name of the father, son and holy spirit, or that he taught that any ritual could be a required rite of passage into Christendom or heaven. Two significant considerations in forming this conclusion are:

- Jesus' other teachings on what one must do to enter the kingdom of heaven do not involve a water baptism ritual, but state that other actions suffice. As discussed earlier, these things differ depending on whether you believe the synoptic gospels alone or also believe the Johannine and/or the Pauline doctrines. However, none of these bases make the water baptism sacrament the predominant requirement. Rather, faith, repentance, and a life of generous self-sacrifice to follow the way, persevering until death is required. With John's gospel, Acts, and the Pauline doctrines, this also requires being born of a spirit – an internal spiritual transformation, rather than an external ritual.

- The water baptism sacrament, as practised in the Roman Catholic, Eastern Orthodox, Anglican and some other denominations, bears little resemblance to the water baptism Jesus endorsed. The baptism practised by John the Baptist was a public gesture by a consenting adult who chose to repent of their sins and live a righteous life; not a ritual practice performed on infants.

The Didache provides some assistance in understanding how the practices of the Roman Catholic and Orthodox Church evolved from early Christian practices. As discussed in Chapter 2, the Didache or '*The Lord's teaching through the twelve apostles to the nations (or Gentiles)*' is the earliest extant example of church orders and the earliest extant written description of Christian sacraments. Chapter 7 of the Didache reads:

"And concerning baptism, baptise in this way: Having first said all these things, baptise in the name of the father and of the son and of the holy spirit in living water [flowing water]. *But if you have no living water, baptise into other water; and if you cannot do so in cold water, do so in warm. But if you have neither, pour out water three times upon the head in the name of the father and son and holy spirit. But before baptism let the baptiser fast, and the baptised, and whoever else can; but you shall order the baptised to fast one or two days before."*

So, already by the end of the 1st century CE, the church was creating ritual requiring certain components not mentioned at Jesus' baptism. The practice of baptism was evolving, and continued to evolve to what it is today, with some components removed and others added, giving us many variants across different denominations. For example, Roman Catholicism holds that undergoing its Baptism ritual (which involves sprinkling of water), not only cleanses a person from sin, but also initiates them into the church and fills them with the holy spirit. We can immediately see how different this was from what occurred in the time of the first apostles. In Acts 11:16, Peter recalls Jesus saying, *"John baptised with water, but you will be baptised with the holy spirit"* (Acts

11:16). Also in Acts, Paul is recorded as teaching some people who had already been baptised in the way Jesus had been that *"'John baptised with the baptism of repentance, telling people to believe in him who was coming after him, that is, in Jesus.' When they heard this, they were baptised in the name of the lord Jesus. And when Paul laid his hands upon them, the holy spirit came on them, and they began speaking with tongues and prophesying"* (Acts 19:4-6).

So, Acts teaches there are clearly two baptisms: One is the water baptism Jesus underwent, signifying repentance, and the other resulted from the baptiser *"laying hands upon them"* to induce the holy spirit and (at least in this instance) speaking in tongues. Perhaps this signifies a distinction between water baptism and the baptism performed here by Paul in the name of Jesus (significantly, not in the name of the father, son and holy spirit). In any event, this is vastly different from the ritual practised in the Roman Catholic church and many other Christian denominations.

Today, water baptism is a common, but not universal, Christian practice, about which beliefs vary. Baptism as practised by John the Baptist was simply a symbolic gesture in which a person chose to demonstrate their decision to turn from sin and live a righteous life.

In Chapter 2, I raised concerns about the suspicious extent of alignment between some of the miraculous details in the gospel accounts of Jesus' baptism, and about the apparently out of place exhortation at the end of two of the gospels to go into the world to baptise people of other nations. By the time the gospels were written, water baptism within Christendom may have evolved from a symbolic personal declaration by an individual, into a required ritual when one is accepted into membership of Christendom. This would explain the apparent editing of the gospel accounts to give this practice added emphasis. Jews were Jewish by birth, but Christians needed another mechanism to transition from being outside God's blessing to entering his new covenant (Jeremiah 31:31-34), particularly after the Council of Jerusalem at which Christianity renounced the requirement for circumcision (Acts 15).

Although sacraments, such as Baptism, might not be necessary for salvation, Jesus clearly valued the utility of allegory and symbolism. He frequently taught using parables and metaphors, and to make a point he used symbolic acts such as water baptism and the sharing of bread and water during the Jewish Passover festival.

EUCHARIST (HOLY COMMUNION)

Roman Catholic and Eastern Orthodox Christians hold that Jesus commanded his followers to eat his flesh and drink his blood literally, and that this is necessary to enter God's kingdom. To justify this claim, they refer to John 6:48-58, verse 54 of which quotes Jesus as saying, *"He who eats my flesh and drinks my blood has eternal life, and I will raise him up on the last* day." To enable this consumption of Jesus' flesh and blood to occur, they hold that the bread and wine which they use during their Eucharist ritual mystically transforms into Jesus' actual flesh and blood after a blessing by the priest. Let's unpack this idea.

Soon before Jesus' crucifixion, he shared a final meal with his disciples. This meal was part of the Jewish festival of Passover. This tradition celebrated the historic event recorded in Exodus 12, where God sent a *"destroyer"* to kill all the Egyptian first-born children. In that event, God's destroyer passed over the houses of the Jews who had eaten lamb and unleavened bread and painted their doorframes with the lamb's blood to ward off the destroyer.

The gospels record Jesus' final meal with his disciples. During this meal he broke the bread and passed it to his disciples, in most manuscripts saying, *"this is my body which is given for you; do this in remembrance of me"*, then he poured wine into a cup saying, *"this is my blood of the covenant, poured out for many"*. In saying these things, Jesus gave part of the Passover tradition a new symbolic meaning, foreshadowing his imminent death.

Many Christians continue the ritualised sharing of bread and wine, following Jesus' instruction to *"do this in remembrance of me"*. This tradition was later labelled as the sacrament of Eucharist (or Holy Communion). Both Roman Catholicism and Eastern Orthodoxy hold that during their sacrament of Eucharist, the bread is transformed into the body of Jesus, and the wine is transformed into his blood. Roman Catholicism refers to this as the miracle of 'transubstantiation'.

These denominations hold the position that literally eating Jesus' flesh and drinking his blood is necessary to enter God's kingdom. They justify this claim by referring to John 6:48-58, verses 53 and 54 of which read, *"So Jesus said to them, 'Truly, truly, I say to you, unless you eat the flesh of the son of man and drink his blood, you have no life in yourselves. He who eats my flesh and drinks my blood has eternal life, and I will raise him up on the last day.'"* To enable this consumption of Jesus' flesh and blood to occur, they hold that the bread and wine they use during their Eucharist ritual mystically transforms into Jesus' actual flesh and blood after a blessing by the priest. To justify this belief, they refer to Matthew 26:26-28 (The Last Supper) *"While they were eating, Jesus took some bread, and after a blessing, he broke it and gave it to the disciples, and said, 'Take, eat; this is my body.' And when he had taken a cup and given thanks, he gave it to them, saying, 'Drink from it, all of you; for this is my blood of the covenant, which is being poured out for many for the forgiveness of sins.'"*

I find this interpretation far from credible. In John 6:47, immediately before speaking of himself as being the "bread of life", Jesus is quoted as saying "*Truly, truly, I say to you, the one who believes has eternal life.*" As discussed earlier, for this to be true, when Jesus then went on to talk about himself as being the bread of life, he must have been speaking allegorically, as was his usual teaching practice. For both John 6:47 and John 6:54 to be true, when Jesus said you must eat his body and drink his blood, he must have meant you must believe (πιστεύων - pisteuō) God. To reinforce this interpretation, in John's gospel we read Jesus saying, "*Truly, truly, I say to you, the one who hears my word, and believes him who sent me, has eternal life, and does not come into judgement, but has passed out of death into life.*" (John 5:24)

Jesus also teaches that to find life we must deny ourselves, take up our cross daily and follow him (Luke 9:23; Matthew 16:24). For both this teaching and the teaching in John 5:24 and 6:47 to be true, the belief Jesus talks about must mean more than simply having an opinion on the veracity of what he taught. The verb translated from the original Greek as 'believe' (πιστεύων – pisteuō) in John 5:24 and 6:47, clearly means the deeper impact discussed above – having faith and entrusting one's spiritual well-being. The teaching to deny ourselves, take up our cross daily and follow him emphasises the extent to which we must trust him – total self-sacrificial commitment.

Also, in John Chapter 6, immediately before his teaching on 'Bread of life', Jesus had just fed a large crowd with only five barley loaves and two fish. So, the obvious interpretation of the 'bread of life' teaching is that Jesus was acting in a way that was consistent with his usual style of his ministry, using allegory and symbolism to make a point. Having just demonstrated he could miraculously feed people 'in the flesh', he then began teaching that he was the *"bread of life"* (John 6:48), able to feed people spiritually. This teaching also aligns with his teaching that he is the Way, the Truth and the Life (John 14:6) and that those who would enter heaven must deny themselves, take up their cross daily and follow him (Luke 9:23; Matthew 16:24-26). Therefore, claiming that the bread and wine used when remembering Jesus transforms into his actual body and blood, draws a long bow that lacks credibility. Understandably therefore, denominations that are freed from the 'succession of authority' doctrine and who are permitted to *"work out their salvation"* (Philippians 2:12), all tend to abandon the 'transubstantiation' doctrine.

At the Last Supper, Jesus was still present in the flesh when handing out the bread with his actual body, so he clearly didn't mean the bread he was handing out was literally his body. Also, his blood at that time had not yet been spilled. Today, for recipients of the bread and wine shared with them during the Eucharist ritual, these substances still taste like bread and wine; no measurable transubstantiation has occurred. So, this supposed miracle of transubstantiation bears no resemblance to recorded miracles of Jesus, such as turning water into wine, healing the sick or raising the dead, all of which produced observable outcomes.

Although Anglicanism holds that both water baptism and Eucharist are *"generally necessary to salvation"* (1662 Catechism), they do not hold to the notion of transubstantiation but instead hold that the bread and wine undergo a spiritual transformation. Whereas such a notion of dead material items undergoing some sort of spiritual transformation may seem extreme to people not brought up with such beliefs, as outlined in Chapter 1, it is not unusual for the human brain to come up with apparently farfetched ideas to support beliefs already held. Fortunately, we do not need to create a notion of transubstantiation. Jesus actually gave the reason for taking the symbolic actions he did at the last supper: He wanted his disciples to remember him each time they ate, because he knew he was about to die. The significance of what he would shortly endure to sacrifice himself for them was weighing heavily on his mind.

Again, the Didache can help us understand how Jesus' teachings as recorded in the Gospels have evolved to the Eucharist sacrament as practised today. Chapter 9 of the Didache reads:

> *"Now concerning the Eucharist, give thanks this way. First concerning the cup:*
>
> *We thank you, our father, for the holy vine of David your son, which you made known to us through Jesus your son; to you be glory for ever.*
>
> *And concerning the broken bread:*
>
> *We thank you, our father, for the life and knowledge which you made known to us through Jesus your son; to you be glory for ever. Even this broken bread was scattered over the hills, and was gathered together and became one, so let the church be gathered together from the end of the earth into your kingdom; for yours is the glory and the power through Jesus Christ for ever.*
>
> *But let no one eat or drink of your Eucharist, unless they have been baptised into the name of the lord; for concerning this also the lord has said, Give not that which is holy to the dogs."*

Chapter 10 then goes on to make it clear that the Eucharist was an actual meal, because it gives instruction on how one should *"pray after Communion, after you are filled"*.

Of note, in this earliest record of how the early Christians practised the Eucharist, they prayed to the father and saw both Jesus and King David as sons of the father. (Some translations say servants, but the same Greek word is used for both.) Also of note, the apostles referred to the bread as symbolic of all the followers of Jesus being geographically spread, rather than anything about transubstantiation of Jesus' body.

So, do such weaknesses in the beliefs and practices of denominations such as Eastern Orthodoxy and Roman Catholicism mean that all their members will not get into God's kingdom? No, that does not follow, but it does follow that some things they believe are false and that practising such rituals and requirements is not enough for salvation. Fortunately, scriptures on the teachings of Jesus about what is necessary for salvation are extensive and supported by different sources, as discussed earlier.

Potentially more significantly, because it affects all Christian denominations, I find it interesting that the Codex Bezae record of the last supper in Luke 22 omits verse 20, *"which is given for you. Do this in remembrance of me.' And likewise the cup after they had eaten, saying 'This cup that is poured out for you is the covenant in my blood'"*. This passage appears in other manuscripts, which may therefore be interpolations. Verses 17 and 18 refer to Jesus talking about the cup and passing it to the disciples. Verse 19 then refers to him talking about and passing the bread to the disciples. The cup was already dealt with, yet most manuscripts reinsert Jesus again talking about the cup after the disciples had eaten. This seems out of place; the Codex Bezae account seems more credible; even more so if we also note that in Jewish fashion, the cup precedes the bread. Codex Bezae does however include the equivalent of verse 20 in Mark's gospel, which Luke drew from in writing his. If this possible interpolation is removed, the passage reads well. Therefore, considering all this conflicting evidence together, it is inconclusive whether Luke 22:20 is an interpolation.

If we do accept that the narrative recorded in Luke 22:20 is an interpolation, then by also considering the Didache record of what should occur in the Eucharist, modern understandings and practices in the Eucharist would seem to have been invented by the church, rather than what Jesus or the first apostles practised or instructed. If we practised the Eucharist as instructed by the apostles, we would be thanking God for his *"son David"* whom Jesus descended from and thanking God for the life and knowledge which his *"son Jesus"* made known to us.

The Last supper occurred in the context of a Jewish ritual practice. The thought of drinking blood in a Jewish context is unthinkable; consuming blood is not kosher (Leviticus 17:10-16). Such practices do occur in other pagan practices. In 1 Corinthians 11:23-27 Paul is more explicit about the meaning of the practices associated with the Eucharist. It may be that the associated beliefs are a Pauline doctrine that were later added into the gospels.

3.4 SUMMARY

Throughout his ministry, Jesus used many different analogies to teach the same message. The overarching theme running through his teaching is that God wants our heart, rather than our compliance with ritual rules and practices; he wants us to seek, love, and trust him. Prophets before Jesus gave a similar message (Hosea 6:6; Ezekiel 36:26-27; Jeremiah 31:33). Jesus used symbolism, but did not impose mitzvahs (ritual acts of religious duty), and in fact taught that mitzvahs (the law) in the Tanakh were misunderstood and being used to oppress people.

Various ways Jesus conveyed this message include:

- He was critical of the Pharisees for burdening the people with mitzvahs (Matthew 23:4).

- He contravened a mitzvah and, when criticised for it, gave examples of King David and priests doing likewise. He then told his critics that the sabbath (Shabbat) was made for man, not man for the sabbath (Mark 2:23-28; Matthew 12:1-8).

- At the moment of his death on the cross, the curtain in the temple that separated the people from the inner sanctum, known as the 'Holy of Holies', where God was said to dwell, was torn in two. This rip is interpreted by many as symbolising God's permission and desire for us all to approach him directly, rather than through priests (Matthew 27:51).

- He taught that the greatest commandment is to love God with all your heart (Mark 12:28-30; Matthew 22:37-38; Luke 10:27; Deuteronomy 6:5).

- He taught that we should show compassion to each other (Luke 7:13; Luke 10:30-37; Matthew 15:34; Matthew 22:39; Mark 12:31).

- He taught we should repent and turn away from a selfish life, which he referred to as living in the flesh (Matthew 4:17; Matthew 6:24; Matthew 16:24; Luke 13:3; John 6:63)

We have seen throughout history how humans find it easier to substitute laws, mitzvahs, and sacraments, rather than giving God what the scriptures show he wants from us, which involves worshiping him in spirit and in truth (John 4:24), presenting our entire being as a living sacrifice (Luke 9:23; Romans 12:1-2). We organise ourselves into groups – our churches – that create and operate the mechanisms by which we normalise this perversion of Jesus' teachings, creating a belief that it is by faithfully practising laws and sacraments that we will satisfy God.

I conclude from the Gospel accounts that Jesus did not require the sacraments. These were created by the church and evolved over time to become increasingly ritualised. For many, these rituals have taken the place of the devotion that Jesus taught God wants. Some people misinterpret Jesus in John 3:5 as commanding water baptism as a necessary rite of passage to enter heaven. However, other scriptures seem to conflict with that interpretation. The structure of the chapter more readily suggests Jesus' purpose in referring to being born of water was to contrast physical birth from a mother's womb with the spiritual birth required to enter God's kingdom. He equates being born from a mother's womb (vs 4) with being born of water (vs 5) and born of the flesh (vs6); these all mean the same thing.

The concept of God requiring a spiritual birth rather than legal compliance is a difficult concept to grasp and accept if one's religious leaders have always taught that their religion requires mitzvahs, as Nicodemus' religion had required of him, and as so many Christian and Islamic denominations and sects require of them. Christianity's mitzvahs are its sacraments, and Islam has its five pillars and Sharia.

Why do humans do this? It is not the purpose of this book to answer this question, but I encourage you to explore. To get you started, I offer three theoretical perspectives to consider[65]:

- **Religious perspective:** Could it be because God has chosen only a few to know the mysteries of heaven (Matthew 13:11)? If the political

---

[65] Note: I am not necessarily advocating any of these perspectives; they are just to get you thinking.

powers require all people to follow a religion, not all are going be the chosen few, so they need to come up with another formula.

- **Political perspective:** Governance at a national, sub-population, or organisation level, requires legitimacy to be able to govern. So, if an organisation or a political power wants to use Religion to control the masses, it must create a narrative and associated practices that the majority will follow and that legitimise the authority of the ruler.

- **Sociological perspective:** People establish and seek to maintain cultural identity through social norms that incorporate rituals and practices peculiar to their cultural group, thereby distinguishing them from other groups. (Consider this perspective as we enter the next chapter.)

CREDIBLE?

4. JESUS FULFILLING THE LAW

"For you are not a true Jew just because you were born of Jewish parents or because you have gone through the ceremony of circumcision. No, a true Jew is one whose heart is right with God. And true circumcision is not merely obeying the letter of the law; rather, it is a change of heart produced by the Spirit."

Romans 2:28-29

4.1 WHAT DO CHRISTIAN SCRIPTURES SAY ABOUT THE LAW?

Jesus approached Jewish religious laws from the perspective of Judaism, which believes religious laws were given by God through Moses, as part of a covenant with God. In this covenant, God promises land and his protection on the Jewish people so long as they obey his laws. As a sign of accepting this covenant, Jewish parents have their sons circumcised when they are 8 days old. Circumcision symbolically signifies belonging to God as part of the covenant community. The most well-known of Judaism's laws are the 10 Commandments (Exodus 20), which Exodus 31:18 records as being inscribed on two tablets by God on Mount Sinai. Christians and Jews both support the 10 commandments. However, the Torah also contains numerous other very detailed laws, particularly in the book of Leviticus, which it records as having been given to Moses by God (Leviticus 1:1). By Jesus' time, Judaism's religious leaders had added further rules to the laws of Moses. Jesus was critical of these.

Matthew 5:18 records Jesus in his Sermon on the Mount saying, *"For truly, I say to you, until heaven and earth pass away, not an iota, not a dot, will pass from the law until all is accomplished"*. Most Jews and Christians take this verse to mean that Jesus was affirming the laws of Moses, as recorded in the Torah. Jews hold that Jesus was commanding people to continue obeying all the laws in the Torah. However, the Jewish prophets had been telling the Jewish people for hundreds of years that God did not want their ritualistic laws, such as animal sacrifices and festivals. Instead, he wanted them to repent from sinful living, humble themselves, love him, and love each other (Psalm 50:9-15; 51:16-17; Hosea 6:6; Micah 6:6-8; Isaiah 1:11-15; Jeremiah 7:22-23). So, Jesus may have been referring more broadly to what God had been commanding his people.

As we will see, these messages from the Jewish prophets are consistent with the teachings of Jesus. Also, Christianity holds that it is impossible for humans to never break one of the laws, so a penalty for breaking the law was required. Christianity holds that Jesus' death on the cross paid that penalty for us all (Romans 8:3-4). They refer to Jesus as 'the lamb of God', referring to the Jewish practice of sacrificing lambs as a sin offering to God. In this chapter I will explore evidence for the credibility of this idea.

Some Christians hold that, because Jesus affirmed the law, the old covenant still exists for Jews whereby God promises land and protection to the Jewish people if they obey his commandments. However, as discussed in Chapter 3, Christians also believe that this is insufficient for people to be able to enter the Kingdom of God. At the Last Supper before his crucifixion, Jesus also spoke of his death ushering in a new covenant (Luke 22:20; 1 Corinthians 11:25). Christianity holds that Christians are now under this new covenant, rather than the old Jewish covenant. Chapter 8 of The New Testament epistle to the Hebrews discusses this new covenant and how it makes the old Jewish covenant obsolete. This narrative draws on the Jewish prophet, Jeremiah, who in Jeremiah 31:31-34 prophesied a new covenant.

In the new covenant, we are expected to love each other – even natural enemies and classes of people generally rejected by proper society. Jesus modelled this behaviour by interacting with Samaritans, Romans, tax collectors, lepers, gentiles and the demon possessed. He treated everyone the same, irrespective of their social class identity. Rather, he judged those who were humble, broken, and caring more highly than those who were rich, powerful, and pious.

4.2 JESUS' RESPONSE TO ACCUSATIONS OF BREAKING THE LAW

Jesus was often accused by the Jewish leaders of breaking religious laws, but he always challenged them on this, saying things like he was fulfilling the law, and making it clear that:

- the intent behind the law was more important than the letter of the law, and

- that the law was for the benefit of man rather than a yoke put on man.

He gave the example of David eating consecrated food from the temple when no other food was available (Matthew 12:3-8), he healed people on the Sabbath (Mark 3:1-6) and he said it was OK to pull a donkey out of a ditch on the Sabbath rather than leave it there (Luke 14:5). In other words, although there is a place for symbolic practices, they are not paramount.

He said, for example, *"The Sabbath was made for man, and not man for the Sabbath."* (Mark 2:27) Throughout his ministry, Jesus frequently expressed concern that the law had become paramount, rather than the reason for the law, which was about loving God and one's neighbour.

4.3 JESUS AS THE LAMB OF GOD

THE CHRISTIAN NARRATIVE

The Christian narrative about Old Testament Jewish laws is that they were merely shadows of things to come (Colossians 2:16-17). For example, the Torah commanded animal sacrifices as an atonement for sin, *"For the life of the flesh is in the blood, and I have given it for you on the altar to make atonement for your souls, for it is the blood that makes atonement by the life"* (Leviticus 17:11). This is because God is understood to be a holy god with whom no relationship is possible if a person is sinful. *"You are to be perfect, as your heavenly father is perfect"* (Matthew 5:48). However, both Judaism and Christianity hold that animal sacrifices could never atone for all sin permanently. Judaism therefore held that such sacrifices needed to be repeated. Accordingly, every day, priests slaughtered lambs, bulls, goats, pigeons and turtle doves, because Judaism required sacrifice for forgiveness of sins. Also, every year on the Day of Atonement (Yom Kippur) in the Jewish calendar, the high priest performed a special sacrifice ritual for forgiveness of the sins of the Jewish nation as a whole (Leviticus 16).

In the Christian New Testament, John the Baptist declared Jesus to be "*the lamb of God who takes away the sin of the world*" (John 1:29). Through Jesus' sacrifice on the cross, he supposedly fulfilled the law, reconciling us with God who now no longer requires animal sacrifices (Romans 3:25 & 5:10-11). Although the Christian narrative is consistent with the Jewish Day of Atonement narrative, claiming that Jesus' death fulfils the law, and replaces it, is an audacious claim. To support such a claim, historical evidence is required in addition to the Christian narrative. As I will show, such evidence exists in the Jewish Talmud.

HISTORY OF JEWISH SACRIFICIAL PRACTICES

Historically, Jewish faith revolved around animal sacrifices at the temple. However, even though Jews do not accept Jesus was from God, they no longer make animal sacrifices and have not done so since his crucifixion. The reason typically given for why animal sacrifices ceased is that the temple was destroyed by the Romans in 70 CE, it has never been possible to rebuild the temple, and animal sacrifices are only permitted to be made at the temple. As I will show, it is significant that the destruction of the second temple occurred 40 years after Jesus' crucifixion.

The first temple (Known as Solomon's Temple) was built around 1,000 BCE. After its construction, animal sacrifices were only permitted to be made at the temple. Solomon's Temple was later destroyed by the Babylonians in 586 BCE. However, the Tanakh records Jews resuming animal sacrifices prior to construction recommencing on the second temple (Ezra 3:6). Also, the practice of animal sacrifices began before Solomon's Temple was constructed. At that stage, Jews set up temporary tabernacles made from tent material. So, the credibility of the argument justifying ceasing animal sacrifices because the temple was destroyed, seems weak to me.

I find it interesting that in the Mishna, which is the earliest and most central part of the Rabbinic Talmud, we find the following passage:

> "*During the tenure of Shimon HaTzaddik, the lot for God always arose in the High Priest's right hand; after his death, it occurred only occasionally; but during*

the forty years prior to the destruction of the Second Temple, the lot for God did not arise in the High Priest's right hand at all. So too, the strip of crimson wool that was tied to the head of the goat that was sent to Azazel did not turn white, and the westernmost lamp of the candelabrum did not burn continually. And the doors of the Sanctuary opened by themselves." (Yoma 39b)

Understanding the symbolic significance of this record requires some knowledge of the context – Yom Kippur. This annual Jewish ritual sacrifice prescribed in Leviticus 16 of the Torah, involved two goats. What would happen to them was decided by lots:

- One goat was 'for God'. This goat would be sacrificed and its blood taken by the high priest into the 'Holy of Holies' behind the curtain in the temple (the part of the temple where God was said to dwell). The priest would select the two lots, one in each of his hands. If the lot 'for God' came up in his right hand, this was considered a good omen of God's acceptance of the sacrifice that year.

- The other goat 'for Azazel' (possibly a wilderness area) was known as the scapegoat and would be set free in the wilderness after the peoples' sins had been symbolically loaded onto it by speaking over it and tying a strip of red wool to its head. The red colour in the wool faded to white after being out in the weather for a time. This fading from red to white symbolised the peoples' sins being washed clean following the atonement ritual.

THE MISHNA CORROBORATES THE GOSPEL

Most scholars estimate the year of Jesus' crucifixion as 30 CE. We read in the synoptic gospels that at the moment of Jesus' death the curtain in the temple symbolically separating God (in the Holy of Holies) and humans (outside the Holy of Holies) was torn in two from top to bottom (Mark 15:38). Also, as recorded above in the Mishna, in that same year the doors of the sanctuary containing the Holy of Holies opened by themselves and numerous other synonymous symbolic things happened.

Given what we know of Jesus' death from the accounts in the Gospels, I find the passage in Yoma 39b of the Mishna to be strong corroborative evidence that God rejected Judaism's system of atonement from the point in history when Jesus dies on the cross. The gospel account of the curtain separating the Holy of Holies being ripped in two and the Mishna account of the self-opening doors to the sanctuary containing the Holy of Holies are symbolically consistent. They both symbolise the same thing – the barrier between God and man being taken away at the moment of Jesus' death. It is not credible to assume these two accounts from sources on opposite sides of the argument are coincidence, particularly since the account in the Mishna almost certainly post-dates the account in the Gospels. Furthermore, the final verse in the chapter of the Torah requiring this annual sacrifice for the sins of the people (Leviticus 16), reads "'*Now you shall have this as a permanent statute, to make atonement for the sons of Israel for all their sins once every year.' And Moses did as God commanded.*" Rabbinic Judaism no longer includes what is perhaps the most important ritual of the Torah – the one that preserves the Jewish people in relationship with God. These days, Yom Kippur practices instead conform to new rules and traditions created by Rabbis in their Talmud, seemingly in direct disobedience to the command in Leviticus 16:34 of the Torah.

4.4 WHAT DOES JESUS MEAN BY 'FULFILLING THE LAW'?

In the previous chapter I provided numerous instances of Jesus teaching that to fulfil the law a person's heart must be right with God and toward people. Jesus said that, if ones heart is in the right place, the behaviour and actions God wants from us will flow out from us. The implication of this teaching is that one fulfils the law by putting one's heart in order, rather than by following laws literally. As written (possibly by Paul) in the epistle to the Jews: "*For the law is only a shadow of the good things to come, not the realities themselves. It can never, by the same sacrifices offered year after year, make perfect those who draw near to worship*" (Hebrews 10:1). This narrative aligns with records of Jesus' teaching and death, so passes the consistency test.

Jesus' behaviour demonstrates his abhorrence of hypocrisy and what the Jewish rituals had become. For example, moneylenders in the temple court angered Jesus because they were exploiting people (Matthew 21:12-13). He also frequently criticized the Jewish Religious leaders for burdening their people with mitzvahs (religious commandments or laws) rather than guiding them into right relationship with God and their fellow man (Matthew 23:4-7). Compliance with mitzvahs had become the primary requirement of Jewish faith, rather than loving God and other people. Religious leaders used their knowledge of laws to boost their own social status in comparison with ordinary Jewish people. Jesus saw this as the antithesis of what they were supposed to be doing.

The Jewish people had been looking for a Messiah to free them, they thought from Roman oppression, but what Jesus showed them was that they needed to be freed from spiritual oppression. When challenged to take a political stand, Jesus refused (Mark 12:17). He taught instead that whatever situation people find themselves in – slave or free – rich or poor – powerful or powerless – how we behave towards God and the people we encounter in life is what is truly important. Jesus was the antithesis of a 'social justice warrior', fighting political causes through advocacy. He didn't teach slaves to disobey their masters; he didn't teach equity and redistribution of wealth; he didn't teach workers to overthrow their bosses. Jesus taught that such an agenda missed the point. Instead, he challenged the individual about their own personal demonstration of love. This remains a radical idea, far removed from what humans naturally gravitate to.

The Jews in the second temple period had been captured by the agenda of their cultural, religious, and ethnic identity with its social norms of behaviour. Jesus challenged those who piously reject shunned classes of people (e.g. Samaritans; tax collectors; lepers). This is not so different from today, where identity politics drive much self-righteous contention amongst humanity. Rather than be part of that way of living, Jesus calls people out of that very human state and into a right relationship with God and our fellow man instead. Jesus' message therefore cuts across time and cultures. In his time, people were looking for Jesus to support political positions, both secular and religious (Mark 12:14-27; Matthew 9:10-13; Matthew 20:1-6). However, he instead taught how you individually should relate to God and the person in front of you, whoever they are.

4.5 SUMMARY

The evidence that Jesus fulfils the law is at least coherent and still relevant. His life and teachings are internally inconsistent and consistent with the historical Jewish narrative.

The corroboration between the symbolism recorded in the Mishna and Gospels coinciding historically with Jesus' death is compelling. In particular, the evidence is strong that his death fulfilled the requirement that Judaic law previously sought to fulfil through animal sacrifices. However, does this mean we can dispense with all traditional religious laws? Is following Jesus sufficient instead? It would be easier to believe this if we can be confident that he is the long-awaited Messiah prophesied in the Tanakh who would save the people.

CREDIBLE?

5. IS JESUS THE MESSIAH?

"Who has ascended into heaven and descended? Who has gathered the wind in his fists? Who has wrapped the waters in his garment? Who has established all the ends of the earth? What is his name or his son's name? Surely you know!"

Proverbs 30:4

5.1 COMPARING MESSIANIC BELIEFS

The Christian gospels record Jesus claiming to be the Messiah and others who knew him recognised him as such (Matthew 16:15-17; Mark 14:61-62; Luke 4:17-21; John 4:25-26; John 11:25-27). Christianity holds that Jesus is the Messiah prophesied in the Old Testament (Tanakh), that he came once 2,000 years ago, and that he will come again at the end of time when he will rule over the earth and judge the nations (Matthew 25:31-46). Judaism holds that the Messiah has not yet come and that he will only come once. So, both Judaism and Christianity currently await a coming of the Messiah, even though Christianity holds he has already come once before.

Islam accepts both the Jewish belief that there were prophecies about the coming of the Messiah, and the Christian belief that the Messiah was Jesus, son of Mary. They also believe he will come again at the end of the world and slay the anti-Christ (Sahih Muslim 41:7023). However, unlike Christianity, Islam holds that Jesus was not the son of God, nor was he crucified (although Islam claims someone else was substituted for Jesus on the cross). Islam considers the term Messiah as a kind of honorific title, in a similar way to how Muslims consider Messenger of God (Rasul Allah) to be an honorific title referring to Muhammad.

I found far less attention given by Islamic scholars to studying evidence about whether Jesus is the Messiah than I found from Jewish and Christian scholars. Islam holds Jesus was a prophet, and one whom God granted miraculous powers, including resurrection and ascension. God did not grant such powers to Muhammad. However, Muslims treat Muhammad with much greater reverence. This conflict between the relative level of God's blessing/power on each of these 'prophets' and the relative level of reverence and focus given to them by Muslims, supports my earlier conclusion in Chapter 2 – that the creator(s) of Islam only included mention of Jesus, the Messiah, and other Jewish prophets in their Qur'an as a device to increase the chance of their narrative appealing to Jews and Christians.

5.2 WHICH PASSAGES IN THE TANAKH PROPHESY JESUS AS THE MESSIAH?

Various Christian scholars cite numerous verses from the Old Testament (Tanakh), which they claim are prophesying Jesus coming as the Messiah. Most of these prophecies can be divided into two categories: Those which seem to prophesy Jesus (possibly as the Messiah) coming 2,000 years ago and those which seem to prophesy the Messiah coming at the end of time. I will focus more on the prophecies relating to Jesus' life 2,000 years ago, because the coming of the Messiah at the end of time has not yet occurred. We cannot yet compare what was prophesied with events that have not yet come to pass.

Challenges exist in verifying Messianic prophecies. Many contain insufficient information or specificity to be confident about whether they refer to Jesus. Others prophesy additional things that either don't seem to relate to Jesus or that did not occur at the same time as other parts of the prophesy. Because Jews expect the Messiah to come only once, one reason they give for denying Jesus is the Messiah is that the end-times aspects of the prophecies have not yet occurred.

As I read through the different passages in the Tanakh cited by different scholars as referring to the Messiah, it is not always obvious that the passage refers to the Messiah. Many such passages consist of short statements buried within a longer monologue that seems more likely to relate to someone else. For example, some of King David's psalms seem to relate more to King David's own situation than to that of Jesus or another future Messiah. Therefore, they may not actually be Messianic prophecies. Not all scholars cite the same passages as being Messianic prophecies.

I include below some of the passages which Christians often cite as referring to Jesus as the Messiah. Jewish scholars will concur that some of these passages are likely to be Messianic prophecies and would dispute that others are.

Potential Messianic prophesy	How this might be prophesying Jesus
Deuteronomy 18:18 "*I will raise up a prophet like you for them from among their fellow Israelites. I will put my words in his mouth and he shall speak to them everything I command.*"	• God telling Moses that he will raise up another prophet like Moses. This foretells of a future prophet but provides no information to assess whether this is Jesus. • Some Islamic scholars hold this verse prophesies Muhammad. This opinion is not supported by the verse itself, because it says the prophet will be a *"fellow Israelite"*, which Muhammad was not.
Psalm 2:1-12 "*Why are the nations in a rage and the people plotting in vain? The kings of the earth and the rulers conspire together against God and his anointed Messiah, saying 'Let's tear their shackles apart and free ourselves from their ropes!' He who sits in the heavens shall laugh, the lord scoffs at them. Then he will speak to them in anger and terrify them*"	• Prophesies God installing a king whom he designates as his son. • Prophesies this king being given the nations – a possible reference to other peoples than Jews. Christianity spread to other nations, even though it started amongst Jews.

in his rage, saying 'I have installed my king upon the holy hill of Zion. I will announce the decree of God: He said to me, 'You are my son, today I have begotten you. Ask of me, and I will certainly give the nations as your inheritance, and the ends of the earth for your possession.' You shall break them with a rod of iron, you shall smash them like earthenware. Now therefore, you kings, take the warning, you judges of the earth. Serve God with reverence and rejoice with trembling. Kiss the son and heir, so that he does not be angry and you perish on the way, for his wrath may ignite quickly. How blessed are all who take refuge in him!"

- Where the passage concludes with "*How blessed are all who take refuge in him*", Christians believe their refuge is in Christ Jesus who saves them.

Isaiah 7:14 "*Therefore the lord himself will give you a sign: Look, a virgin will conceive and give birth to a son, and she will name him Immanuel.*"

- The gospels record Jesus being born to a virgin. The term Immanuel means 'God with us', which Christians interpret as one of the titles referring to Jesus, as opposed to a given name.

Isaiah 9:1-7 "*But there will be no more gloom for she who was in anguish. In earlier times he treated the land of Zebulun and the land of Naphtali with contempt, but then he will make it glorious, by way of the sea, on the other side of the Jordan, Galilee of the gentiles. The people walking in darkness will see a great light; The light will shine on those who live in a land of deep darkness. You will multiply the nation, increasing their joy; they will rejoice in your presence like with the joy of harvest, as people rejoice when they divide the plunder. For you*

- Refers to Galilee, the region Jesus grew up in and commenced his ministry in.

- Jesus preached about bringing light to the world, partly through his teaching and partly through the hope of salvation by breaking the power of sin and death.

- Jesus challenged the yoke of the Pharisees – the burdensome obligations they were loading onto the people.

break the yoke of their burden and the staff on their shoulders, the stick of their oppressor, as at the battle of Midian. Indeed, every boot of the marching warrior in the roar of battle, and every garment rolled in blood will be burn as fuel for the fire. For a child will be born to us, a son will be given, and the government will rest on his shoulder, and his name will be called wonderful counsellor, mighty god, everlasting father, prince of peace."	• This passage seems to be saying that a child born human will be called mighty god. Jesus was born human and Trinitarian Christians claim he is God. The gospels record Jesus saying that those who have seen him have seen the father.
Isaiah 11:1-2 *"Then a shoot will grow from the stem of Jesse, and a branch from his roots will bear fruit. The lord's spirit will rest on him, the spirit of wisdom and understanding, counsel and might, knowledge and the fear of the lord."*	• Matthew's gospel records Jesus as being descendent of Jesse. • All four gospels record the spirit of God descending and resting on Jesus in the form of a dove at his baptism. • The gospels record Jesus as possessing amazing knowledge of the scriptures, being wise and understanding of people of different stations in life who may not have felt understood by others.
Isaiah 35:4-6 *"Tell those who are anxious, 'Be strong! Fear not! Look, your god comes to avenge! With God's retribution he comes to deliver you.'* *Then blind eyes will open, deaf ears will hear. Then the lame man will leap like a deer, the mute tongue will shout joyfully; for water will flow in the wilderness; streams in the desert."*	• Jesus is recorded as performing many miracles including healing blind, deaf, mute, and lame people.

Isaiah 40:3 "A *voice cries out, 'Clear the way for the lord in the wilderness; make a straight highway in the desert for our God.'"*	• All four gospels claim this verse refers to John the Baptist. • John the Baptist lived in the wilderness; he preached repentance and identified Jesus as the one he had prophesied who was much greater than he, so much so that he would baptise people with the holy spirit.
Isaiah 42:1-9 "*Look, my servant whom I uphold; my chosen one in whom my soul delights. I have placed my spirit on him; he will bring forth justice to the nations. He will not cry out nor shout, nor make his voice heard in the street. A broken reed he will not break, and a dimly burning wick he will not extinguish; he will faithfully bring forth justice. He will not faint or be discouraged until he has established justice on the earth; and the coastlands will wait expectantly for his law. This is what mighty God says, who created the heavens and stretched them out, who spread out the earth and its offspring, who gives breath to the people on it and spirit to those who walk in it: I, God, have called you in righteousness, I will take hold of your hand and watch over you, and I will make you a covenant to my flock, as a light to the nations, to open blind eyes, to release prisoners from dungeons and those who dwell in darkness from prison. I am God, that is my name; I will not give my glory to another, nor my praise to idols. Look, the former things have come to pass, now*"	• All four gospels record the spirit of God descending and resting on Jesus in the form of a dove. • Jesus remained silent for much of his trial. • Jesus is recorded as performing many miracles, including healing blind people.

I declare new things. Before they start, I proclaim them to you."

Isaiah 52:13-53:12 *"Look, my servant will prosper, he will be high and lifted up and greatly exalted. Just as many were shocked at you, so his appearance was marred he no longer looked like a man, and his form beyond the sons of mankind. Therefore, he will sprinkle many nations; Kings will shut their mouths because of him: For that which they had not been told, they will see, And that which they had not heard, they will understand. Who has believed our report? And to whom has the arm of God been revealed? For he grew up before him like a tender bud, and like a root from dry ground. He has no stately form or majesty that we might look at him, nor an appearance that we would take pleasure in him. He was despised and abandoned by people, a man of sorrows and familiar with sickness. And like one from whom people hide their faces, he was despised, and we did not respect him. However, it was our sicknesses he bore and our pains that he carried, yet we assumed that he had been afflicted, struck down by God, and humiliated. But he was pierced for our transgressions; he was crushed for our iniquities. The punishment for our well-being was laid upon him, and by his stripes we are healed. All of us, like sheep, have gone astray; each to his own way; But God has caused the iniquity of us all to be placed on him. He was oppressed and*

One of the strongest prophecies pointing to Jesus because it includes numerous aspects that could be associated with the account of his crucifixion:

- Christians believe 'lifting up' refers to both Jesus' crucifixion and his exaltation for being willing to be sacrificed for our sakes.

- His appearance being marred beyond that of a man could refer to the results of his being beaten by the Romans prior to his crucifixion.

- Reference to him sprinkling many nations, and kings shutting their mouths because of him, may refer to the subsequent spread of Christianity and the influence of the church over different countries.

- Growing up like a tender bud and a root from dry ground fits his upbringing in an ordinary family in Nazareth.

- Being "*despised and abandoned by people, a man of sorrows*", describes what happened following his apprehension and subsequent crucifixion, when even his disciples abandoned him.

- Bearing our sickness, carrying our pain, crushed for our iniquities and having the punishment laid on him for our *afflicted, yet did not open his mouth. Like a lamb led to slaughter, and like a sheep silent before its shearers, so he did not open his mouth. After oppression and judgement, he was taken away, and as for his generation, who was concerned that he was cut off from the land of the living, stricken for the wrongdoing of my people? And his grave was assigned with wicked people, yet he was with a rich man in his death, because he had done no violence, and there was no deceit in his mouth. But God desired To crush him, causing him grief. If he gives himself as a guilt offering, he will see his offspring, he will prolong his days, and the pleasure of God will prosper in his hand. Out of the anguish of his soul, he will see and be satisfied. By his knowledge the righteous one, my servant, will justify the many, for he will bear their iniquities. Therefore, I will assign him a portion with the great, and he will divide the spoils with the strong, because he poured out his soul unto death, and was numbered with wrongdoers. Yet he bore the sin of many and interceded for the wrongdoers."*

well-being fits the Christian narrative about Jesus taking the punishment for the sins of the world to redeem us.

- Jesus was pierced during his crucifixion, both with a crown of thorns that the Romans placed on his head and by the spear they stabbed him with to see if he was dead.

- Jesus was crucified alongside two common criminals, after which his body was placed in a rich man's tomb.

- Jesus' days were prolonged through his resurrection, and his offspring are those who choose to follow the way he taught.

Isaiah 61:1-2 *"The Spirit of the Lord is upon me, because he has anointed me; he has sent me to preach glad tidings to the poor, to heal the broken-hearted, to proclaim freedom to the captives, and recovery of sight to the blind; to declare the acceptable year of the Lord, and the day of recompence; to comfort all that*

- Jesus claims this refers to him, as quoted in Luke 4:18.

- The gospels record Jesus healing blind people.

mourn.'[66]

Jeremiah 23:5 "*Behold, the days are coming, says God, when I will raise up for David a righteous branch; he will reign as king and act wisely and will do justice and righteousness in the land.*"	• Jesus preached righteousness and is a descendant of King David.
Jeremiah 31:31-34 " '*Behold the days are coming*', *says God*, '*when I will make a new covenant with the house of Israel and the house of Judah, not like the covenant that I made with their fathers on the day I took them by the hand to bring them out of the land of Egypt, my covenant which they broke, although I was a husband to them*' *declares God*. '*For this is the covenant which I will make with the house of Israel after those days*', *says God*: '*I will put my law within them and write it in their hearts; and I will be their god, and they will be my people*' "	This prophesy strongly aligns with the teaching of Jesus: • Christians hold that, through what Jesus did, God made a new covenant with his people (Jews and gentiles). Here, Jeremiah is prophesying such a new covenant that will be different from the old covenant Jews previously had. (Luke 22:20; 1 Corinthians 11:25) • Whereas the old covenant involved complying with various laws, Jeremiah prophesies that in the new covenant, God will write the law on peoples' hearts. This seems to fit the teaching of Jesus, who taught what comes out of a person defiles them, rather than the food that goes in (Mark 7:15; Matthew 15:11). • Jesus taught that the law, prophecies and righteousness are fulfilled by getting one's heart right with God and fellow man. After this new covenant of the heart is in place, the relationship that

---

[66] This translation is based on the Septuagint. As discussed in Section 2.2, the Masoretic Text omits *"and recovery of sight to the blind"*.

	God wants with people will be restored.
Daniel 9:26 "*Then after sixty-two weeks, the anointed one will be cut off and have nothing, and the people of the prince who will come will destroy the city and the sanctuary. Its end will come with a flood; even to the end there will be war; desolations are determined.*"	• A commonly cited prophesy that suggests the anointed one [Messiah] will be cut off [killed?] before the destruction of the city [Jerusalem?] and the sanctuary [temple?] by the prince who will come [son of the Roman emperor?]; there will be a war and desolation. • Historical evidence shows that Jesus was crucified in 30 CE or soon after, Jerusalem and the temple were then destroyed in 70 CE by Titus, son of the Roman Emperor Vespasian (i.e. a prince); the desolation to both Jerusalem and its people was extreme. • 300 years after Jesus' resurrection, Eusebius posited that Jesus' ministry lasted three and a half years. However, he is known to get some other facts wrong in his writings. Scholars are uncertain of the duration of Jesus' ministry. Estimates typically range between 1 year and 3.5 years. It is possible that 70 weeks elapsed between Jesus' baptism and the coming of the holy spirit recorded in Acts 2. If so, the period of 62 weeks mentioned in this passage may refer to the period of Jesus' active ministry.

Micah 5:2 "*But you, Bethlehem Ephrathah, too little to be among the thousands of Judah, from you one will come forth to me to be the ruler in Israel. His times of coming forth are from long ago, from ancient days.*"	• The gospels record Jesus being born in Bethlehem.
Micah 5:4 "*And he will arise and shepherd in the strength of God, in the majesty of the name of the lord his god. And they will remain, because at that time he will be great to the ends of the earth.*"	• Jesus spoke of himself as being the "good shepherd" (John 10:11). The gospels record Jesus providing 'pastoral care' to his disciples and guidance to thousands of others who came to hear him speak.
Zechariah 9:9-11 "*Rejoice greatly, O daughter of Zion! Shout, O daughter of Jerusalem! Look, your king is coming to you; He is just, having salvation, humble and mounted on a donkey, upon a colt, the foal of a donkey. And I will cut off the chariot from Ephraim and the horse from Jerusalem, and the battle bow will be cut off. He will speak peace to the nations, and his dominion will be from sea to sea, and from the river to the ends of the earth. As for you also, because of the blood of my covenant with you, I have set your prisoners free from the waterless pit.*"	• In the week prior to his crucifixion, Jesus entered Jerusalem on a young donkey. That said, Jesus would have been aware of this prophesy, so it is possible he could have chosen to ride a donkey to be seen to fulfil this prophesy. • The gospel account and Christian narrative describes Jesus as a sacrificial lamb. His willing act of self-sacrifice created a new covenant in which those who follow him will be set free spiritually.
Zechariah 12:10 "*And I will pour out on the house of David and upon the inhabitants of Jerusalem, the spirit of grace and of pleading, so that they will look at me whom they pierced; and they will mourn for him, like one mourning for an only son, and they will weep bitterly for him like the bitter weeping over their firstborn.*"	• Jesus was from the house of David and ministered in Jerusalem where he was crucified. • Jesus was pierced during his crucifixion. • Paul writes of Jesus being the firstborn of all creation

	(Colossians 1:15) and the firstborn of many brothers (Romans 8:29); Revelation speaks of Jesus as being the firstborn of the dead (Revelation 1:5).
Malachi 3:1 "Behold, I will send my messenger, and he will clear the way before me. And the lord, whom you seek, will suddenly come to his temple. The messenger of the covenant, in whom you delight, behold, he is coming, says the lord of hosts."	• This could be interpreted as God announcing Jesus or John the Baptist, clearing the way for Jesus (the lord) to arrive.

Additional prophetic passages exist in the Tanakh which could be interpreted as referring to Jesus. However, the above references alone contain considerable specific details consistent with Jesus' life. Throughout the gospels, Jesus says and does things that communicate he is the Messiah. He also claims that title directly. For example, when he asks Peter who Peter thinks he is, and Peter says Jesus is the Messiah, Jesus praises him for getting it right and instructs the disciples to tell no one (Matthew 16:13-20). Also, in Mark 9:41, Jesus tells his disciple John that anyone who gives you a cup of water because you are a follower of the Messiah (himself – implied) will be rewarded. Finally, when the Jewish High priest asks Jesus if he is the Messiah, Jesus acknowledges this recognition (Matthew 26:63-64). Therefore, when considered alongside the prophecies in the Tanakh, the available evidence supporting the claim that Jesus is the Messiah is extensive.

5.3 SUMMARY

Having listened to the perspectives of numerous Jews and Christians, my impression is that Christians are so confident Jesus is the Messiah that they struggle to entertain the possibility he might not be; conversely, Jews have been so conditioned to oppose the possibility of Jesus being any more than a deluded teacher, that they tend to put more faith in arguments against the possibility than warranted by the strength of those argument.

A particular sticking point for Jews is believing that God could have meant the peace that had been prophesied to accompany the Messiah would be an internal spiritual peace, rather than a military peace. Jesus did not bring a military peace for the nation of Israel, but many Christians have attested to him bringing peace within their lives and the New Testament epistles repeatedly speak about the peace Jesus brings.

Some of the prophecies seem to match Jesus closely. Could it be that Jesus was prophesied, but not as the Messiah – at least not yet? Is it possible that some of the passages interpreted by some to be Messianic prophecies may not be, but may be prophesying Jesus, nevertheless? For example, it is easy to recognise in Isaiah 52:13-53:12 many things about Jesus. However, this passage does not talk so much of the coming of a king who will defeat enemies and rule in the way other Messianic prophecies do; it talks of God's servant.

Christians commonly point to Isaiah 53 as the most obvious prophesy in the Tanakh pointing to Jesus. However, from an evidential perspective, if one accepts Daniel 9:26 as referring to the Messiah, this would be more compelling because it appears to include significant historically verifiable events – the destruction of the temple by the son of who will rule after this event. The only point in history that fits this description is the destruction of Jerusalem (and the temple in it) by Roman Emperor's son, General Titus, in 70 CE, only 40 years after Jesus' crucifixion. Although this would make Jesus the most likely candidate for Messiah, even if the Messiah was someone else, this verse suggests the Messiah has already come and "been cut off". However, Judaism holds that the Messiah has still not yet come.

I found more Jewish arguments against the Christian interpretation of Daniel 9:26 than against any other verse. I encountered a variety of different arguments, which suggests that a single clear interpretation is not obvious. However, one recurring item amongst these arguments is the interpretation of the word מָשִׁיחַ (mā-šî-aḥ) which literally means 'the anointed one' (or similar). Jewish arguments frequently point out that elsewhere in the Tanakh, this word in Hebrew is not used to refer to the Messiah, but to people, such as priests, kings or other people God has specially blessed or called to perform a task for him. In contrast to the variation in Jewish arguments, Christian arguments almost always interpret this particular instance of this word to be referring to the Messiah, due to the context of this verse.

Given the potential significance of this verse, a strong conflict of interest exists for both Jewish and Christian scholars. Personally, if I treat the interpretation of this word in the context of Daniel 9:26 as unclear, I still find it intriguing that the rest of the verse so closely aligns with the destruction of the temple that we know occurred in 70 CE.

Conclusion: No single prophesy when considered in isolation definitively points to Jesus. This is partly due to their tendency to be somewhat vague or cryptic and partly because each prophesy in isolation contains only limited details. However, collectively, the volume that contain aspects that align with the life of Jesus and the overlap between some of these, strongly supports a case that Jesus was foretold in the Tanakh, possibly as the first appearance of the Messiah. It is possible that the picture Jews have built up of the Messiah being a military commander rather than a spiritual one is mistaken and built on assumptions that evolved into part of their tradition.

The above passages that Christians claim prophesy Jesus as the Messiah, suggest the Messiah will be a servant, prophet and king. These aspects can all be seen in his life. Having now covered how Jesus lived and died, what he taught and what prophecies may refer to him, what can we infer from all this about who he is?

6. WHO IS JESUS?

"I know him, because I am from him, and he sent me."

John 7:29

Jesus is the key protagonist within Christianity. Therefore, as expected, Christian writings provide the most detail on him. However, because of the impact Christianity has had on Judaism and Islam, these religions have something to say about him too. So, before delving into the details provided within the Christian narrative, let us make ourselves aware of the perspectives of Judaism and Islam on the question of who Jesus is.

6.1 JUDAISM'S PERSPECTIVE

Most Jews accept, or can be persuaded, that Jesus was a Jew whose Hebrew name was Yeshua and who lived during the second temple period; many will even accept he was a Jewish teacher, but that he did not intend to start a new religion. Christianity also holds that he did not intend starting a new religion, but claims he came with a new covenant and that much of his teaching was a 'course correction' for what Judaism had become. However, Judaism holds that he is neither a prophet (as Islam holds) nor divine (as Christianity holds), and that he was not resurrected.

So strong is the rejection within Judaism of Jesus' teachings and of what Christians believe about him, that Judaism rejects Jews who believe Jesus is the Messiah, often viewing them either as being no longer Jewish or as apostate.

This strong aversion of Judaism to acknowledging any possibility of Jesus having any divine status or sanction is understandable. The Christian Church – particularly before the European Renaissance – influenced a negative and discriminatory impact of Jews lasting centuries.

In Chapter 2, I identified probable edits in the Masoretic Text that have the effect of weakening the alignment between Messianic prophecies in the Tanakh and Jesus' life. To further prevent assertions Jesus might be the Messiah or even a prophet, Judaism holds that the prophetic era ended centuries before Jesus, denying that God would ever send any more prophets. The Rabbinic phase of Judaism that properly formed in the 7th century CE subsequently created other mechanisms by which Judaism has evolved its canon: Rabbinic debate and the Talmud.

6.2 ISLAM'S PERSPECTIVE

The Qur'an makes numerous statements about Jesus that align with the Christian New Testament, including that he:

- was the Messiah (3:45), but it doesn't expand on what this means;

- was born to Mary (3:45) who, at the time, was still a virgin (3:47; 19:20);

- was a messenger to the children of Israel (3:49);

- healed lepers and the blind, and raised the dead (3:49; 4:158; 5:110);

- ascended to heaven (4:158).

The Qur'an also makes numerous statements that contradict the Christian New Testament, including that:

- Jesus was not crucified; someone else was substituted for him (4:157);

- God taught Jesus the Torah and the Gospel (3:48; 5:46; 5:110), as if the Gospel was a book that could be taught to Jesus rather than the record of his life and teachings, and the spiritual implications of his death and resurrection;

- he made a clay bird come to life (3:49);

- he was only a messenger like prophets who came before him (4:171; 5:75);

- he spoke while still a baby in the cradle, saying that he was a slave of God who had given him the book and appointed him a prophet (19:30);

- he prophesied the coming of Muhammad (61:6).

The Qur'an is light on detail about the events of Jesus' life and teachings. Islam holds that Jesus is not God or the son of God, but that he will return, and he will judge the people (4:157-159, Sahih al-Bukhari 3448).

I find it interesting that the Qur'an ascribes miraculous powers to Jesus, and states that God caused his ascension to heaven. However, Islam attributes no such power or ascension to Muhammad, even though Muslims revere him more. This inconsistency makes me wonder if the Qur'an tells us more about humanity than it does about God.

6.3 SON OF GOD OR MAN?

Christians refer to Jesus as 'the son of god'. This term is found in the Christian gospels associated with the identity of the Messiah. When Jesus asked his disciple, Peter, whom he thought Jesus was, Peter responded, "*You are the Christ, the son of the living God*" (Matthew 16:16). Similarly, When Jesus was asked by the high priest, "*Are you the Christ, the son of the Blessed?*"[67], he responded, "*I am, and you shall see the son of man sitting on the right hand of power and coming in the clouds of heaven*" (Mark 14:61-62). In response to this statement, the high priest accused Jesus of blasphemy. This may be because he recognised a reference to the prophesy in Daniel 7:13 which speaks of the son of man arriving with the clouds of heaven for an audience with God[68].

In most manuscripts, the first verse of Mark (probably the earliest gospel) reads, "*The beginning of the Gospel of Jesus Christ, the son of God*". However, the earliest manuscript containing a complete copy of Mark's gospel (Codex Sinaiticus) ends the sentence without saying "the son of God" (υἱοῦ θεοῦ), which is consistent with a number of other early manuscripts (described by Origen, Epiphanius and Victorinus), but not with Vaticanus, Alexandrinus and the

---

[67] Translators note in the NASB 2020 states that the term "Blessed" as used here by the high priest was a common way for Jewish leaders to refer to God.
[68] In Daniel 7:13, the Aramaic expression used for God is 'Ancient of Days'.

more verbose Western and Byzantine manuscripts. This omission from some early manuscripts creates uncertainty as to whether the original gospel contained this term. Reinforcing the possibility that it did not, I find it interesting that in Mark's gospel, neither Jesus nor any of his disciples directly refer to Jesus as the son of God. This term is only used by his enemies: High priests, demons, and the Roman centurion at the crucifixion. Instead, Jesus most commonly refers to himself as the son of man. It may be that Jesus' followers only began thinking of him as the son of God after the impact of his crucifixion and resurrection sunk in.

In is epistle to the Colossians, Paul says of Jesus, *"He is the image of the invisible God, the firstborn of every creature: for by him were all things created that are in heaven and that are on the earth, …"* (1:15-16a). At first glance, this passage appears to say Jesus is a created being who then participated in the creation of everything else. However, it may instead be a poetic expression intended to signify Jesus' authority over creation[69].

Christians since the middle ages, particularly in formal church settings within older branches of Christianity, commonly bestow on Jesus the title "God the Son". This title (ὁ θεὸς ὁ υἱός in Koine Greek) does not appear in the Christian scriptures but does appear in one late medieval manuscript[70]. Scholars accept this appearance is an error because it conflicts with all other manuscripts[71]. The earliest expression I have found that is similar to 'God the Son' is θεὸς θεοῦ υἱὸς – meaning 'God the son of God'. This appears in 'Dialogue with Trypho', a 2nd century CE writing by Justin Martyr. Therefore, use of the title 'God the Son' to refer to Jesus, appears likely to have been an innovation by Christians, perhaps beginning as early as the 2nd century CE[72].

---

[69] The Greek is a little ambiguous in Colossians 1:15. It uses the word πάσης which can mean 'of every', 'of every kind of' or 'of everybody', so can be translated 'the firstborn of everybody' (or 'of every creature' – KJV). However, most translations translate it more generically as 'firstborn of all creation". The NET Bible translators suggest this genitive form of the adjective suggests subordination. Accordingly, they translate the clause as, 'firstborn **over** all creation". This concept would be consistent with the family structure in that time, whereby the firstborn son inherited the authority of the father.

[70] Galatians 2:20 of the Manuscript that Gregory numbers 1985, and Tischendorf and Scrivener number 395ᴾ

https://www.skypoint.com/members/waltzmn/MSConv.html Accessed 3 July 2025

[71] https://en.wikipedia.org/wiki/God_the_Son Accessed 3 July 2025

[72] Hick, John (1993). *The Metaphor of God Incarnate: Christology in a Pluralistic Age (2ⁿᵈ ed.).* Westminster John Knox Press. p31

English usage of the term 'God the Son' may have derived from the Latin term 'Deus Filius'. This term appears in the Athanasian Creed, which is a strongly Trinitarian creed. This creed may have been named after Athanasius because he was the key protagonist in establishing the doctrine of the Trinity within church dogma at the Council of Nicaea in 325 CE. However, it is unlikely Athanasius wrote this creed because there is no evidence of its existence until centuries later[73]. Augustine of Hippo also used the term Deus Filius in his early 5th century CE writing 'On the Trinity'. Later, in 1530 CE, the Lutheran Augsburg Confession adopted the term.

In the Christian gospels, Jesus did not refer to himself as the son of god. Instead, he frequently used the term 'son of man'. However, he did refer to God as 'the father'. He prayed subserviently to the father and claimed he was sent by the father to do the father's will. So, by implication, if God is his father, he is God's son. He also taught his disciples to refer to God as their father, so effectively claimed not to be God's only son. He may have referred to God as his father as an example to his disciples to do the same. The gospels clearly show his own sense of identity was not equal to the father yet was primarily as a heavenly being sent to earth on a mission from God (Matthew 10:40; 12:18; Mark 14:61-62; Luke 4:17-21; John 17; 20:21).

One possible explanation for Jesus choosing to refer to himself as the son of man is that being born into a human body differentiates him from the other sons of god referred to in the Old Testament (Gen 6:2-7; Job 1:6; Job 2:1; Dead Sea Scrolls 4QDeut^j). Some people believe these scriptures refer to angels, but the scriptures do not make this clear; these are obviously heavenly beings who converse with God. The term son suggests they come from the father, perhaps created by him, or having less status or power than him.

The term 'son' when used to refer to heavenly beings should not be understood in quite the same terms as a human son, which is a biological product of a reproductive act by a man and a woman. Given that we cannot be clear on its meaning when applied to Jesus, I will make little use of the titles or concepts 'son of god' and 'son of man'.

---

[73] Krueger, Robert (1976). *The Origin And Terminology Of The Athanasian Creed*, Western Pastoral Conference (Lutheran) of the Dakota-Montana District, October 5-6, 1976 http://essays.wisluthsem.org:8080/bitstream/handle/123456789/2744/KruegerOrigin.pdf?sequence=1 Accessed 3 July 2025

6.4 SON OF MARY

Luke's gospel records that Jesus was born to an engaged woman as a result of the holy spirit coming upon her and enveloping her in a shadow or haze of brilliancy (Luke 1:35). Jesus' mother, Mary, remained a virgin until after Jesus was born (Matthew 1:18-25, Luke 1:26-38). This account is consistent with the prophesy in Isaiah 7:14 "*Therefore the Lord Himself will give you a sign: Behold the virgin[74] will conceive and give birth to a son, and she will name him Immanuel.*"[75]

Therefore, if one believes the gospel account, Jesus was not formed from a sexual act and its resultant mechanism of merging the chromosomes of a man and a woman. Rather, God planted him into Mary's womb. Roman Catholicism holds that Mary was so holy that she was protected from 'original sin'[76] and remained a virgin her whole life[77]. However, most denominations do not believe this 'perpetual virginity' notion about Mary. They hold that her lowly status is an important point God was making in the message he gave us. In fact, it is significant that God selected Mary and the birthplace of Jesus to both be of lowly status. To raise either to a more elevated status would seem to undermine the point God made through how Jesus was born in humble conditions, having to be laid in an animal feeding trough because there was no room for the family in the local inn (Luke 2:7).

In Luke 1:28 we read of the angel Gabriel informing Mary that God had favoured her (presumably by choosing her to bear Jesus). However, in Matthew 12:46-50, we read of Jesus making the point that Mary's status was not so holy that she met the criteria for being part of his divine family – He rejects her, along with her other sons when he was busy preaching. When Jesus was told they were outside, wanting to talk to him, he told his listeners that his biological family was not his real family, but those who did the will of his heavenly father were.

---

[74] As discussed in Section 2.2, although the Septuagint clearly says 'virgin', the Masoretic Text of the Tanakh substitutes 'young woman' for 'virgin'. It is uncertain whether this was deliberate or a euphemistic term for virgin at the time it was written.
[75] 'Immanuel' isn't necessarily a given name but means 'God with us'. The name Yeshua (Jesus) means 'salvation', 'rescue' or 'to save'. It is a contraction of the name Yehoshua (Joshua), which means 'YHWH saves' or 'The Lord is salvation'.
[76] McKim, Donald K. (1996). *Westminster dictionary of theological terms.* Westminster John Knox Press. *p197 ISBN 0664255116*
[77] Declared at the 5th Ecumenical Council in Constantinople in 553 CE then subsequently confirmed by Pope Martin 1

Emphasising this point, Luke 14:26-27 records Jesus saying, "*If anyone comes to me and does not hate his own father, mother, wife, children, brothers, sisters, yes, and even his own life, he cannot be my disciple. Whoever does not carry his own cross and come after me cannot be my disciple.*" Reading on, Jesus gives metaphors to illustrate what he means by this bold statement. Rather than actually hating people, Jesus is using the word hate to give emphasis to the point he wants to make – that the level of commitment required to be his disciple involves prioritising this commitment over everything else, including the things people normally value most, such as family, friends and even one's own life.

From available evidence, it seems the Eastern Orthodox and Roman Catholic churches make an unfounded claim that Mary was a virgin before, during and forever after her pregnancy with Jesus. The evidence from scripture seems clear that Mary only remained a virgin 'until' (ἕως) Jesus was born (Matt 1:25), and that she had 4 other sons and at least 2 daughters. Jesus' brothers were James, Joseph, Judas and Simon. His sisters' names are not given in scripture, but they lived in Galilee (Mark 6:3; Matt 13:55; John 7:3-5; Acts 1:4; Matt 12:46; Matt 13:55-56; Mark 3:31; Mark 6:3; Luke 8:19; John 2:12; John 7:3-10; Acts 1:14; Galatians 1:19).

Eastern Orthodoxy and Roman Catholicism hold that these people whom the gospels refer to as Jesus' brothers and sisters (ἀδελφοί – adelphoi) were his cousins. This idea may have arisen because the Latin word for brother (frater) found in the Vulgate, can also mean cousin[78]. The Vulgate is a Latin translation of the Bible in use at the point in history when the notion of the perpetual virginity of Mary entered church dogma (553 CE). So, it is easy to see how this translation could have been used to support this idea which is unsupported in the Greek scriptures.

In addition to scriptural references, early writers Flavius Josephus[79], Hegesippus (Five books – via Eusebius of Caesarea)[80], Clement of Alexandria[81] and Origen[82] wrote about James being Jesus' brother, becoming Bishop of Jerusalem and being stoned for his faith. Jerome, author of the Latin Vulgate, wrote that Jesus' mother Mary had a sister who was also called Mary, and it was she who was James' mother. This claim seems unlikely to be true, first because it is unlikely Mary's parents would give two daughters the same name; more

---

[78] Bush, A. C., & Cerutti, S. (1986). *A Use of the Term Frater in the "Pro Caelio."* The Classical Journal. v82(1), pp37–39
[79] Josephus, *Antiquities* 20.9.1
[80] Eusebius, *History of the Church* 1.23.3-19
[81] Clement, *Hypotyposeis* [lost], through Eusebius, *History of the Church 2.1.3-6*
[82] Origen, *Against Celsus*, 1.47b-d; 2.13

significantly because numerous other writers attest to James (and others) being the sibling(s) of Jesus. Jerome also mistranslated Luke 1:28 in a way that some in the early church took to mean Mary was born sinless. These two writings by Jerome suggest he may have esteemed Mary, contributing to her elevation of status in comparison with other contemporaries of Jesus. However, Jerome also recorded that Hegesippus said regarding James, that *"This one was holy from the womb of his mother"*[83], implying he came from the same womb as Jesus.

In the 4th century CE church orders known as the Apostolic Constitutions, we read: *"And I, James, brother of Christ according to the flesh, and servant of the only begotten son as of God, and bishop handpicked by Christ himself and by the apostles of Jerusalem, say these things: When it has become evening, O bishop, assemble the church; and, after the speaking of the psalm at the lamplighting, the deacon shall sound out [for prayers] for the catechumens, the energumens, the illuminated, and those in repentance, as we said before."*[84]

The above evidence when considered together provides a compelling case that James was indeed the biological brother of Jesus, from Mary's womb. I therefore confidently reject the notion of Mary's perpetual virginity. James was Jesus' brother 'in the flesh' (as opposed to just in faith).

Throughout Roman Catholic history, the status of Jesus' mother, Mary, has progressively increased. In 1854, Pope Pius IX, declared that, unlike all other humans (excluding Jesus), she was free from 'original sin'. This claim is known as the 'Immaculate Conception'. More recently, in 1950, Pope Pius XII declared that Mary, like Jesus, ascended to heaven alive.

There is no sound scriptural basis for such claims. However, a book written in the 2nd century CE, known as the Infancy Gospel of James, makes claims that position Mary as holy. This book seems to be the primary source for this notion. It fills in extra unsubstantiated details about the life of Mary, her cousin Elizabeth (the mother of John the Baptist), and Elizabeth's husband Zechariah. In particular, it claims Mary, like Jesus, was conceived without her parents having sexual intercourse.

Because the Infancy Gospel of James post-dates the gospels, includes direct quotes from Luke's gospel, and has no corroborating evidence for its elaborations, it is likely a work of fiction. Given the significance of its claims, I would expect it to have been included in the gospels if a credible belief had existed in the time of Jesus. However, the Gelasian decree of the church around

---

[83] Jerome, *On Famous Men 2*
[84] Apostolic Constitutions Century IV.8.35.1-2

500 CE rejected the Infancy Gospel of James, classifying it as an apocrypha text, including it in a list of books that should be avoided by Catholics.

Nevertheless, numerous Catholics liked the idea of venerating Mary, so debates continued between different factions of Roman Catholicism throughout history, at one stage almost coming to war between the Franciscan and Dominican orders. Thomas Aquinas – arguably the greatest medieval Roman Catholic scholar – strongly opposed the idea[85], helping it to stay out of official Roman Catholic dogma until 1854, by which time, the level of Mary's veneration within the Roman Catholic church had reached such a peak that Pope Pius IX made the Immaculate Conception part of Roman Catholic dogma.

In 1894, Pope Leo XIII addressed the (Eastern) Christian Orthodox church in his encyclical Praeclara Gratulationis. In response, in 1895, the (Eastern) Ecumenical Patriarch Anthimos replied with an encyclical approved by the Constantinopolitan Synod in which he stigmatised the dogmas of the Immaculate Conception and Papal Infallibility as *"Roman novelties"* and called on the Roman church to return to the faith of the early centuries.

6.5 OVERRIDING THE EVIDENCE

Before leaving the topic of Mary the mother of Jesus, permit me a short aside from exploring the question of who Jesus is. We can use the example of Roman Catholic dogma about Mary to explore why a religion, or more accurately, a religious power structure such as a denomination, sect or organisation, might avoid forming evidence-based beliefs, and instead construct perilous logic to retain disproven ideas. I discuss this issue at this stage of the book, because it follows on nicely from the previous section.

I will start with the answer then illustrate through examples. The answer is the macro-level equivalent of the confirmation bias that occurs with individuals, as discussed in Chapter 1. At the level of the organisation, denomination or sect, it is more about maintaining legitimacy. I am not suggesting Roman Catholicism is the only movement subject to such weaknesses, but the above example of their beliefs about Mary provides a ready illustration of this concept.

Superficially, it is difficult to fathom why Roman Catholicism would cling so strongly to ideas about Mary that are unsupported by the most credible

---

[85] McGrath, Alister E. & Thomas, Matthew J. (2025) *Christian Theology An Introduction*, Wiley Blackwell, 7th ed. p37

evidence. Two factors may be (i) an early mistranslation of the Greek language the New Testament was originally written in and (ii) the notion of papal infallibility (the idea that the pope can't make mistakes – an extension of the succession of human sovereignty idea discussed in Chapter 1). Having made a decree one way, reversing the decision when stronger evidence becomes available would amount to confessing that popes can make mistakes. So instead, to retain legitimacy as the authoritative source of doctrine, new arguments are created to justify the now disproven claim.

To illustrate this point, consider the history of the version of the bible that Roman Catholicism used to create most of their canon. In 382 CE, Jerome was commissioned by Pope Damasus I to produce an updated Latin translation of the Gospels. Jerome's resultant translation (which he later extended to the whole bible) is known as the Vulgate. This translation progressively became the dominant translation used within the Western church. However, during the 16th century European Renaissance, knowledge of biblical (Koine) Greek had advanced, and Greek language scholars thought more accurate translations would be possible if the bible was translated into other languages directly from the original Greek. Resultant new translations revealed inaccuracies in the Vulgate and weaknesses in the bases for some church beliefs based on that translation.

For example, based on the Vulgate, Matthew 4:17 would say '*Do penance, for the kingdom of heaven is at hand*'. One of church's seven sacraments, Reconciliation, uses this verse as a basis for its practice of priests requiring a member who has confessed a sin to then have to perform an act of penance for the sin to be absolved. However, 16th century CE Greek scholar, Erasmus of Rotterdam, pointed out that a more accurate translation of the original Greek would be '*Repent, for the kingdom of heaven is at hand.*' The church practice of requiring penance was revealed to be an innovation created by the church, rather than a command of Christ (i.e. a sacrament). However, because the church held to the notion of papal infallibility, they doubled down, criticising Erasmus and convening a council (the Council of Trent) to make various decrees supporting existing church dogma. One of these decrees was to require that only the Vulgate translation could be used in the church's 'mass', which is the regular ritualistic event in which their sacrament of Eucharist is practised.

Similarly, proponents of the notion that Mary was sinless used the Vulgate translation to help justify this idea. Luke 1:28 tells the story of the angel Gabriel announcing to Mary that she would become pregnant. Based on the Vulgate translated into English, this verse would say, '*And the Angel being come in, said unto her: Hail, full of grace, the Lord is with thee: blessed art thou among women*'. The church interpreted the phrase '*Hail, full of grace*' to imply Mary was sinless. However, a better understanding of the Greek reveals that it is not saying '*Hail, full of grace*', but something more like '*Greetings, favoured one*' (NASB) or '*be calm, you have been graced with special honour*' (My own literal translation. '*Be calm*' was used as a greeting in Mary's time. Jerome translated this expression as 'Hail'). These more accurate translations imply that God has shown Mary favour rather than that God has declared her to be free of sin.

Prominent Oxford University Historical Theologian, Dr Alister McGrath, concludes, *"These developments undermined the credibility of the Vulgate translation and opened the way to theological revision on the basis of a better understanding of the biblical text in the Western church. It also demonstrated the importance of biblical scholarship in relation to theology.* **Theology could not be permitted to base itself upon translation mistakes!**'[86]

The examples I have given of translation errors show how doctrines can form based on a misunderstanding of the evidence. However, because of the politics of legitimacy, authority, and power, the church locked into a position of claiming itself to be the sole authority on doctrine. Any acceptance of democratisation of interpretation based on independent scholarly expertise was seen as a threat to its power. Claiming a divine mandate based on succession of sovereignty allowed it to suppress the truth that evidence revealed.

To avoid developing mistaken understandings, one question a member of any religion, sect, or denomination should ask themselves is '*What are the evidential bases for our beliefs?*' The purpose of this book is to help us ask ourselves this question, and be able to accept the answers, even if they invalidate some of our existing beliefs.

Here endeth my aside. Thank you or your indulgence.

6.6 THE WAY, THE TRUTH AND THE LIFE

Uniquely in John's gospel, Jesus is quoted as saying *"I am the way, the truth, and the life. No one comes to the father except through me"* (John 14:6). The Greek word translated here as 'through' can also mean 'because of'. To enhance credibility beyond that of a single author, I would have liked this quote to appear in one

---

[86] McGrath, Alister E. & Thomas, Matthew J. (2025). *Christian Theology An Introduction*, Wiley Blackwell, 7th ed. p42

of the synoptic gospels as well. So, given its uniqueness in John's gospel and its significance to Jesus' divinity, its credibility may be seen as plausible but far from certain.

If we accept John's account as true, the meaning of *"No one comes to the father except through me"* is still not clear. I consider three possibilities:

- except by following his teaching,

- except because of his sacrifice for our sin, or

- some more mystical direct encounter with him or intercession by him.

In the absence of additional context, the first interpretation would be the simplest and apparently most plausible. Jesus taught us to be righteous, selfless, devoted to God and caring of others. Given God's abhorrence for sin, evident throughout the Old Testament, this makes sense. However, the counter argument is that this isn't enough because people have a sinful nature and cannot stop themselves from sinning; they would therefore need some sort of divine intervention or assistance.

The second interpretation (sacrifice for our sin) is consistent with Jewish custom, as recorded in the Torah, of an unblemished animal sacrifice being made as an atonement for sin. A sinless Jesus sacrificing himself for our sin would clearly be of higher value – a more significant sacrifice, particularly if this had been directed by God and if Jesus was his son. Although we may struggle to comprehend why such a sacrifice would be necessary, it is very consistent with God's values as recorded in Jewish scripture. The idea is that, for some reason, God requires a penalty of death for sin and will accept the death of a perfect and innocent life to pay the price for someone who is guilty. Supporting this notion in both the Jewish and Christian tradition, not only did God establish in the Torah the practice of sacrificing animals as an atonement for sin, but he also blessed Abraham for his willingness to sacrifice his son, Isaac. Admittedly, God did not require Abraham to go through with this child sacrifice, but it appears Abraham's willingness to do it was what was important to God (Genesis 22).

That 'sacrificing one life may save another' is a challenging concept to understand and accept; intuitively, this interpretation therefore seems weak. However, from a consistency point of view, it does align with Jewish belief and tradition, so would have resonated strongly with the people of Jesus' day. This internal consistency adds to the credibility of this interpretation. For us to accept this interpretation, we need to go beyond tradition and accept that God knows some things we don't as to why this is necessary, because it is unfathomable to humans. As I stated at the outset, the amount we know is far superseded by the amount we don't. So, this interpretation retains plausibility on the basis of consistency, even if we may struggle to understand how and why this mechanism works.

If one is to subscribe to the third interpretation – mystical encounter with, or intercession by Jesus – his resurrection becomes particularly important. Although the teachings of a dead man may live on and have a powerful and transformative effect on peoples' lives, with a resurrected Jesus it is easier to subscribe to an interpretation requiring a direct encounter with Jesus.

At various times throughout the gospels, Jesus seems to be associating the 'kingdom of God' with himself. For example, at the start of his ministry, Jesus teaches in Galilee, saying "*The time is fulfilled, and the kingdom of God is at hand; repent and believe in the gospel*" (Mark 1:15); In response to questions by the Pharisees about when the kingdom of God was coming, he tells them "*Behold, the kingdom of God is in your midst*" (Luke 17:21b); In response to questioning by Pontius Pilot, the Roman governor, Jesus says "*My kingdom is not of this world. If my kingdom were of this world, then my servants would be fighting so that I would not be handed over to the Jews; but as it is, my kingdom is not of this realm*" (John 18:36).

If we continue to follow the interpretation of John 14:6 which positions a personal encounter with, or intercession by Jesus as the route to salvation, the question then arises as to how this encounter or intercession would be effected. The writings of Paul say much on this, most of which was not taught directly by Jesus – certainly not in the synoptic gospels. It does not follow that Paul was necessarily wrong, but the weight we give to the writings of Paul, who did not come into the picture until after Jesus' death, should be less than the weight we give to the synoptic gospels which meet more of the criteria for credibility as an account of what Jesus taught.

So, what happens when one does approach Jesus in the way he requires? As discussed earlier, Chapter 3 of John's gospel records an account of a Pharisee, Nicodemus, coming to consult with Jesus by night – possibly because he did not want his colleagues to know. In that conversation, Jesus talks of a need to be born of spirit if one is to enter the kingdom of God. John the Baptist had earlier prophesied that Jesus baptises with the holy spirit (Mark 1:8). Later, when Paul baptised people in the name of Jesus, the holy spirit came on them (Acts 19:1-7). So, an explanation for how Jesus might be the only way into the kingdom of God that is at least consistent across these records, is that Jesus is the one who effects the birth in the spirit required to enter the kingdom of God.

Judaism and Islam do not cover this ground; they emphasise instead the need to follow their laws, which they claim were established by God. Because I am primarily examining conflicts between the doctrines of Judaism, Christianity and Islam, I will leave to you any further research on how Jesus might provide the way by which a person comes to god the father (John 14:6). My main purpose in outlining the above three possibilities is to provide context for considering other questions.

6.7 IS GOD A TRINITY?

Most Christians are 'Trinitarians' – holding that three divine persons – father, son and holy spirit – make up the godhead. On the face of it, this belief seems at odds with the claim that the Christian religion is monotheistic (having only one God). In the various arguments from Judaism and Islam that I have read against the doctrine of the Trinity, I note that followers of Judaism tend to differ from followers of Islam in their arguments. Islamic polemics focus on arguing that God is just one being, so cannot be made up of more than one person. This may seem like the simplest argument, however Jewish polemics are more likely to know that in the Shema (a prayer based on Deuteronomy 6:4), where God is talked of as being 'one', the Hebrew word used is 'אחד' (echad). This can be used to denote the number one but can also be used to express the concept of oneness, whether numerically or in the sense of harmony and unity. It is used elsewhere in the Tanakh in this way. For example, in Genesis 2:24 we read that "*a man shall leave his father and mother, and be joined to his wife, and they shall become one* (echad) *flesh*" They don't actually become one person; rather they formed a close harmony where even the distinction of their identities was not important for certain purposes, such as property ownership. In Genesis 41:25, Joseph tells Pharaoh that different dreams he had were actually one (echad). Although each dream was distinct, they had the same meaning. In Exodus 24:3 "*all the people answered with one* (echad) *voice*" (i.e. in unity). In Ezra 3:1 we read that "*the people gathered together as one man* (echad) *to Jerusalem*" (i.e. in unity). In Ezra 3:9 we read "*Then Jeshua with his sons and brothers stood united (*echad*) with Kadmiel and his sons*".

Had the Shema simply said there is one God, this would be clearer. However, rather than say this, it instead says God is one (echad), opening alternate possible interpretations. God may be saying '*We whom you know of as God are united and in harmony*'. Such an interpretation includes the possibility of there being more than one entity in the godhead or that God is a defined person in the sense a human is. Deuteronomy 6:4 does not, therefore, preclude the

Christian belief about the Trinity. However, neither does it confirm it. If there is a plurality to God, this may be different from the Christian concept of the Trinity.

One reason for Christians believing Jesus is part of a Trinity god is that in John 14:7-11, Jesus is recorded as saying that if you have known and seen him, you have known and seen the father. He goes on to say he is in the father and the father is in him. These claims reflect a connectedness and harmony that could be interpreted as aligning with the use of the descriptive for God – (echad) – recorded in Deuteronomy 6:4. However, the notion that God consists of three persons – father, son and holy spirit – did not initially seem clear. We can see across various historical records, the evolution of this concept over the first few centuries of Christendom.

In the early church, beliefs varied between different leaders on some points of doctrine. Although all agreed Jesus was at the core of Christianity and came from God, differences of opinion existed on whether he was actually God showing himself to us in human form, a different person but equal with 'god the father' or created by and therefore of lower status than 'god the father'.

The Roman Emperor Constantine became concerned that such differences could threaten peace within his empire, so applied pressure to church leaders to reconcile their different beliefs into a unifying creed. The doctrine of the Trinity was adopted (at the Council of Nicaea in 325). Any other opinion was deemed "anathema"; dissenters were declared to be heretics and excommunicated from the church (Christendom).

However intuitively likely or unlikely you think the concept of the Trinity, an important factor in assessing credibility of evidence is conflict of interest: The decision to adopt the doctrine of the Trinity by the church was driven by political pressure for a single creed that the church leadership could agree on. It is difficult to conceive of Jesus foreseeing and endorsing such a decision mechanism. Either Jesus was just a man and could not foresee the future or I am forced to conclude that the church's deciding that he was God was not important to Jesus.

This conclusion may, at first, not seem obvious. However, if we look at the teachings of Jesus himself, it becomes evident that his message was less concerned with getting people to focus on an accurate distinction between the father and himself, and more on encouraging people to turn from selfishness and sin towards loving God and other people. The gospel accounts of what Jesus said provide evidence that he was sent by the father as an enabler for this to occur, in part, by revealing what God was like.

Much of church history has been intertwined with political leadership and power. Such political pressures drove the adoption of the doctrine of the Trinity in its creed. Ritualised practices were introduced to reinforce this doctrine. The need for such ritualistic reinforcement is understandable because the Trinity is intuitively difficult to believe for people outside the church. Also, throughout history, many within the church have come to reject it, often resulting in schisms within Christendom.

The primary debate at the Council of Nicaea in 325 CE was between two positions, one holding that Jesus was equal with the father and the other that he was a created being. Other possibilities were not debated. What if heaven exists in eternity, past, present and future, and that Jesus is a heavenly being? What if creation is only relevant to our physical universe? If Jesus is from heaven, he could be eternal, existing before the creation talked about in Genesis 1:1 and yet be the perfect son of God, fully supporting the father, sent to earth as his long-promised Messiah and given the father's authority over the earth. Such a doctrine would reconcile better with the scriptures.

If Jesus was sent by god the father to teach us and make a way for us to reach heaven, surely he would have made this clear through what he said. Our most reliable sources for what he said are the synoptic gospels. In the synoptic gospels, Jesus did not teach that it is necessary to have an accurate and detailed knowledge of the correct doctrine to enter the kingdom of heaven. Rather, he said "*Truly I say to you, unless you change and become like children, you will not enter the kingdom of heaven*" (Matthew 18:3). Later Jesus rebuked his disciples for trying to keep children away from him, saying, "*Leave the children alone, and do not forbid them to come to me; for the kingdom of heaven belongs to such as these*" (Matthew 19:14). Earlier, in his sermon on the mount (Matthew 5 and Luke 6), Jesus said "*Blessed are the poor in spirit, for theirs is the kingdom of heaven*" (Matthew 5:3). Some translators have translated 'poor in spirit' as "*devoid of spiritual arrogance*" (Amplified version) and "*recognise they are spiritually helpless*" (God's Word version). The implication of these teachings is that a simple understanding and a humble desire are required ingredients.

The fact that the church leaders at the council of Nicaea and subsequent councils debated complex points of doctrine about which their beliefs differed from each other is telling. The existence of differing beliefs by such learned people is evidence that the answers had not been clearly revealed by God. The reason the church councils made their decisions on what creed they would share was because of political pressure rather than divine direction. From Jesus' teachings, God was clearly comfortable that humans did not need to know the answers to all questions about heaven. In compromising to political pressure, the Christian church became an instrument of the state, used to maintain peace across the empire, rather than a fellowship of disciples of Jesus, following the way he taught to the kingdom of God.

I conclude that the bases for forming the doctrine of the Trinity are evidently flawed on many levels, including:

- likely modifications to the scriptural accounts we have today,

- the way the doctrine of the Trinity was formally created under Emperor Constantine, and

- the fact that Jesus did not teach it but taught another way.

Therefore, on balance, the evidence suggests the doctrine of the Trinity is not correct as we understand it.

6.8 THE QUESTION OF JESUS' DEITY

JOHN'S GOSPEL

At first glance, parts of John's gospel appear to position Jesus as being God and other parts suggest otherwise. An oft-quoted verse that Trinitarian apologists use to make the claim that Jesus is God is the first verse of John's gospel, which says, *"In the beginning was the word, and the word was with god and the word was God."* Later, in verse 14 of the same chapter, the author implies that when he says the *"word"*, he is talking about Jesus, *"And the word became flesh and dwelt among us; and we saw his glory, glory of the only son from the father, full of grace and truth"*. The argument for Jesus' deity is that, if Jesus was the word who became flesh and dwelt among us, and this word was the same word referred to in verse 1, then Jesus is God.

I note that John Chapter 1 does not actually quote Jesus attesting to his own deity. Rather, it is the author of John's gospel making a series of indirect assertions which, when coupled together, seem to imply Jesus is God. So, what does the same gospel record Jesus himself saying about his identity?

In Chapter 5 Verse 19 of John's gospel, Jesus is recorded as saying, *"Truly, truly, I say to you, the son can do nothing of himself, unless it is something he sees the father doing"*, suggesting he can only copy the father. Then in Verse 30 of the same chapter, Jesus is recorded as saying, *"I can do nothing on my own. As I hear, I judge; and my judgement is righteous, because I do not seek my own will but the will of him who sent me."*

If Jesus was an omnipotent god, he would not be saying that he can do nothing on his own; neither would he be deferring to the will of the one who sent him.

Later in John 14:28, Jesus is recorded as saying *"the father is greater than I."* Towards the end of the gospel, Jesus is quoted as saying *"I am ascending to my father and your father, my god and your god"* (20:17b). So, Jesus has a god – the one whom he calls the father, and that is who our god is too. Therefore, if we accept that John's gospel records Jesus accurately, then we need to accept that by his own testimony, Jesus is less than the father, who is his God. If the author of the gospel did mean to imply in Chapter 1 that Jesus is God, he may have been confused.

Alternatively, the author of John's gospel may not be confused – this apparent confusion may simply be to do with language. Words don't always translate simply from one language to another. Hebrew terms for God/god is a clear example of this. The author is likely to have been Jewish. In the Jewish scriptures, different words are used to refer to God. YHWH (יהוה) always means the single monotheistic deity; Adonai (אֲדֹנָי) means Lord or Master; Elohim (אֱלֹהִים) is also often used to refer to God. As discussed in Chapter 1, Maimonides, the most influential Torah scholar of the Middle Ages, wrote *"I must premise that every Hebrew knows that the term Elohim is a homonym, and denotes God, angels, judges, and the rulers of countries ..."*[87]. All these Hebrew words could be translated into Greek as θεός (god). So, the author may have been thinking Elohim (אֱלֹהִים) when he wrote καὶ θεὸς ἦν ὁ λόγος (in English: *'and the word was god'*), in which case he may have meant something like *'and the word was a heavenly being'*. If so, this would remove the confusion, making John's gospel more internally consistent.

Later in the same gospel, John records Jesus saying, *"I am the way, the truth and the life; no one comes to the father except through me"* (John 14:6). Although in this verse Jesus is not saying he is God, he is claiming a special role in enabling people to reach God.

THE SYNOPTIC GOSPELS

I find it telling that none of the synoptic gospels provide corroborative accounts of the initial superficial interpretation of John 1:1 I presented above, which is that Jesus may be God (יהוה). They do, however, record him claiming to be the Messiah (Mark 14:61-62; Luke 22:67-70), sent by God to do a job given him by God (Luke 4:18-19) – a claim I explored in Chapter 5. They also record Jewish

---

[87] *Guide for the Perplexed*, by Moses Maimonides, Friedländer tr. [1904], at sacred-texts.com

religious leaders accusing Jesus of claiming he is from God, but Jesus never confirms this assumption and often challenges them.

I have heard Christian arguments that Jesus is God because he manifests attributes of God such as miraculous power, or because he says things that identify himself as the Messiah or manifest characteristics traditionally associated with God. They claim the Jewish religious leaders of Jesus' time accused Jesus of claiming to be God (יהוה) (Matthew 26:65; Mark 14:64). However, Jesus did not claim or imply that he was God. In Matthew 26:63-65, Jesus is recorded as saying, *"But I tell you, from now on you will see the son of man sitting at the right hand of the power and coming on the clouds of heaven"*. The high priest would have recognised this as a prophetic quote from Daniel 7:13, where the 'son of man' is escorted into the presence of God. The high priest's reaction was in response to Jesus claiming he was this 'son of man', not God. Also, in John 10:36, Jesus uses a rhetorical question, asking if they say: *"You are blaspheming', because I said, 'I am the son of God'?"*, highlighting their refusal to consider the possibility that he might be the Messiah, prophet or heavenly being.

In John 8:19 we read Jesus telling people. *"If you knew me you would know my father also"*, and in John 14:9 we read where Jesus tells his disciple, Philip, *"Whoever has seen me has seen the father"*. However, from the disciplines of Philosophy, we recognise a belief that Jesus is God because he is like God, to be a propositional fallacy known as 'affirming the consequence'. To illustrate, I have two ducks living in a river on my property. They look identical and behave the same; I can't tell them apart. However, I know they are distinct from each other. Just because one resembles the other, it does not follow that he is the other.

THE EPISTLES

Paul, in his epistle to the Colossians, provides an interpretation of the apparent dilemma of Jesus revealing God without actually being God. We read in Colossians 1:15, *"He is the image of the invisible God, the firstborn of all creation"*. In other words, in seeing Jesus, we are not actually seeing God but seeing what God is like – an *"image"* of God. In the first of John's epistles, we also read, *"No one has ever seen God"* (I John 4:12). So, if we believe both accounts, in seeing Jesus, we are not actually seeing God.

Furthermore, if one interprets John 1:1&14 as the author of John's gospel saying Jesus is God, then this conflicts with 1 John 4:12. To resolve these conflicting statements, it is necessary to either reinterpret John 1 as not suggesting Jesus is God or accept that the author of John's gospel had a different belief about Jesus from the author of 1 John (which would reinforce the idea that they are different authors).

As shown in Chapter 2, Paul distinguishes between Jesus and God in his epistles. Another example of this is in his second epistle to the Corinthians: *"Now all these things are from God, who reconciled us to himself through Christ and gave us the ministry of reconciliation."* (2 Corinthians 5:18). So, although Paul's writings indicate that Paul did not see Jesus as God, neither did he see him as just an ordinary human. Rather, Jesus was sent by God, he reflects God, and he provides a way to God.

Some Trinitarian scholars of biblical Greek argue that the wording of two short passages should be interpreted as Paul and Peter declaring that Jesus is God. These passages are as follows:

- *"...looking for the blessed hope and the appearing of the glory of our great god and saviour, christ Jesus".* (Titus 2:13) which in Greek is as follows:

  προσδεχόμενοι τὴν μακαρίαν ἐλπίδα καὶ ἐπιφάνειαν τῆς δόξης τοῦ μεγάλου θεοῦ καὶ σωτῆρος ἡμῶν Ἰησοῦ Χριστοῦ

- *"Simon Peter, a bond servant and apostle of Jesus christ, to those who have received faith of the same kind as ours, by the righteousness of our god and Saviour, Jesus christ."* (2 Peter 1:1) which in Greek is as follows:

  Συμεὼν Πέτρος δοῦλος καὶ ἀπόστολος Ἰησοῦ Χριστοῦ, τοῖς ἰσότιμον ἡμῖν λαχοῦσιν πίστιν ἐν δικαιοσύνῃ τοῦ Θεοῦ ἡμῶν καὶ σωτῆρος Ἰησοῦ Χριστοῦ

Note that in the Greek, both passages end with a similar grammatical structure, the word order of which is as follows:

- Titus: glory (of)the (of)great (of)god and (of)saviour our (of)Jesus (of)Christ

- 2 Peter: righteousness (of)the (of)god our and (of)saviour (of)Jesus (of)Christ

This word order appears to fit one of six observations (rules or principles) about Koine Greek grammar made by Granville Sharp in 1798.[88] Scholars

---

[88] 1803. *Remarks on the Uses of the Definitive Article in the Greek Text of the New Testament: Containing Many New Proofs of the Divinity of Christ, from Passages Which Are Wrongly Translated in the Common English Version*, Verner and Hood, London

subsequently found examples that disprove five of these. The remaining 'rule' is as follows:

> *"When the copulative kai connects two nouns of the same case, [viz. nouns (either substantive or adjective, or participles) of personal description, respecting office, dignity, affinity, or connexion, and attributes, properties, or qualities, good or ill], if the article 'ho', or any of its cases, precedes the first of the said nouns or participles, and is not repeated before the second noun or participle, the latter always relates to the same person that is expressed or described by the first noun or participle".*

Granville Sharp used this rule to claim that eight verses of the New Testament were mistranslated.[89] This rule came under considerable criticism. Scholars showed that the rule does not work with six of the eight verses suggested by Granville Sharp. However, the balance of scholarly opinion seems to support it for the remaining two instances in Titus and 2 Peter given above.

Therefore, deferring to the Greek grammar expertise of these scholars, I conclude that, on balance, looking at these two passages in isolation from other writings by their authors, their most likely interpretation is that they are declaring θεοῦ[90] and Jesus Christ are one in the same person. However, like the author of John's Gospel, the authors of Titus and 2 Peter were also Jewish. So, when they wrote θεοῦ, they may have meant Elohim (אֱלֹהִים) and not YHWH (יהוה). Also, these are stand-alone statements by each of these authors; corroborative evidence from other statements made by the authors of these passages does not exist. In fact, other writings by Paul indicate he did not hold the belief that Jesus is YHWH (יהוה). Also, when Jesus asked Peter who he thought Jesus was, Peter declared he was the Messiah but did not declare he was also God. (Mark 8:29)

In the opening of the epistle of James, the author acknowledges the lordship of Christ, but distinguishes his identity from God, saying, *"James, a bond-servant of god and of the lord Jesus Christ"* (James 1:1a). This listing of God and the Lord Jesus as distinct from God, rather than saying the father and the son occurs commonly throughout the New Testament. I find it telling that the title 'God' is typically associated with the father and rarely with Jesus.

---

[89] Ephesians 5:5, 2 Thessalonians 1:12, 1 Timothy 5:21, Titus 2:13, 2 Peter 1:1, Jude 4, Acts 20:28, 2 Timothy 4:1
[90] The genitive form of θεὸς

JESUS' PRAYER BEFORE HIS ARREST

Returning to John's gospel, Chapter 17 amounts to a statement from Jesus himself that provides evidence about his identity. It records Jesus' prayer to the father shortly before he was arrested and crucified. In this prayer, Jesus gives insight into his relationship with the father. He makes it plain that it is the father who has given him authority over all mankind (vs2), rather than such authority being intrinsic to him as its source. The father's purpose in giving Jesus this authority was to enable Jesus to give eternal life to those people the father had given him (vs2). Jesus described this eternal life as knowing the only true God and knowing Jesus, the Messiah whom God sent (vs3). (Note his differentiation between God and himself: He identifies as the Messiah.)

Through verses 6-8 we learn that Jesus has revealed what the father told him to share with those the father had given him and, as a result, they now understand that Jesus came forth from the father who sent him (which could explain the 'son of god' expression). In verses 9 and 10 Jesus goes on to say those people are both his and the father's because all things that belong to him belong to the father. These people whom the father had given him are not of the world, just as Jesus is not of the world (vs14). The world hates them. Jesus asks the father to protect them from the evil one and to set them apart for sacred use through truth (vs15-17).

In verse 4, Jesus says that he glorified the father (not himself), having accomplished the work which the father gave him to do. Then, in verse 5, Jesus asks the father to restore the glory he had with the father before the world existed (eluding at least to his status as a heavenly being, if not deity). Therefore, through these verses Jesus makes it plain that (a) the father is in command and he is the father's servant, (b) he existed with the father before the world existed, (c) glory he previously experienced before the world existed had subsequently been removed, and (d) it is the father, not himself, who has the power to restore his glory. Through all this, he effectively states he is not God but was sent from God to achieve a purpose of God.

In the same prayer, Jesus tells the father that he has given the glory that the father gave him to those the father gave to him, to enable them to be one just as Jesus and the father are one (vs21-23). To better understand how Jesus and the father are one, we should therefore reflect on what it means to say that people who have come together with a common identity and purpose are one. People remain distinct organisms but their unity in identity and purpose perhaps creates a closer level of trust in, and support for, each other. Jesus talks of wanting the love that is in him and the father also to be in those people to whom he taught about the father (vs26).

The implications of Jesus' prayer on Christian doctrine are profound, revealing that Jesus may not be who the church has always claimed him to be. In fact, different branches of modern Christianity vary in their beliefs, not only about who Jesus is, but also about what he wants us to do.

A CLUE THROUGH HOW JESUS EARNED THE NAME 'SON OF GOD'

In Matthew 28:18 we read of God giving Jesus all authority in heaven and on earth. The power wasn't innately his; God gave it to him. This is entirely consistent with Jesus' prayer in John 17. It is also consistent with Daniel 7:13-14, a prophetic passage that refers to the 'son of man', the most common term Jesus used to refer to himself:

> *"I saw in the night visions, and, behold, one like the son of man came with the clouds of heaven, and came to the ancient of days, and was escorted to him. He was given dominion, honour, and a kingdom, so that all people, nations, and languages, should serve him. His dominion is an everlasting dominion, which shall not pass away, and his kingdom is one that shall not be destroyed."*

The writer of the epistle to the Hebrews, in Chapter 1, expands on who Jesus was before God (the Ancient of Days) gave him this honour and power:

> *"¹God, who at different times and in various ways spoke in the past through the prophets to the fathers, ²has in these last days spoken to us by his son, whom he appointed heir of all things, by whom also he made the world; ³Who being the radiance of his glory, and the express image of his person, and upholding all things by the word of his power, when he had by himself purged our sins, sat down on the right hand of the Majesty on high. ⁴Thus he became much better than the angels, to the extent that he inherited a superior name to theirs. ⁵For unto which of the angels did god ever say, You are my son, today have I begotten you? And, I will be to him a father, and he shall be to me a son? ⁶And again, when he brings the first born into the world, he says, 'And let all the angels of god worship him'. ⁷And of the angels he says, 'He makes his angels spirits, and his ministers a flame of fire.' ⁸But to the son he says, 'Your throne, god, is for ever and ever, and the sceptre of righteousness is the sceptre of your kingdom. ⁹You have loved righteousness and hated iniquity; therefore god, your god, has anointed you with the oil of gladness above thy fellows.'"*

Interestingly, this passage tells us that because Jesus *"purged our sins"*, God promoted him above the angels. The term 'angels' is sometimes translated as 'messengers' and at other times as 'heavenly beings'. Here it doesn't appear to mean 'messengers', but heavenly beings who are Jesus' fellows/companions/associates/sharers/partners[91] (v.9), of which Jesus was one, then he "*became so much better than*" them (v.4).

If we read the Greek superficially, in verse 8, Paul appears to be saying that God refers to Jesus as God. In doing this, Paul is quoting from Psalm 45:6 which is usually translated, "*Your throne, god, is forever and ever*". However, the Psalms were written in Hebrew, which uses many different words that can mean God, but that each have a different meaning from each other. All these words tend to be translated into Greek as θεός (god). Greek uses this one generic word for god because it doesn't have the range of names Hebrew does. In this instance, Psalm 45:6 does not use the word 'YHVH' (Yahweh or Jehovah) which would mean God, but 'Elohim', which we have learned can mean 'angel' or 'ruler' rather than 'God'.

So, it is important to appreciate that we must treat the word θεός (god) in the New Testament very carefully, particularly when it is part of a quote from the Old Testament. However, even in Greek, we should take into account the fact that, in the time of Christ, the Middle East had been strongly Hellenised (which is why the New Testament was written in Greek). The Greeks had a pantheon of gods, with Zeus being the supreme god, yet other heavenly beings were also referred to as gods. The Greek word θεός was used for all.

SO WHAT ARE WE TO BELIEVE?

The term 'Trinity' is not recorded in the New Testament. It likely arose in the writings of 2nd – 3rd century CE theologian Tertullian in his treatise Against Praxeas (132)[92]. The idea developed from there, even though Tertullian believed the son and the spirit were subordinate to the father.

Some Christians may reconcile Jesus' obvious subservience to the father by accepting Jesus was less than God whilst on earth and aligning with Paul's belief that the father exalted him above other people because of his willingness to die on the cross to purge sins (Philippians 2:8-9). However, others align with the superficial interpretation of John 1, arguing that Jesus was always equal with the father and either just another dimension of God (Modalism), "the word" or another person in the godhead.

To me, the evidence suggests two alternative hypotheses seem more likely. The first and simplest of these is that Jesus, whether a divine being or not, is not

---

[91] μετόχους in Greek, which is a translation of the Hebrew word מְחַבְרֶיךָ: used in Psalm 46:7 from which this verse is translated.

[92] https://www.tertullian.org/articles/evans_praxeas_eng.htm Accessed 19 June 2025

Almighty God but subservient to him. The second, which is consistent with numerous testimonies of near-death experiences, is that human form limits the spiritual being inside us, which is why we are not experiencing what is going on in spiritual realms. So, in his human form, Jesus felt his limitation and saw the wisdom of following the father's will even though his human experience of frustrations and anticipation of his imminent painful death was distressing for him as a human.

Of note, John 3:16 says *"For god so loved the world that he gave is only begotten son, that whoever believes in him should not perish but have eternal life."* However, in both Genesis and Job we read of other sons of god. John 3:16 might mean Jesus is a son of god in a different way, but this is not clear without making assumptions.

Alternatively, because this extremely important quote does not appear in any of the synoptic gospels, we cannot dismiss the possibility that Jesus may not have said this at all. It may be a fabrication or a story that evolved amongst early Christians, possibly just within the Johannine school of thought.

John 3:1-21 is possibly the most significant passage of scripture about the role of Jesus in effecting salvation. This passage includes the suggestion that **belief** in Jesus is the primary criteria for achieving salvation (verse18). 'Believers' subsequently became a common term Christians used to refer to themselves. This way of identifying oneself exists in stark contrast to the Jewish tradition, which was more about commitment to what you do and how you live your life.

I find it somewhat concerning that such a critical passage to the foundation of Christian doctrine and identity should only appear in John's gospel and none of the synoptic gospels. Even more so, given that Jesus' teachings throughout the synoptic gospels were about what we should do more than about what we believe. However, the word 'believe' behind the label 'believer' is a translation of the Greek word pisteuō (πιστεύω). As discussed in Chapter 3, this word can mean more than simply accepting something as true; it can mean to place one's trust in someone, or even to commit one's life to them[93].

THINKING LATERALLY

So, let us return to John 1:1, the most cited verse Christian apologists use to support their claim that Jesus is God. I have shown that the author may have intended to refer to Jesus as a heavenly being, rather than God (Elohim rather than YHWH). It may also be relevant that Genesis 1 does not describe the

---

[93] Robinson, Maurice A. & House, Mark A. (2012). *Analytical Lexicon of New Testament Greek*. Hendrickson Publishers. ISBN: 978-1-59856-701-4 p283

creation of the universe; just the creation of Earth. This event is what the expression *"In the beginning"* refers to in Genesis 1:1. It is possible that beings who were in existence with the father at that time were not necessarily in existence at the beginning of time itself, which may have pre-dated the beginning of the earth. This is a point some scholars often miss, assuming that the expression *"In the beginning"* in John 1:1 refers to the beginning of the universe. However, although John's gospel was written in Greek and Genesis was written in Hebrew, given that Jews wrote both books in a continuous tradition, it seems more likely that this use of *"In the beginning"* was referring to the same point in time, in which case this must be referring to the beginning of the terraforming of the Earth. If so, this leaves open the possibility that Jesus is a created being without conflicting with John 1:1.

Alternatively, other scriptures I quoted above suggest Jesus may be an eternal being. Perhaps we are too; not created in time as the earth was, but each existing on earth in human form at different times for some purpose we have not been permitted to know. After all, originally humans weren't even permitted knowledge of good and evil (Genesis 2:17). We refer to humanity's action to discover forbidden knowledge as 'The Fall' which resulted in eviction from the Garden of Eden and curses to be placed on us.

So, right from the start, scripture makes it clear that it is not God's will for us to know everything. Because of the heated debate about the status of Jesus by learned people throughout the history of Christendom, it is obvious that his full status is one of those things that we simply do not know with certainty. This may be hard to accept, given his core role in influencing Rabbinic Judaism, Christianity and Islam. We naturally feel a need to hold a position on such a central fact.

Jesus' apparent lack of concern to clarify his divine status is telling. This implies that it is not necessary for us to think of him as God. His role is that of a teacher and possibly a sacrificial lamb that mystically atones for our sin, thereby opening a way for us to enter the kingdom of heaven. Such things perhaps should make us revere him, but do not mean he is God. However, I guess the power and authority God gave him can be seen as making him 'a god' if we take the Classical Greek sense of the word.

6.9 HOW TO RESOLVE THIS QUESTION?

The question of Jesus' deity is one the early Christian church grappled with, coming to crisis point at the Council of Nicaea in 325 CE. Under pressure from the Roman emperor, church leaders were forced to formally decree a position, even though their beliefs differed. The position they settled on was the confusing one that Jesus was *"begotten from god the father"* before everything else was made, emphasising he was *"begotten not made"* and that he is *"true God from true God"*[94]. Later councils sought to clarify church creed and strengthen the Trinity concept, explicitly stating that God is a Trinity whose members each have coequal immeasurable power[95].

So, to what extent can this idea be supported in scripture? As we have seen, the balance of evidence from the Old and New Testaments would suggest Jesus is a heavenly being. Scriptures tell us he was with God before the world was created, he was involved in the creation of the earth, and God gave him authority over the earth. The miracles recorded throughout all four gospels attest to such authority. However, the author of Matthew's gospel recognises Jesus as the servant of God foretold by the prophet Isaiah (Matthew 12:18), as does Paul's letter to the Philippians which speaks of Jesus being obedient to God (Philippians 2:8). Because Jesus cleansed us of our sins, he became better than his fellow heavenly beings, so God anointed him above his companions, giving him a more excellent name (son of god?) (Hebrews 1:1-9; Philippians 2:9; Daniel 7:13-14). This all points to Jesus' divinity, but a divinity that is subservient to god the father – Elohim but not YHWH. It appears, therefore, that the writers of the Christian Scriptures did not hold the concept of the Trinity that church councils later developed.

Perhaps the question should not be whether Jesus is or is not God, because this presumes we know what God is. Doctrinal debates such as those related to the notion of the Trinity show that we do not really know, and perhaps we do not need to know, everything about God. What if being Christian instead meant doing what Jesus taught us to do?

To understand what this requires, we should refer to the most credible and comprehensive accounts of Jesus' life and teachings – the three synoptic

---

[94] From the Nicene Creed, despite Jesus himself referring to the father as *"the only true God"* (John 17:3)
[95] See the Athanasian Creed

gospels. To understand how Jesus wants us to live, it may also be helpful to examine the way his first followers lived.

From available records, Jesus' initial followers most likely originally referred to themselves as followers of the way (Acts 9:1-2; Acts 19:9&23; Acts 19:23; Acts 22:4; Acts 24:14&22). The term 'the way' may have been an abbreviated form of "the way of righteousness" referred to by Jesus (Matt 21:32) and Peter (2 Pet 2:21).

Although early Christians referred to themselves as followers of the way, they may have been known by others as Nazarenes (Acts 24:5). The first non-biblical reference to the term 'Christians' did not occur until the early 2nd century CE in Antioch.

Reference to 'the way' may also have meant following the way Jesus taught people to live. As discussed above, John 14:6 records Jesus saying, *"I am the way, the truth and the life; no one comes to the father except through me"*. The epistle to the Hebrews, provides what might be an explanation of this claim. Its author writes, *"We have confidence to enter the holy places by the blood of Jesus, by the new and living way that he opened for us through the curtain, that is through his flesh"* (Hebrews 10:19-20).

Such verses helped establish a doctrine about Jesus that became a core feature of Christendom. As discussed in Chapter 4, Judaism practised regular blood sacrifices of animals in the temple to atone for their sins. The author of Hebrews is saying that Jesus' death was a sacrifice for the sins of mankind for all time, and that this sacrifice is necessary for us to reach the father. We also read that God does not desire animal sacrifices and that the blood of animals cannot take away sins (Hebrews 10:4).

Later in the same chapter, Verse 20 mentions a curtain that may refer to the curtain in the Jewish temple separating sinful people from the innermost place where God appears, known as the 'holy of holies'. This interpretation would align with an event recorded in Matthew 27:51 and Luke 23:45 that occurred the moment Jesus died on the cross: *"the curtain of the temple was torn in two"*. The symbolism of this curtain being torn in two the moment Jesus died is significant in that it removed the barrier separating people from God. Powerful though this symbolism is, its significance is its reinforcement of the notion that Jesus opened a way to God, rather than that he is God.

Is 'the way' that Jesus opened to God accessed simply by adhering to his teachings, or is something spiritual required as well? John's gospel records Jesus promising to send the holy spirit as a helper. So, what is this 'holy spirit' and what does it do?

7. WHAT IS THE SPIRIT OF GOD?

"They are asking you about the spirit. Say, the spirit is by command of my lord, and of knowledge you have been given only a little."

Surah 17:85

Christian Trinitarians hold that there are three persons in the godhead – father, son, and spirit. The father is generally seen as the first person in the Trinity – the unseen creator of the universe. As shown, various early Christian writers frequently referred to the father as God (Mark 13:32; John 1:18; 1 Philippians 2:8-11; James 1:27; Jude 1:1). The father is the person in the godhead who most closely aligns with the concept of God in Judaism, Islam and Christian Unitarianism. However, Judaism and Islam profess different beliefs from Christianity and each other about the nature and requirements of God.

As discussed in Chapter 1, the second person in the Trinity is referred to as the son of god, who took on the human form of Jesus of Nazareth, being the Messiah prophesied by John the Baptist and in the Tanakh, and to whom God gave authority over the earth (Matthew 9:5; Mark 3:15; John 17:2; Philippians 2:10-11). Judaism, Islam and Christian Unitarianism hold that Jesus is not God. However, Islam and Christian Unitarianism hold that he is the Messiah sent by God.

Except perhaps within the Pentecostal branch of Christianity, the least discussed member of the Trinity is the spirit, who shows up in different ways and is often also referred to by various scriptural authors as the 'holy spirit', 'the 'spirit of god' or the 'spirit of the lord' (Genesis 1:2; Isaiah 11:2; Luke 1:35; Matthew 3:16; John 14:26; Acts 5:3; Acts 19:6; Romans 8:14-15; 1 Corinthians 3:16). In Muhammad's time, Christendom's stronger focus on god the father, Jesus and Jesus' mother (Mary) was such that Muhammad thought the third person in the Trinity was Jesus' mother rather than the holy spirit (Surah 5:116).

Before examining Christian beliefs more closely, let us consider what Judaism and Islam believe about the spirit of god.

7.1 JUDAISM'S PERSPECTIVE

In Christianity, the terms 'holy spirit' and 'spirit of god' are generally understood to be interchangeable. Adherents of Judaism, although negatively disposed towards Christianity's claims about Jesus and the holy spirit being distinct divine persons, do accept that the holy spirit is referred to in their Tanakh.

The Tanakh refers once in Psalms and twice in Isaiah to רוח הקודש (ruach ha-kodesh), which can be translated into English as holy spirit:

- In Psalm 51:11, King David prays to God, *"Do not cast me away from your presence, and do not take your **holy spirit** (ruach ha-kodesh) from me."*

- Isaiah (63:10-11) writes of God (יהוה), *"But they rebelled and grieved his **holy spirit** (ruach ha-kodesh); therefore, he turned himself to become their enemy, he fought against them. Then his people remembered the days of old, of Moses. Where is he who brought them up out of the sea with the shepherds of his flock? Where is he who put his **holy spirit** (ruach ha-kodesh) in the midst of them"*.

More frequently, the Tanakh refers to the spirit of god:

- Genesis 1:2 speaks of the **spirit of god(s) (אלהים - elohim)** hovering over the surface of the waters during creation.

- 1 Samuel 16:13 speaks of the **spirit of God (יהוה - YHWH)** rushing upon David from that day forward.

- In Psalm 143:10, King David prays to God, *"Let **your good spirit** lead me on level ground"*.

- As discussed in Chapter 5, Christians see Isaiah 42:1 as a Messianic prophesy referring to Jesus where it says, *"Behold my servant whom I uphold; my chosen one in whom my soul delights. I have put **my spirit** upon him; he will bring forth justice to the nations."*

- Isaiah writes (44:3b) that God *"will pour out **my spirit** on your offspring, and my blessing on your descendants."*

- Joel; (2:27-28) prophesies, *"So you will know that I am in the midst of Israel and I am the lord your god and there is no other and my people will never be put to shame. It will come out about this that I will pour out **my spirit** on all mankind and your sons and daughters will prophesy, your old men will have dreams, your young men will see visions."*

So, the Tanakh speaks of the 'holy spirit' and 'spirit of god' in similar ways. The two authors who use the term holy spirit, also elsewhere also refer to god's spirit (David the king: "your spirit"; Isaiah the prophet speaking for God: "my spirit"). Like the Christian perspective, it seems that in Jewish scripture the terms are interchangeable.

In Psalm 51, King David is concerned about God separating himself from David by taking one of two particular actions: casting David away from his presence and taking his holy spirit away from David. David expresses these fears in the same verse, suggesting some association in his mind. It may be that David is saying the same thing in two different ways. Alternatively, casting someone out and removing a spirit from someone could be two distinct acts, suggesting that God's spirit is a distinct entity from God.

Rather than being a spirit, David may instead be using the term figuratively to refer to an anointing or blessing that God gave him through Samuel and which remained on him from that day forward. This is similar to Isaiah's prophesy in 42:1 of God putting his spirit on his servant in whom his soul delights. The dove descending on Jesus during his baptism is believed by Christians to symbolize an anointing of the holy spirit on him. Scriptures reveal God anointing various people throughout history – most notably his prophets, who appeared to subsequently experience a relationship involving communication with God, and sometimes miraculous powers.

In Psalm 143:10 where King David prayed for God to let his spirit lead him on level ground, his use of the word spirit may mean God's nature or will. However, it may also mean the spirit of God. Isaiah 63:10 speaks of grieving God's holy spirit. It is not clear whether this should be interpreted as referring to a distinct spirit or is just an expression meaning 'upset God' (i.e. sadden his spirits). If the latter, this suggests a possibility that God and the holy spirit are one in the same spirit; If the former, it could be a distinct entity from God who is grieved, which would suggest the holy spirit is a distinct person from God.

Some passages write of God 'pouring out the holy spirit' upon people or 'removing the holy spirit from' people. The benefits to people of the holy spirit's actions seem to include providing direction, blessing, and awareness of its presence.

These accounts of the holy spirit do not conflict with how Christians think of the holy spirit. Christianity, however, adds more, as I will discuss below. Before doing so, it is worth considering more recent teachings within Judaism.

Subsequent to the Tanakh being written, the concept of 'shekhinah' (שכינה) arose within early Rabbinic Judaism, meaning god's presence amongst his people. This idea is repeated throughout the Talmud. For example, in Pirkei Avot within the Mishna, we read that if two people sit together and share words of Torah, the shekhinah abides among them. This is similar to the Christian concept articulated by Jesus, as recorded in Matthew 18:20, *"For where two or three have gathered in my name, I am there in their midst"* and in John 14:16-17 where we read of Jesus talking about sending a helper who is the spirit of truth from the father that will dwell in Jesus' followers. Paul also wrote in 1 Corinthians 3:16, *"Do you not know that you are the temple of God and that the spirit of God dwells in you?"*

Although Christian tradition understands the spirit of God as living within individuals, Judaic tradition understands it more to be able to dwell in the midst of God's people. The concept of the spirit of God 'dwelling', is somewhat aligned with the Judaist concept of shekhinah, whose Hebrew root word means 'to dwell'.

Within the Judaic mystical tradition known as Kabbalah, shekhinah takes on a feminine quality, being compared to a mother, sister, daughter or bride. Sefer ha-Bahir (the book of brilliance) says regarding righteous people that, *"shekhinah rests among them, and through their deeds she rests in the bosom of the holy one, and makes them fruitful and increases them."*

7.2 ISLAM'S PERSPECTIVE

The holy spirit in Islam is not God. It must therefore be a creation of God's, which leads many to believe it to be synonymous with the angel Gabriel, as alluded to in other places in the Qur'an

The Qur'an makes numerous references to the holy spirit:

- In Surah 16:102 and 26:193 we read of the holy spirit delivering revelations from God.

- Surah 2:87&253 when talking about Jesus says, *"we strengthened him with the holy spirit"*.

- Surah 4:171 speaks of *"Jesus son of Mary"* as being (i) the Messiah, (ii) only a messenger of Allah, (iii) Allah's word conveyed to Mary, and (iv) a spirit from Allah.

- Surah 17:85 is guarded about revealing information about the spirit. It reads, *"They are asking you about the spirit. Say, the spirit is by command of my lord and acknowledge you have been given only a little."*

- Other Surahs also refer to the 'spirit' or the 'true spirit' bringing down messages (from heaven?)

So, whereas in the Tanakh, the spirit is closely linked to God himself, pouring out power and blessings upon people, it is more restrained in the Qur'an. Here (i) the spirit acts as a messenger, (ii) the spirit is one who strengthens Jesus the Messiah, and (iii) possibly Jesus himself is a spirit. However, the Qur'an is also guarded about the identity of the spirit. It may be that Muhammad was aware of the Jewish and Christian concept of holy spirit but did not do much research into it or see the need to write much on it due to it not being one of his greatest concerns about Jewish and Christian doctrines. His misunderstanding of the Christian belief that the holy spirit is part of the Trinity would have reduced his interest in it; consequently, he may not have felt he needed to write much about the spirit.

7.3 CHRISTIANITY'S PERSPECTIVE

At this stage, we can recognise that the concept of the 'holy spirit' or 'spirit of god' shares some similarities across Judaism, Christianity and Islam. Christianity has more to say.

Mathew 4:1, Mark 1:12 and Luke 4:1 record Jesus being led by the spirit into the wilderness following his baptism. Later, in Luke 10:21, we read that Jesus *"rejoiced greatly in the holy spirit"*. So, the holy spirit appears to be able to influence Jesus.

In the gospels of Matthew and Luke, we read of Jesus, in his sermon on the mount saying, *"If you then, who are evil, know how to give good gifts to your children, how much more will the heavenly father give the holy spirit to those who ask him."* (Luke 11:13; Matthew 7:11) This passage being repeated almost word for word in these gospels, but absent from Mark's gospel, supports the idea that the authors sourced it from the common independent source 'Q' discussed in Chapter 2.

The synoptic gospels say that when the spirit of God lives in someone, it will give them words to say if they are arrested and required to defend themselves (Matthew 10:19; Mark 13:11; Luke 12:12).

John's gospel adds much to what is recorded in the synoptic gospels, including various quotes of Jesus:

- *"It is the spirit who gives life; the flesh provides no benefit; the words that I have spoken to you are spirit and are life."* (6:63)

- *"I will ask the father, and he will give you another helper, so that he may be with you forever."* (14:16)

- *"But the helper/advocate* (παράκλητος - paráklētos), *the holy spirit, whom the father will send in my name, he will teach you everything and will remind you of all that I said to you."* (14:26)

- *"But I tell you the truth: It is to your advantage that I am leaving; for if I do not leave, the helper/advocate* (παράκλητος – paráklētos) *will not come to you; but if I go, I will send him to you. And when he comes, he will convict the world regarding sin, and righteousness, and judgement: Regarding sin, because they do not believe in me; and regarding righteousness. Because I am going to the father and you will no longer see me; and regarding judgement, because the ruler of this world has been judged."* (16:7-11)

Additionally, as discussed earlier, John Chapter 3 includes much about the 'spirit', with significant doctrinal implications. However, it does not explicitly use the terms 'holy spirit' or 'spirit of god'. Christians tend to believe that most references to 'spirit' in John 3 relate to the holy spirit.

The book of Acts gives numerous examples of the holy spirit imparting power to people:

- *"And they were all filled with the holy spirit and began to speak with different tongues, as the spirit was giving them the ability to speak out."* (Acts 2:4)

- *"Then they* [Peter and John] *began laying their hands on them, and they were receiving the holy spirit."* (Acts 8:17)

- *"And when they had prayed, the place where they had gathered together was shaken, and they were all filled with the holy spirit and began to speak the word of god with boldness."* (Acts 4:31)

John the Baptist also spoke with boldness in his ministry. Luke 1:15 says that he was filled with the holy spirit while still in his mother's womb.

The author of Jude encourages people to pray in the holy spirit to build up their faith (Jude 1:20), and Peter writes of people who were moved by the holy spirit to speak from God (2 Peter 1:21). However, Paul has the most to say about the holy spirit.

Paul taught that the holy spirit lives within the saints (ἅγιος – hagios) which means 'holy ones'. These are the people who have been chosen/called by God and sanctified (ἡγιασμένοις – hēgiasmenois), which means 'made holy' (1 Corinthians 1:2). In Greek, the words 'saint' and 'sanctified' are derived from the same route word. Sanctification is the mechanism by which a person is cleansed of sin and separated for God – the mechanism by which a person is made holy. People undergoing such sanctification are saints. The mechanism of sanctification frees people from being slaves to *"desires of the flesh"* and produces righteous *"fruit of the spirit"* (Galatians 5).

Most scholars believe that Paul is speaking about all 'believers' when he uses the term 'saints'. However, the Roman Catholic church and Eastern Orthodox church reserve the term 'saint' for a special category of deceased believers whom their church leadership has explicitly declared to be saints. The process of declaring someone to be a saint involves an investigation after the person's death. That investigation seeks to determine whether the candidate for sainthood demonstrated exceptional virtue and whether miracles have been attributed to them. These denominations hold that miracles provide evidence of a person's holiness and their ability to advocate to God on behalf of others. Accordingly, they practise praying to saints, whereas most other denominations follow the teaching of Jesus to pray directly to the father and that the holy spirit, rather than other saints, is our intercessor (παράκλητος – paráklētos) (Romans 8:27).

The evidence across Paul's epistles suggests a broader definition of 'saints' than that held by the Roman Catholic church and Eastern Orthodox church. In various of his epistles, Paul calls different groups of people 'saints', including *"all who are beloved of God in Rome"* (Romans 1:7), *"the congregation of God which is in*

Corinth" (1 Corinthians 1:2), *"the saints who are at Ephesus and are faithful in Christ Jesus"* (Ephesians 1:1), *"all the saints in Christ Jesus who are in Philippi, including the overseers and deacons"* (Philippians 1:1), and *"the saints and faithful brothers in Christ at Colossae"* (Colossians 1:1). Therefore, Paul's concept of saints is not just a select few deemed as particularly special by the church leadership, but rather the general host of people who have been transformed by Christ and are being sanctified by the holy spirit. The restriction of the term 'saints' to a small proportion of believers whom the church leadership designates with this term after their death, is a later innovation. It is not biblical, most Christian denominations do not consider it valid.

The Author of the epistle to the Hebrews (possibly Paul) wrote that by God's will *"we have been sanctified through the offering of the body of Christ once for all time"* (Hebrews 10:10; 13:12). The spirit of God is involved in effecting the sanctification process (1 Corinthians 6:11; 1 Peter 1:2; 1 Thessalonians 4:7-8) over time, rather than instantaneously (2 Corinthians 3:18; Philippians 2:13).

Paul believed we each have our own spirit within us, and this spirit knows our thoughts. He uses this concept to illustrate that, in the same way, the spirit of God knows the thoughts of God. So, because the spirit of God lives within saints, they can know the things God has given them (1 Corinthians 2:11-16). If a person does not have the holy spirit, he does not belong to Christ (Romans 8:9).

Paul taught that the holy spirit intercedes with God on our behalf *"with groanings too deep for words"* because *"we do not know what to pray for as we should"* (Romans 8:26-27). He also taught that the holy spirit has power that gives saints special gifts and abilities (1 Corinthians 12&14; Ephesians 1:17).

Paul reminds people that they received the spirit by hearing and by faith, rather than by following religious laws and rituals. He is critical of saints[96] who fall back from this teaching into relying on laws and rituals instead. No one is justified by following laws and rituals (Galatians 5). Rather, you will know if you have the spirit of god in you because you will experience your life being led by the spirit of god, you will not be living in fear, you will experience a close relationship to God as a child to its father (literally 'Daddy'– Ἀββᾶ), and the spirit of God will tell you (Romans 8:14-16) that you are a child of God.

So, Paul is unequivocal: If you have the spirit of God living in you, you will have been transformed, showing both 'fruit of the spirit' and 'gifts of the spirit',

---

[96] As discussed above, 'saints' is a term Paul commonly used for Christians/believers/brothers and sisters in Christ

aware of a personal relationship with God as his child. However, if you are relying on following church laws to receive the spirit of God, you have missed the point.

7.4 SO, WHAT TO CONCLUDE?

The scriptures of all three religions agree on the existence of a 'holy spirit' or 'spirit of God'. These scriptures all speak of the spirit of God upholding or strengthening people and conveying messages from God, although Islam holds that such messages were only given to prophets and there can be no more prophets after Muhammad. From Judaic and Christian scriptures in particular, the spirit of God seems to be God's mechanism for reaching through from 'heaven' (where he exists) to anoint/empower certain people on earth throughout history.

Beyond this, I have found it difficult to assess the credibility of differences in their beliefs on this issue because this spirit, by its nature, is somewhat elusive and different from the tangible world of 'the flesh' that provides opportunities to measure evidence.

In general, Judaism and Christianity see God's spirit as more universally available. In their shared scripture (which the Qur'an, although not Muslims, upholds), Isaiah says that God *"will pour out **my spirit** on your offspring, and my blessing on your descendants."* (Isaiah 44:3b). Jews generally hold that the word 'descendants' refers to the Jewish race so refers to them, whereas Christians often hold that it refers to descendants of God's message and covenants, so refers to them.

Early Christian history, as recorded in Acts, is replete with accounts of miracles and personal transformations that fit the narrative about the holy spirit given in the gospels and epistles. I did not find any substantive conflicts in Christian scriptures about the holy spirit, which of course includes the Tanakh.

Regarding the conflict within branches of Christendom regarding designating certain deceased followers as saints and praying to them to intercede on behalf of others (living or dead), scripture does not support this practice; it is clearly a later innovation. Roman Catholicism and Eastern Orthodox traditions permit such innovation because they permit their leadership to develop canon. However, on this particular question, their positions are evidentially weaker than the Protestant position. First, this position relies on the succession of sovereignty argument I discussed and dismissed in Chapter 1. Second, imposing designated deceased saints between God and man contradicts the teaching of their own bible. The bible teaches that, although we might not know how to pray, we should still pray directly to God and rely on the holy spirit living within us to intercede in the way God requires.

If a person has experienced being *"born of the spirit"* (John 3:6) so that the holy spirit subsequently *"lives within"* them (1 Corinthians 6:19) who is *"testifying with our spirit that we are children of God"* (Romans 8:16; 2 Corinthians 1:22; 5:5; Ephesians 1:13-14), they will of course, be in no doubt that they have no need of praying to saints. These scriptures provide a possible explanation for why certain groups of Christians might develop such a custom as praying to deceased saints: If one either does not believe these scriptures or does not have the holy spirit living within them in this way, praying to others to intercede on their behalf is understandable.

In talking with Christians who claim to have experienced transformation in their life that they refer to either as being 'born again' or 'baptised in the holy spirit', they tend to attest to a personal experience that aligns with the narrative supported by these scriptures.

In talking with traditionalist Roman Catholics, I have found they tend to rely on a belief in following practices their religious leaders have prescribed: That the sacramental processes Roman Catholics and Eastern Orthodox Christians submit themselves to as part of their faith (in particular, water baptism), will have effected the holy spirit coming to live within them. Even though they may not have experienced any transformational change in their life as Paul describes in Romans 8, they have faith that the process they underwent through baptism, along with subsequent processes associated with other sacraments, will suffice to ensure their redemption.

From a human sense, I can understand this perspective. It is the easiest path to follow if one has been brought up that way. It would take a major catalyst to move to the alternative ('born again') belief. In listening to those who have done so, their accounts vary in what influenced them to change. However, one universal theme emerged in all accounts: They read the scriptures for themselves, genuinely seeking to find out what they teach. This resulted in (a) a change in their understanding of what scripture teaches and (b) a personal sense of encounter with God (typically expressed as the holy spirit) which they describe as a sense of conviction and a growing awareness of the holy spirit speaking to them, sometimes with words; usually not.

It is easy to see the connection between Judaic and Christian ideas about the holy spirit, with Christianity providing an evolution of concepts in the Tanakh.

Even though Islam is a more recent innovation, its understanding seems however, to have dropped back to a far simpler concept, revolving around the theme of a messenger. To help us understand why this is, let us explore the life of the primary messenger of Islam.

CREDIBLE?

8. WHO WAS MUHAMMAD?

"For those who live according to the flesh set their minds on the things of the flesh, but those who live according to the spirit set their minds on the things of the spirit. For to set the mind on the flesh is death, but to set the mind on the spirit is life and peace."

Romans 8:5-6

8.1 SOURCES

Our primary sources of information about Muhammad are the Qur'an, Hadiths and historical records about the period and locations where he lived. Islam holds that the Qur'an is a collection of revelations from God given to Muhammad via visitations from the angel Gabriel. However, after Muhammad's death, his followers found that the Qur'an omitted guidance on many problems within their religion and life in society.[97]

Hadiths helped fill this gap. They are collections of sayings attributed to Muhammad, written after his death by various of his followers to record what he said so it wouldn't be lost. In this way, Hadiths are similar in nature and purpose to the Gospel of Thomas regarding Jesus. However, unlike the Gospel of Thomas, which is not conventionally considered part of the Christian canon,

---

[97] Jeffrey, Arthur (1958). *Islam: Muhammad and his Religion*. Bobbs-Merrill, Indianapolis

for most Islamic sects, Hadiths constitute an essential part of their faith and are heavily relied upon in determining Islamic law.

Originally, Hadiths were just Islamic oral tradition, but they were eventually compiled into distinct written collections by scholars. Hadiths are popular with Muslims in part because they are accessible in their own native languages, whereas many believe the Qur'an should be read in Arabic, which most Muslims do not know.

The Hadiths of Sunni and Shi'ite Muslims differ. Sunni Hadiths include words and practices attributed not only to Muhammad, but also his companions, whereas Shi'ite hadiths include words and actions of Muhammad and his family.

Not all Muslim sects believe Hadiths are divinely revealed. Some treat only the Qur'an as divine guidance. However, the Qur'an does not provide clear guidance on many practical matters, so most Muslims like to integrate into their practices how Muhammad lived his life, believing that he is the best example of what a person should be. Consequently, Hadiths constitute an important part of what most Muslims believe and about the laws that should govern them. Over time, various attempts were made by learned jurists to work out an Islamic legal framework (e.g. Abu Hanifa; Malik b. Anas; ash-Shafi'i; Ahmad b. Hanbal).

Although understanding the nature of Hadiths is helpful to explain the basis for Islamic law, Hadiths constitute a less important source than the Qur'an. Most Muslims consider the Qur'an of greater importance than Hadiths. So, I will draw primarily on the Qur'an. However, where certain Hadiths add useful evidence, I will refer to these and historical records of the period.

8.2 MUHAMMAD'S FAMILY

The man we know as Muhammad the prophet of Islam was born in 570 CE in Mecca. Muhammad may not have been his birth name. Some Muslim scholars claim he was named Muhammad at birth. Other scholars believe Muhammad was a title and his birth name was Qutham ibn Abd Al-Lat, which means Qutham the son of the slave of Al-Lat. Al-Lat was the name of the Moon Goddess, worshipped in Arabia around the time Muhammad was born. Al-Lat was also one of three daughters of the pagan god Allah. It is also the feminine form of the name 'Allah'[98].

---

[98] Fahd, T., "al-Lat", in Bosworth et al. 1986, p692

Egyptian Islamic scholar, Dr Youssef Ziedan, Director of Manuscripts at the Library of Alexandria in his book Hayat Mohammad (p.39) and author Dr Muhammed Hussein Haykal state that Qutham kept this name until he was over 40 years of age, which is when he started claiming he had received revelations from God through the angel Gabriel and changed his name to Muhammad.

Muhammad's father, Abd al-Muttalib, died before Muhammad was born and his mother, Amina bint Wahb, died when he was only 6 years old, after which he was sent to live with his father's kin in the Arabian desert. Muhammad's mother was a member of the Quraysh tribe in Mecca. The Quraysh was a polytheistic Arab tribe, one of whose gods was Allah, the god Muhammad later declared was the one true god.

Having been orphaned, Muhammad was fortunate when he obtained employment from a rich female caravan merchant, Khadija bint Khuwaylid. They later married in 592 or 595 CE when Muhammad was around 22 or 25 and Khadija was 40 or 41. This marriage boosted Muhammad's wealth and status. Khadija is believed to have been a strong and positive influence on him, supporting him emotionally and financially. The couple had six children during a stable period for the family. Muhammad remained monogamous until Khadija's death in 619 CE. It was only in the last decade of their marriage that Muhammad started sharing his 'revelations'.

After the death of Khadija – particularly after he fled to Medina – Muhammad's followers and personal power grew. No longer under her strong positive influence, he progressively turned to a life of carnal pleasures – food, conquest, and women. The Qur'an and Hadiths show he always justified his actions, thinking that God would want to bless his messenger with such carnal pleasures (in stark contrast to all God's prophets before him). Muhammad's power was such that no one would challenge his appetite for young girls, or his having concubines or more wives than other men were allowed. Two of his wives were controversial. The first of these was Aisha bint Abi Bakr, who was only around 6 years of age when they married and 9 when they consummated the marriage. This occurred in 623 CE, when Muhammad was over 50 years old and living in Medina.

The second was Zaynab bint Jahsh who was Muhammad's first cousin and the wife of Muhammad's stepson, Zayd ibn Harithah. When Muhammad decided he wanted Zaynab for himself, Zayd responded by divorcing her so this could happen. Muhammad conveniently had a new Qur'anic 'revelation' (33:36-37) allowing him to do whatever he liked and particularly specifying he could marry Zayd's wife if Zayd had divorced her.

Zayd had been a slave of Muhammad's late first wife. Muhammad had freed Zayd and adopted him as a son. Zayd would have been careful to appease Muhammad, even if this meant giving his wife to Muhammad. Given this history, combined with Muhammad's 'Messenger of God' status, wherein Muhammad could make whatever decrees he wanted as if they were God's word, Zayd's willingness to give up his wife is understandable. Such an action would have been necessary for his self-preservation. Gratitude to Muhammad for his earlier emancipation may also have played a factor.

Islam forbids a man marrying more than four wives (Surah 4:3), and Muhammad is known on at least two occasions to have forced men who had more to get rid of some of them. However, Muhammad claimed a revelation from Allah allowing him an exception (Surah 33:50). He had a total of at least 11 wives. Scholars debate whether two additional women were also his wives or just concubines.

8.3 A NAME SUITABLE FOR GOD'S MESSENGER

Muslims greatly revere Muhammed. To those outside Islam, Muslims seem to almost deify him with their level of reverence. For example, they always say a blessing ("Peace be upon him") whenever mentioning Muhammad's name and they have often reacted violently to anyone drawing pictures of him[99] [100]. The most common explanation given by Muslims for such a reaction is that drawing pictures of Muhammad is idolatry. However, Muslims don't react similarly to pictures of anyone else, even of Allah. Also, if someone who rejects Islam draws a picture of Muhammad, they obviously won't be doing this to create an idol of someone, because they don't revere Muhammad.

The argument against drawing images of Muhammad is therefore flawed. Instead, it signals that Muhammad is treated by Muslims as God-like. Cartoon images can be used in humour or to ridicule someone, as often occurs with cartoons of Jesus, God, popes, bishops, rabbis, politicians and celebrities. Permitting cartoons to be drawn of Muhammad would expose him to becoming the subject of similar humour and ridicule. It seems, therefore, that

---

[99] Brian Trench (2016). *Charlie Hebdo, Islamophobia and Freedoms of the Press*. Studies v105(418) pp183-191
[100] https://en.wikipedia.org/wiki/Jyllands-Posten_Muhammad_cartoons_controversy Accessed 14 June 2025

Muslims take greater offence at potential criticism of Muhammad than Allah because he is the true centrepiece of their religion. If he were to be revealed to be flawed, the entire Islamic house of cards would come tumbling down. Islam therefore simply cannot afford to take that risk.

Consistent with this level of reverence for Muhammad, the name Muhammad means praiseworthy, which is a name one might give to someone who has achieved great things, rather than to a baby. However, to some, it seems incongruous within Islam to give anyone a title of Praiseworthy other than their God. I have heard some ex-Muslims questioning the wisdom of calling yourself Muhammad because that would be committing the sin of 'Shirk', which is putting yourself in the place of God. This is somewhat similar to the accusation the Pharisees made against Jesus of associating himself with God (Luke 22:69-71).

Although we cannot be certain of what Muhammad's birth name really was, in a pagan culture that worshipped a moon god, Qutham slave of the moon god's daughter seems a more likely choice of name for a baby than Praiseworthy. However, being named as a slave of a pagan goddess in a polytheistic culture is obviously unsuitable for someone claiming to be the greatest and final prophet of a monotheistic religion. So, if Qutham ibn Abd Al-Lat was his birth name, he clearly had a motive to change it.

His choice of name – Praiseworthy – is telling. Researchers who have studied offenders' lives are familiar with a common theme amongst violent offenders, in particular. They have frequently suffered embarrassment, low self-esteem or disrespect earlier in life[101]. It is easy to imagine that being named the slave of a pagan god in a polytheist culture would cause a child to (a) suffer a negative emotional impact on his psyche, (b) resent such a belief system, (c) be conditioned to believe followers of a god are slaves of that god, and (d) change things about himself (such as his name and identity) to enhance his own self-image.

This understanding may help explain why we see repeated evidence in the Qur'an and Hadiths of Muhammad's loathing of polytheists, and of his positioning Muslims as slaves of God, rather than as beloved children of God, as Judaism and Christianity do[102]. A child with such an unflattering name, would

---

[101] James Gillian, (2003). *Shame.* Social Research. v70 pp1149-1180

[102] Note: Some Greek scholars identify a self-identification label δοῦλος (doulos) often used by Christians in the New Testament can mean 'slave'. However, most scholars identify it has a broader meaning including servant or bond-servant, implying a choice. *The Greek-English Interlinear ESV New Testament* (2018). Crossway. pg xxii

have been driven to create a personal narrative that boosts his ego. We see much evidence in the Qur'an and hadiths of such an ego, possibly extending to narcissism. In the 7th century CE, Muhammad destroyed the temple of Al-Lat[103], an act that is consistent with despising and wanting to bury the association with her that his name had given him for the first 40 years of his life.

It is interesting that Muhammad chose to retain use of the name of the pagan god Allah, father of Al-Lat, for his monotheistic god. He may have done this to appeal to other Arabs at that time who were familiar with Allah. Allah was seen as chief among the pantheon of gods and goddesses. By retaining Allah, Muhammad was not throwing out the entire religion of his people but just claiming that people had falsely believed in polytheism, creating lesser gods to worship. Rather than inventing a completely new religion that no one would have any connection with, he took the tactical option of linking his religion to a well-known monotheistic religion, transplanting his name 'Allah' for the name of their god. The Qur'an clearly demonstrates that Judaism and Christianity had been major influences of Muhammad's belief system. He also adopted sufficient material from these religions to appear to be building on them, but rejected doctrines and practices he did not believe in, substituting new ones that served him better.

8.4 THE TURNING POINT IN MUHAMMAD'S MINISTRY

In Mecca, for the first few years following his initial 'revelation', Muhammad's teachings were more benign and tolerant than they later became after his flight to Medina in 622 CE (known as the Hijra). He had initially been concerned with widows and orphans, possibly influenced by his own childhood. He spent around 13 years in Mecca trying to recruit people to his religion, but failed, managing only to recruit family and friends. By 622 CE the Quraysh in Mecca had become fed up with him and were making life difficult for him, so he fled to Medina with his followers.

Medina contained a Jewish community, so Muhammad would have been exposed to Jewish people, beliefs, and practices. Muhammad reasoned that if he could persuade the Jews to accept his religion, that would engender respect

[103] Tabari, Al (25 Sep 1990). *The last years of the Prophet (translated by Isma'il Qurban Husayn). State University of New York Press. p46, ISBN 978-0-88706-691-7*

and stature amongst his own people, who might then be more likely to accept his claims. Muhammad's earlier writings in the Qur'an say positive things about the 'people of the book'[104]. However, as can be seen in his later Surahs, after they refused to accept him and acknowledge him as the last of the prophets, he turned on them.

This is the point in time when Islam evolved from being a religious movement into a political movement cloaked in religion. Muhammad's 'revelations' became more aggressive, advocating violence and intolerance. As shown in Chapter 2, these new revelations often over-rode his earlier revelations. Having left his wealth in Mecca, with his new army he began robbing caravans of the Quraysh, confiscating their property and disrupting the flow of wealth to his enemies. In 624 CE during the holy month of Rajab in which Arab culture forbade bloodshed, one of his victims was killed in one of these raids, causing a huge public outcry. Seriously embarrassed by this unexpected public reaction, Muhammad initially refused to touch the loot from the raid until the public reaction died down. However later, when public anger receded, he claimed to receive a reassuring message from Allah. He then took a fifth of the loot for himself and shared the rest with his followers. He also shared in the same proportion the ransom money from two prisoners he had taken in the same raid. Some scholars note that, at that time, many of the men of Medina became interested in joining Muhammad's raids purely for the prospect of such financial benefits[105].

The taking of personal wealth and material benefits '*of the flesh*', differentiates Muhammad from Jesus and other Jewish prophets. This marks him out as not being from the same prophetic line but instead being driven by personal factors concerning his own psyche and material benefit.

Two years before his death, after Muhammad's military strength grew beyond that of the Quraysh tribe in Mecca, he returned with his army to Mecca. The Quraysh people, knowing they had by now become militarily weaker than Muhammad, surrendered without a fight and converted to Islam to save their lives from the slaughter Muhammad's religion decreed for non-Muslims.

---

[104] Jews and Christians
[105] Kelen, B. (1975). *Muhammad the Messenger of God*. New York: Thomas Nelson

8.5 MUHAMMAD'S DEATH

Having murdered a Jewish woman's family, the woman (Zeynab bint Al-Harith) fooled Muhammad into eating food she had poisoned (Sahih al-Bukhari 3169; Sahih Muslim 2190), causing him to endure a slow and painful death which he described as like having his aorta severed (Ibn al-Qayyim's Zad al-Ma'ad 4/111). Interestingly, earlier Muhammad had recited in the Qur'an that if he ever invented false sayings, God would sever his aorta (Surah 69:44-46). Whereas we know poison would not actually sever an aorta, clearly this was a turn of phrase used by Muhammad, both when his death was near and earlier when he recited it in one of his 'revelations' that ended up in the Qur'an. This notion, that severing one's aorta is how God punishes false prophets, may signify Muhammad was aware he had fabricated his revelations.

At the end of his life Muhammad was a tortured shell of a man, in physical pain and fearful that God would continue to punish him after death with what he referred to as the 'torture of the grave' (Sahih al-Bukhari 6368). Muhammad's life is a sobering lesson to us all about how, as weak humans, we are susceptible, not only to far-fetched ideas, but also to corruption, particularly if we are powerful. Perhaps, in some ways, Muhammad was not so very different from Judaism's Pharisees living in Jesus' time or Christendom's Bishops living around Muhammad's own time.

Armed with modern knowledge of history and humanity, it is clear now who Muhammad was, what drove him, why he came up with the belief system and rules that he did, and why he behaved the way he did. It is far more credible to attribute the things he said and did to the influences on him of the time, place and events in his life, than it is to attribute them to God.

What is more challenging to understand is why people would believe Muhammad is a good example to us and want to follow what his Qur'an teaches. Perhaps most of his followers have not studied his life in detail, engaging with perspectives outside Islamic dogma. Muhammad's religion requires submission if you are to be left in peace. I can appreciate that the cultural conditioning from a society practising such submission may help to explain why people could still believe Muhammad is virtuous and that his 'revelations' are credible.

8.6 MUHAMMAD TO JEWS AND CHRISTIANS

The writings in the Qur'an reveal Muhammad positioning himself in the succession of prophets recorded in the Tanakh[106]. He adopted some Jewish prophets into his religion, possibly to make it easier to persuade the Jews of his new religion, as if he was affirming that the core of their faith was true. However, similar to his approach towards the Quraysh and their gods, such as Al-Lat and the other daughters of Allah, Muhammad did not support what the Jews practised and believed about God and their prophets. He claimed that the Jews were not following what God had revealed to them. (Surah 2:88; 2:121)

Muhammad even claimed Jesus was an Islamic prophet, a decision he likely made to appeal to Christians. However, as discussed in Chapter 2, his claims about Jesus do not align with Christian beliefs. The Qur'an tells an interesting story about Jesus speaking when still a baby (Surah 19:30-33), and Muhammad seems to have completely misunderstood the Christian belief of the Trinity: His writings in Surah 5:116 show he thought the Trinity consisted of Jesus, Mary, and Allah.

Prior to Muhammad's death, he forced Jews and Christians to become second class citizens. They were only permitted to stay alive if they paid the humiliating Jizya – a form of protection tax that Muhammad introduced through one of his most harsh and violent 'revelations' (Surah 9:29). Surah 9 was 'revealed' near the end of his life, thereby abrogating contradictions from his earlier, more benign 'revelations'. It contains the Qur'an's most strident declarations regarding warfare and violent oppression[107]. The monthly ceremony in which Jews and Christians paid the Jizya was designed to humiliate them on their knees. In some locations they were given a necklace to wear to show they had paid their Jizya, marking them out publicly as humiliated second class citizens. Later, this was updated in Iraq during the 9th century CE by the 2nd Caliph to the yellow star that the Nazis later used in their pogrom against the Jews during the 20th century CE.

Under Islam, Jews were prohibited from blowing the shofar; Christians were prohibited from ringing church bells. Both were prohibited from praying publicly, gathering together or building new synagogues and churches. Because they were considered inferior, if a Muslim man or woman walked on the same

[106] Jeffrey, Arthur (1958). *Islam: Muhammad and his Religion*. Bobbs-Merrill, Indianapolis
[107] Spencer, Robert (2021). *The Critical Qur'an*. Post Hill Press, New York. p132

side of the street, the Jew had to cross to the other side of the street so the Muslim could walk and not be dirtied by the filth of the Jew. Christians were made to wear the 'Zunnar', the belt still warn by men in the west[108]. Failure to wear the Zunnar could result in various punishments, including whipping, imprisonment or public humiliation.

The Qur'an prohibits Muslims from making friends with Jews and Christians (Surah 5:51), but some scholars hold that Surah 3:28 and 16:106 permit Muslims to deceive Jews and Christians in order to protect or advance Islam. So, some Muslims believe they may feign friendship in the interests of Islam.

8.7 SUMMARY: SO, HOW SHOULD WE VIEW MUHAMMAD?

The insights into who Muhammad was as a person and the events that influenced him, help explain why he took the actions he did to create Islam and violently suppress all other belief systems. The information surviving about Muhammad's life is sufficient to create a clear picture of what drove him and how his life evolved.

Being orphaned at a young age then married to an older woman who was powerful, successful, and wealthy in her own right would, or course, have shaped Muhammad's psyche. His membership of an influential family likely protected him from poverty and its associated need to focus on survival, instead affording him time to think about spiritual matters. Yet I can imagine his station in life as an orphan and junior marriage partner, likely placed him somewhat outside the comfortable male-dominated structures of stereotypical Quraysh family and spiritual life.

Nevertheless, he lived a moderate life under the shadow and protection of his wife until she died. The death of a long-term stable spouse would, understandably, have caused Muhammad some soul-searching and to ask himself the obvious question: 'What should I now do with my life?' The Islamic narrative describes Muhammad's desire to escape the social ills that characterised Meccan society by spending long hours hiding away in caves thinking about life and spiritual things. It was from one such period of meditation that he emerged with his first 'revelation'. We cannot know the extent to which Muhammad actually believed he had seen an angel of God in

---

[108] https://wikiislam.net/wiki/Zunar_(Islamic_Yellow-Badge_Practices) Accessed 7 June 2025

the flesh, as opposed to experiencing an epiphany. However, from this point in his life, he found a purpose – one which continued to evolve throughout the remainder of his life.

Through his exposure to some of the beliefs and practices within Judaism and Christianity, Muhammad identified doctrines that resonated with him; in particular, the rejection of polytheism and idolatry. However, he also found some beliefs and practices amongst the Jews and Christians he encountered to be confusing and even corrupt. He believed that the word of God had been revealed to Moses and Jesus and that Jews and Christians should follow these revelations. He was critical of Jews and Christians for failing to follow what God had revealed to them through Moses and Jesus.

Muhammad had a point; he would have been exposed to beliefs and doctrinal debates that many modern Jews and Christians would see as far-fetched or heretical, and the lives of Jews and Christians have not always conformed to the virtuous conduct their scriptures indicate their God expects of them.

Muhammad likely anticipated that by weaving key aspects of Jewish and Christian beliefs into the religious narrative he was working out for himself, Jews and Christians would have been more willing to buy into his religion. Unfortunately for Muhammad, he was never likely to succeed in converting them because he had a poor understanding of their scriptures, so made many mistakes in his 'revelations' that would have been obvious to them. Muhammad's frustration at his failure to convert Jews and Christians to his new religion made him angry with them.

Fortunately for Muhammad, Meccan society included corruption and moral weaknesses, such as abuse and neglect of women, idolatry, an unfair balance of wealth, and abuse of people living in poverty. Like the context for most revolutions throughout history, this combination of failings made Meccan society ripe for an uprising of the oppressed to a noble cause with more egalitarian values. Muhammad sought to provide that cause.

We see throughout the Qur'an and Hadiths how, as Muhammad built his power and influence amongst his growing base of followers, he was not immune to the corruption of power that has affected so many other revolutionary leaders throughout history. He not only extended himself extra privileges beyond those of his followers, he also increasingly used violent coercion to grow his power, and he fell to a personal lifestyle that Christianity would describe as 'living in the flesh'.

Aware of his carnal life and moral failings, Muhammad began fearing he would be 'punished in the grave'. This was a common superstition in his culture at the time, but one which may have originated in Jewish culture. Whatever the origin, he began praying he would not be subjected to such torment (Bukhari Hadith 6366). He died an agonising slow death, most likely the result of poisoning by one of the Jewish women he had oppressed. He described his encroaching death as feeling like his aorta was being pulled out from him. I am left feeling sorry for Muhammad; he started life with a desire to improve the world but ended up doing much evil throughout his life and died in a pitiable state.

9. CONCLUSION

"For we know in part and we prophesy in part, but when the perfect comes, the partial will pass away"

1 Corinthians 13:9-10

9.1 WHAT TO BELIEVE

As stated in Chapter 1, I did not set out to tell you what to believe, but only to provide insights into the credibility of evidence behind various beliefs – particularly those where Judaism, Christianity and Islam hold conflicting positions. Specialist theological, apologetic and polemic scholars have examined many of these positions in more detail than I have done herein. My contribution simply offers a different type of perspective – one that tries to make sense out of this based on a secular evidential credibility approach. Now that you have had a chance to consider the implications of such insights, you may choose to retain a belief you previously held or adjust it where evidence suggests a more credible option. The choice is yours; this is Religion after all, not Science or Philosophy, where stricter requirements must be met before forming a conclusion.

I will, however, offer a couple of insights from this journey that I believe may be helpful and that are relevant to all three religions. When reading the various debates surrounding Judaism, Christianity and Islam, I noticed a significant difference between these religious contexts and a Western Justice system context regarding how people respond to evidence. Within the religious contexts, people tend to advocate for a position and, if they are persuaded that their position is not strong, they will switch to a different position and advocate for that. However, in the Justice context, evidence needs to be strong before any position is formed; the zone of uncertainty is much wider. For example, in Chapter 2, I discussed Critical Text versus Majority Text manuscripts. Here I found scholars and religious leaders tend to declare they are either in the Critical Text camp or the Majority Text camp. The evidence suggests both have pros and cons, and that neither can be completely relied upon over the other.

In keeping with this observation, history contains myriad debates between factions who seemed to genuinely believe what they argued. This is telling. **What is evidently clear is that much is not evidently clear.** History is littered with victims of these debates which often contested academic points that did not need to materially affect how one lives. The dominant factions in these debates often shunned or harmed those who held conflicting opinions. The faction we are part of today likely has baggage that ingrains defence of the particular doctrines its forebears contested to defend.

To illustrate this problem, I attended an Evangelical Protestant church service recently in which the preacher gave a sermon that expounded on four categories we should divide our beliefs between. The most serious of these categories he called "*To die for*". Regarding this category, he drew a parallel with the Battle of Thermopylae in 480 BC in which a small army of Spartans was able to defend their position for two days against an onslaught by a much larger invading Persian army. The preacher argued that Christians should demonstrate the same level of commitment to defending Christian Orthodoxy as the Spartans did to defending their families and way of life. He defined Christian Orthodoxy as being what we should put in the "*To die for*" category. He went on to define Christian Orthodoxy as the various creeds and interpretations of "the Church fathers" who were victorious in the debates at councils of the early church throughout the centuries following the first apostles. However, he did not mention that the teachings of Jesus should be in this category, and he made no comment on the status of decisions by the church councils that have continued to occur since Protestantism split off from Roman Catholicism. Also, I have spoken with people of other faiths whose strongest defences were given for the points of doctrinal difference between their 'faction' and others. So, I don't reserve this observation just for Christian Protestants; it is probably a universal human tendency.

My advice in response to this type of problem is to **accept that we do not know everything**. Perhaps it is OK to not lock into a position on a given doctrinal interpretation that someone else who went before you did. Perhaps not everything our forebears debated and fought over has been revealed. This is the approach I have taken personally in examining my own faith.

A second insight that comes more from a sociological perspective is the pattern in humanity where **people seek to create laws and rituals rather than seeking spiritual transformation** as their means to appease a spiritual god. We see this in Judaism whose Torah contains minutely detailed specifications of ritual practices which are still observed today and have subsequently been extended through oral law. This, despite Judaism's prophets speaking out against such practices for centuries, instead telling the people God wants their hearts; these prophets were not heeded (Jeremiah 7:22-26).

Similarly, even though the Christan scriptures also make it clear that God wants hearts, not rituals, Christendom developed religious hierarchy and suites of ritual sacraments, claiming that performing these practices would effect the spiritual objectives. Islam too has its ritual prayers, fasting and Sharia laws that have become the most important requirements of being accepted as a Muslim and avoiding violent sanctions. All this causes me to wonder – Could humanity's desires for religious laws and rituals be more about forming social norms, cultural identity, and political power than about anything spiritual?

In this journey, I haven't covered all doctrines of Judaism, Christianity and Islam. Rather, I only focussed on the evidential basis for material doctrines where significant conflicts exist between and within each of them. This exploration identified weaknesses in the bases for some beliefs within each of the three religions. What you do with these insights is up to you. In the spirit of not telling you what to believe, I will leave to you any conclusion about what you should now choose to believe.

However, because you have chosen to accompany me on this journey, I will offer some insight into how this journey has influenced what I believe personally. This is where the investigative part of this book finishes. What follows are simply my personal thoughts on where this leaves me. I offer these in the hope you may be able to find something helpful amongst them from a fellow traveller.

9.2 A PERSONAL REFLECTION ON MY JOURNEY

Two primary themes emerged to me as I explored the scriptures and history of all three religions and their various denominations and sects:

Knowledge: We simply do not have all the information needed to answer all the questions we might want answers for, and this doesn't matter; I suspect we are not meant to know and do not need to know everything. We will probably make less trouble for ourselves and others if we can simply live with this fact, rather than force concrete positions through a form of Religion that 'makes up facts'.

Spiritual vs physical world: Throughout history, God has sought for us to be in right relationship with him and each other; this requires our heart to be in the right place. If it is, our actions will reflect this and that is all that is required of us; it is not about laws, rituals and sacraments.

However, humanity has revealed across time and cultures that humans want laws, rulers, and rituals to govern and guide our behaviour. Unfortunately, these often deflected us from what God really wants for us.

- We read in the Torah how, in the Garden of Eden, Adam and Eve walked in right relationship with God and each other until they thought they knew better. (Genesis 3)

- We read in the Torah, the people asking God for a king from among them to rule over them. (1 Samuel 8)

- We read in the Nevi'im and Ketuvim that God does not want our sacrifices, but rather a broken spirit and contrite heart, loving-kindness and that we would know him (Psalm 51:16-17; Hosea 6:6; Micah 6:6-8; Isaiah 1:11-15).

- We read in the Torah, New Testament epistles, and other historical records how people sought to practise their faith through mitzvahs, sacraments and customs, rather than praying directly with God and living a life of love in action towards each other.

- We read in the Gospels, Jesus pointing out how pride and 'living in the flesh' prevents us from being what God wants us to be.

- We read in the Gospels, Jesus giving us the way back to God through an internal transformation that places God, rather than our self-interested egos, directly on the throne of our lives.

- We read in the Qur'an, Muhammad's frustration with the many confusing doctrines he was hearing from Jews and Christians.

- We read in the Qur'an, Muhammad's attempt to make sense of all of this and failing miserably with contradictory and violent commands.

- We read in the Hadiths how people sought to plug gaps in the Qur'an, carving out laws to be governed by, based on what they think Muhammad would have done.

I am left thinking that so much of what has been added since Jesus walked the earth has taken us away from his truth. Apart from the few passages I have expressed concerns about, I am inclined to accept the fundamental thrust of the Gospel message recorded in the synoptic gospels, because it strongly supports the two overarching themes identified above.

Although my faith in some doctrines has been reduced because of what I have discovered, evidence uncovered on this journey has also clarified or bolstered my confidence in other doctrines. For example, I always struggled with the concept of Jesus taking on the role of a sacrificial animal to atone for the sin of humanity for all time (John 1:29; Romans 6:10). However, on this journey, I read Yoma 39b of the Mishna about events associated with Yom Kippur that occurred in the temple in the same year Jesus was crucified. This evidence, when added to the New Testament accounts of Jesus' death, prophecies and associated narrative, compels me to accept that God stopped accepting animal sacrifices for all time from the point in time when Jesus was crucified. So, although I still find it difficult to understand how or why such a blood sacrifice can atone for sin, I am forced to concede that the evidence is compelling that Jesus' death did actually stop the practice of further blood sacrifices and that this was God's will. The alignment between the Mishna account and the evidence from Christian sources could not have been fabricated and is too detailed and too strong for this to be merely a coincidence. Whether or not God previously endorsed blood sacrifices, he appears to have wanted to put a stop to them.

Because of its alignment with the message woven through other scriptures, I am also inclined to accept much of John's gospel's account of what Jesus taught about what we need to do. However, in doing so, I am forced to accept that either the author was guessing about the nature of Jesus' divinity, or that concepts conceived in Hebrew have potential to be misunderstood when translated into Greek – In particular, that the author intended some instances of 'THEOS' to mean 'ELOHIM' and not 'YHWH'

For my part, I am left feeling amazed by the life of Jesus and what he taught, both of which have had more impact on my life than everything man has added since. I find his words and life compelling. I am grateful to him for this and have decided to follow what he taught us to do. However, what should this look like in practice?

This does not mean I necessarily adopt the practices and beliefs of other followers of Jesus who came after him. However, from reading about their experiences, struggles and insights, I can relate to much of what they experienced, and I find this helpful. Conversely, there has been much misplaced focus within Judaism, conflict within Christendom, and intolerance within Islam throughout history. Therefore, the probability of the particular denomination or sect any of us were brought up in having all its facts right is miniscule. So, let us abandon that notion as naïve and unlikely, and instead choose to think for ourselves, issue by issue.

Following Jesus means I reject the claimed spiritual authority of those who would try to exert power over people through Religion. Jesus taught us that is not the way to find God and that such authority can be abused, with religious leaders using Religion to increase their own power and prestige. Rather, the way of Jesus is a simple one of servanthood, sacrifice, love and courage.

Regarding prayer, the teaching of Jesus and the symbolic events that occurred at the time of his crucifixion make it clear that when we pray, we should do so directly to god the father. To pray to others such as his mother or saints is to deny the redemptive effect of Jesus' death.

I struggle to accept that believing any particular narrative as the truth will determine whether one gets into heaven or not. How can one's opinion about the veracity of a fact make any difference? This notion seems illogical and unintuitive. Therefore, like James, I do not believe we are saved by faith alone, if by 'faith' we mean belief in any particular set of doctrines. The main theme of one of the most credible sources – the epistle of James – is that only the kind of faith that produces good works has any value; faith alone is inadequate. Similarly, I struggle to accept that we can get into heaven by doing good works or obeying laws, be these those in the Torah, Mitzvah's, Sacraments, Sharia or the '5 pillars' of Islam. Our desire to be ruled by kings, bishops, caliphs and laws is a human trait. The Tanakh teaches instead that God does not want such sacrifices, but rather, he desires things like a broken and contrite heart, loving-kindness and to know him (Hosea 6:6; Psalm 51:16-17). So, how do we do this when our human nature drives us in other directions?

Consistent with what Jesus taught, I can see that how a person speaks and behaves reflects what is going on inside them. As he said, it is what comes out of a person, not what goes in, that makes a person unclean (Matthew 7:16; Matthew 15:11; James 2:18). Sin is an outflowing of one's spiritual state, as are the fruit of the spirit (Galatians 5:22-23). It follows that if we are to be uncorrupted, we must be transformed by the renewing of our mind (Romans 12:2). From my own life's experience, I believe this is impossible to do adequately by ourselves. It requires some sort of spiritual intervention that we don't fully understand but that biblical authors attempted to describe in John 3 and Romans 8.

Personally, I have experienced struggling against my human nature to be a good Christian (Romans 7), failing, then surrendering to God instead and becoming renewed through that act of devotion (Romans 8), after which I find that my actions and even most of my thoughts no longer let me down as they did – unless I get distracted by the cares of this world again. I feel aware of the presence of God in a way I did not before and that I cannot explain. I feel a connection to all other people on a spiritual level that I did not before; I cannot explain that either. This is not something I worked out logically in advance. It is something I experienced, initially after a transformation had occurred in my life, and subsequently as I sought a closer connection with God. Maybe this is what Jesus refers to when he says, "fulfilling righteousness", "seeking righteousness" and the greatest two commandments (Deuteronomy 6:5 and Leviticus 19:18b), which he said summed up the whole law.

I guess if being a Christian requires accepting all Christendom's dogma and church creeds as divine revelations, then I am not a Christian. However, I do believe the evidence is strong that Jesus is the Messiah referred to throughout the Tanakh. I am choosing to follow Jesus – what I believe he taught, and not all the beliefs subsequently added by Christendom. Accordingly, many Christians may not see me as Christian. Perhaps instead, I should see myself as the true Jew Paul spoke about in Romans 2:28-29: "*For a person is not a Jew who is one outwardly, nor is circumcision something that is outward in the flesh, but someone is a Jew who is one inwardly, and circumcision is of the heart by the Spirit and not written in code. This person's praise is not from people but from God.*"

For Christians, being a 'believer' seems to be the defining requirement. However, Jews (including Jesus) are more centred in what they do. I wonder, if early Christians had instead chosen to simply be Jewish followers of Jesus at the outset, would the other Jews who never followed him have been more willing to incorporate the life and teachings of Jesus into their faith? Sure, they would have been up against the religious leaders who felt threatened by Jesus, but this threat only existed because Jesus resonated with so many Jews and was himself a good Jew.

Perhaps he wants us all – Jew and Gentile – to be 'good Jews', as God intended, rather than hypocrites and lovers of money and power. What upset Jesus most when he walked the earth was corruption of God's laws for selfish gain. He made it clear that he wants us to turn away from such corruption, instead turning back to God, seeking righteousness.

So, is Jesus God? Well, like he said, I believe he is from God, sent on a mission from God. However, unlike perhaps for many Christians, in my life Jesus does not displace the pre-eminence of god the father who sent him. The bible refers to the "son of god" 43 times but does not say, "god the son" even once. This concept is clearly a subsequent innovation by the church.

If you are a Christian, I encourage you to look inside yourself and ask who you have a spiritual relationship with; Who are your prayers directed towards? Do you blur the identities of Jesus, the father and the holy spirit in your prayer? I suspect most Christians do. Is it any wonder that Jews and Muslims are at odds with Christianity on its doctrine of the Trinity?

What would it do to your faith if you discovered that Jesus was not equal in power and glory with god the father, but was instead sent from heaven by him and given power by the father to do all the things he did? As evidenced in the synoptic gospels and Didache, although the first apostles revered and loved Jesus, they saw him as the servant of god the father (Isaiah 49:5-7; 53:10-14; Matthew 12:18; Acts 3:26). Would we be wrong to see Jesus as the early apostles did rather than as the subsequent 'machine' of Christendom ended up doing?

If I stop trying to read things into indirect or cryptic passages in scripture but instead give pre-eminence in my faith to the most reliable accounts of Jesus' teachings, I don't think it matters so much whether Jesus is God. If Jesus had thought it important to have an accurate belief on this question, I think he would have made the answer sufficiently clear to avoid the church making it so important that they created schisms all throughout their history over academic questions about various aspects of his nature and identity. Rather, if we instead do what Jesus taught us to do, be what he taught us to be in our hearts and let that flow through to our actions, how can he be disappointed? Throughout the gospels, Jesus pointed us to the father rather than himself, and he taught us to love each other. He said the greatest commandment was to love the lord your god with all your heart, all your soul, all your mind and all your strength (Matthew 22:37; Mark 12:30). In saying this, he wasn't commanding us to love him but to love the father (Mark 12:32-34) – *"the only true God"* (John 17:3).

God in the form of a three-person father, son and holy spirit therefore no longer makes sense to me. The balance of evidence suggests this concept was developed years after Jesus walked the earth. It has been the source of division ever since. On this basis, particularly given that Jesus did not make it clearer, the conventional notion of the Trinity lacks both credibility and materiality. So, in this regard, I understand and accept the Jewish and Islamic criticism of the doctrine of the Trinity. However, I can see in the Torah, God being talked of as some sort of pluralism or intimate connectedness, so maybe classic Christianity is not completely wrong. Perhaps God is bigger than the Christian notion of a Trinity. Perhaps God is also bigger than the Jewish and Islamic restriction that refuses to admit God can show up in the form of a human, even though he does in various encounters given in the Tanakh. Oxbridge Professor John Lennox, a prominent 21st century mathematician, scientist and theologian, has described God as a fellowship, rather than one or more distinct people as Judaism, Islam and Christendom tend to do. Perhaps this is a healthy way to conceptualise God, particularly if we can also accept that there is so much more we don't know than we do know about this universe.

I wonder if God and Jesus have a more intimate relationship than we can imagine from our human experiences where we all exist in separate bodies. Biologically, is a cell in your body part of the person that is you? What if it temporarily departed from your body then re-joined it? Perhaps even we have an intimate relationship with the father, Jesus and each other that we are only capable of getting a hint of in human form. Scriptures talk of some people who walked closely with God. Some people living today seem to walk closer with him than others. I wonder how much more we will realise and experience this relationship after we shuffle off our mortal coils?

Looking beyond the scriptures, we have hundreds of modern-day testimonies of people who have died and come back to life. We call these 'near death experiences'. Many of these accounts testify to experiencing God, love, and others in a profound and intimate way. We should not dismiss these contemporary accounts; they are the nearest thing we have to direct witness statements of what happens after we die. In terms of evidential credibility, they therefore rank higher than the copied and modified manuscripts that have formed our scriptures.

These near-death experience testimonies frequently talk about going to a place like heaven, which the person feels is their true home, and being aware of a powerful loving presence there. These experiences suggest we may be eternal beings ourselves, living with God. We find some evidence for this in scripture too. For example, in Jeremiah 1:5 we read of God telling Jeremiah that he knew him before he was in his mother's womb. God is not saying he knew about Jeremiah, but that he actually knew him, implying Jeremiah existed before he entered his mother's womb. This verse does not mean God knows Jeremiah because he is omniscient; rather it means he knows Jeremiah personally, as a parent knows their child. This understanding reinforces the notion of humans being eternal beings in heaven. Revelation 3:21 also reinforces this notion; it talks about Jesus raising us up to rule with him in heaven.

Due to our lack of complete information, some of my ideas are necessarily somewhat speculative. I guess we will have to wait and see exactly what God is like. In the meantime, I am confident and at peace that I am where God wants me to be and that he loves me. I see this woven through scripture, and I feel this in my heart. This journey has enabled me to identify important choices about how I am to live my life. That is enough for now. I am content to wait until the mirror clears.

"For now we see in a mirror dimly, but then face to face; now I know in part, but then I will know fully, just as I also have been fully known."

1 Corinthians 13:12

10. EPILOGUE: LETTERS TO THE FAITHFUL

As I end this journey of evaluating evidence, I acknowledge, as anticipated, that it didn't prove what is true. It did, however, identify significant weaknesses in some of the pillars of faith for each of the three religions I considered. So, armed with these insights, how would I challenge people of each of these faiths to continue their own journeys?

10.1 TO MY JEWISH BROTHERS AND SISTERS

שמע ישראל
יהוה אלהינו
יהוה אחד
ואהבת את יהוה
אלהיך
בכל־לבבך
ובכל־נפשך
ובכל־מאדך
והיו הדברים
האלה
אשר אנכי מצוך
היום על־לבבך

Shalom,

In this letter, I will be using the name of our lord יהוה, rather than the name Hashem as is tradition, because יהוה instructs us to proclaim his name (Isaiah 12:4; Psalm 105:1). I mean no disrespect to your traditions. However, in obedience to יהוה, I am choosing to do what I believe he wants me to do, even when this conflicts with tradition.

Your people have a long history of experiencing persecution and discrimination from Christendom, Islam, Nazism, Communism and others, yet you have endured. As I have revealed in this book, Christianity and Islam get some things wrong. The persecution you have suffered at their hands is in part due to these errors. I therefore would not expect you to embrace their religions. In fact, because of their history of persecuting the Jewish people, you will understandably be inclined to want to reject their beliefs and practices. Your forebears did. The evidence suggests they not only rejected the practices of the Christians and Muslims, but it is likely they even corrupted parts of the Tanakh to hide evidence that could be interpreted as referring to Yeshua.

As revealed throughout the Tanakh, your ancestors also have a long history of repeatedly complaining and diverting from doing the will of יהוה, whether this be worshiping idols instead of him, failing to believe his promises or rejecting his prophets. The reaction of your forebears to the Christian religion, which was shaped by Roman emperors, likely conditioned them to reject any possibility that the catalyst for forming that religion – Yeshua – may have been sent by יהוה to the Jewish people as so many prophets before him were.

Who are you to tell יהוה that the age of prophets is over and he cannot send another if he sees you straying from his path? Yeshua's teachings were exactly what I would expect יהוה to give you if you had let all your laws, mitzvahs, and sacrifices obscure the reason for them. יהוה communicated this reason through the prophets Hosea and Isaiah, making it plain he doesn't want your sacrifices and offerings (Isaiah 1:11); he wants your love and for you to know him (Hosea 6:6). Even in the Shema, your most revered scripture, YHWH tells you what he wants most: When יהוה, in Deuteronomy 6:8-9, told you to bind his words on your hands, your foreheads and your doorposts, he didn't mean strap written copies of his words in boxes where you can't read them; instead, he was emphasising what he told you in Deuteronomy 6:5-6. Rather than commanding you to literally wear Tefillin, he was telling you he wants your heart.

This is also the message of Yeshua. He gave myriad teachings in the context of the Torah to show that the laws themselves are not the reason for the laws. He walked the talk to the point of sacrificing his life in a symbolic way you would recognise from Leviticus 16, so that you might recognise the will of יהוה for you. Laws are but crutches to symbolise what יהוה wants from you – mere shadows foreshadowing what Yeshua fulfilled. To you I am just a gentile, but I worship your god in the way the prophets revealed. I therefore feel I am the true Jew, the seed of Abraham, a seed through faith and commitment rather than flesh and blood. To me you seem to have an addiction to laws and being ruled. You asked for Kings and in doing so rejected יהוה as your king (1 Samuel 8:6-7). יהוה relented, but it wasn't his idea for you to have kings, it was yours; he wanted you to know him and to love him.

In the Gospels we read of Yeshua repeatedly referring to the Torah and Nevi'im, anchoring his teaching in them. He was not critical of the Torah; rather, he criticised the arrogant religious leaders misusing their education and power to oppress the common Jewish people for their own benefit. If nothing else, Yeshua was a good Jew, devoted to יהוה and caring about people. However, the evidence I explored suggests he is much more. Personally, for me he is more. Engaging with his teachings has transformed my life, bringing me closer to יהוה and transforming me so that I find the essence of his greatest commandments flows out of me without me having to cite a law or rationalise a behaviour. Isn't this what יהוה was after when he commanded us in

Deuteronomy 6:7-9 to write down his commandments all over the place so that we encounter them continuously? The message of this commandment is that we should internalise the word of יהוה and let it transform us. It is not the practice of rituals themselves that is important, but why we would want to do such things. This is the thrust of the difference between Yeshua's teachings from those of the Pharisees. Yeshua did not take away the law; he made it real, rather than just a ritual physical discipline. He fulfilled the purpose of the law.

Yeshua therefore flips the law on its head. As he said, it is not the food that we put into our body that defiles us, but what comes out of us – our words and actions – that reveal whether we are defiled, because they come from the heart. Food is just a physical thing that passes through the body; it is of no spiritual significance (Matthew 15:17-20). Although ritual practices can be helpful reminders, they can also obscure why we do them.

As a Jewish prophet, Yeshua's message was profoundly consistent with history. Could it be that this time, out of his love for his people, יהוה sent someone very precious to him and, although many started to follow him, their leaders, the Pharisees who had become rich and arrogant, felt so condemned and challenged by this mouthpiece of יהוה that they had him killed? I think Yeshua knew this (Matthew 21:33-46; Psalm 118:22), which means יהוה knew it too, but that did not stop him trying, so great is his love for his people. Could it be that when Yeshua said, "*Therefore I say to you, the kingdom of God will be taken away from you and given to a people producing its fruit*" (Matthew 21:43) he meant that when your forebears rejected the message of יהוה, יהוה then opened that message to both gentiles and those Jews who did accept him instead? Looking at the subsequent events in history, this seems to be what happened. If so, this does not mean it is too late for you to get the message that יהוה intended for you through Yeshua; this message is preserved in the Gospels and is woven through the Tanakh.

If you look at the history of Christendom, this truth may be hard to see. After the second temple period, Christendom developed many other beliefs and practices beyond what Yeshua taught. Much of these you can probably safely reject. However, the evidence I have examined suggests your forebears may have rejected too much, throwing the baby out with the bathwater.

I encourage you to read your own Mishna in Yoma 39b. Don't you find it compelling like I do that יהוה stopped accepting sacrifices in the year Yeshua was crucified? The animal sacrifices commanded in Leviticus could never atone for sins permanently. They just gave cover for a year and needed repeating every Yom Kippur. Yeshua, John the Baptist, and subsequent Christian New Testament writers all claim Yeshua was "*the lamb of God who takes away the sin of the world*". This testimony and Yeshua's crucifixion, in combination with what we read in Yoma 39b, is strong evidence that he indeed was.

I don't set out to make you believe all that Christians believe. In fact, different branches of Christianity have widely varying beliefs on many issues. I do, however, encourage you to try stepping beyond the conditioning of your tradition and evaluate for yourself the claim that Yeshua was prophesied in the Tanakh, and that many of the commands in the Torah foreshadowed their fulfilment by Yeshua. There are strong grounds for such a claim, even if Christians may have made up numerous additional 'facts' in forming their belief system. Specifically, I encourage you to examine the evidence in the Tanakh, in combination with the most reliable historical accounts we have about what Yeshua himself said and did. After doing this, if you still struggle to accept Yeshua as Messiah and/or the lamb of God who takes away the sin of the world, I encourage you to do a very Jewish thing and think about what he taught – his interpretations of the law and the implications of those interpretations for your life and the world.

Yeshua was a Jew. He attended the synagogue and temple and spent time teaching and debating the Torah with Jewish religious leaders and teachers. There is much evidence of him teaching from the prophets and on numerous commandments in the law. So, to understand what he was all about, we should study what he said and did, and we should check these against the Torah and the Nevi'im.

Yeshua said that Deuteronomy 6:5 and Leviticus 19:18b are the greatest commandments. He taught that all the Torah and the Prophets hang on these two commandments (Matthew 22:34-40). Although Yeshua's teachings cover many different passages in the Torah and Nevi'im, he repeatedly showed that the commands of the Torah were all oriented towards revealing how to apply these two commandments in our lives.

Regarding the commandment of יהוה in Leviticus 19:18b, who is your neighbour? The first part of this verse warns off vengeance and holding a grudge against sons of your own people. You may therefore have interpreted this to refer to other Jews. However, are we not all created by God? Are we not all sons and daughters of Noah? Does God not want us all to follow what he would instruct us each to do? Yeshua's parable of the Good Samaritan (Luke 10:25-37) teaches what it means to put this commandment into practice. It means an inclusive, generous and compassionate love in action for all humanity.

The letters of early Christians, such as Peter, Paul and John, quoted passages from the Tanakh pointing to Yeshua. Some of this evidence is found in the Septuagint, but is suspiciously missing from the modern-day Hebrew Tanakh, the earliest manuscript of which dates from only one thousand years ago. These differences are unsurprising because Yeshua challenged the teachings and practices of the Jewish religious leaders of his day, particularly the Pharisees. This understandably made the Pharisees want to discredit and even kill him.

The early Christian church grew rapidly, converting many Jews and gentiles from their previous beliefs and practices. This growth created an existential threat to the dominion of the Pharisees. The Pharisees therefore had a motive to suppress belief in Yeshua as the Messiah, just as Christians had a motive to encourage belief in Yeshua as the Messiah. Both sides had a conflict of interest regarding the truth where that truth supported the other side's beliefs. So, I am not surprised that some of the records remaining today have been edited to support each side's narrative.

Tradition can condition us to close our minds to the truth. Just as we are aware in the 21st century of the conditioning that Palestinian Arabs have been subjected to since childhood, so it is that we all, whether Jew or gentile, are exposed to conditioning. Given Yeshua's disdain for the Pharisees, and the fact that Rabbinic Judaism developed from the Pharisaic movement, what would you expect Rabbinic Judaism's tradition to be regarding the possibility of Yeshua as Messiah?

Will you conform to this conditioning rather than research the evidence yourself? Difficult though it may be to do, I encourage you to try to put tradition aside and just look at the Tanakh objectively, including the Septuagint's potential references to the Messiah. The Septuagint is a Greek translation of the Tanakh dating from over 250 years before Yeshua's birth. Greek was the language in common use during the second temple period. Septuagint manuscripts pre-date the oldest remaining Masoretic Text manuscript by over 1,100 years. They even pre-date the birth of Christianity, so could not have been fabricated by Christians. If we look at differences between the Masoretic Text and the much earlier Septuagint, we find the Septuagint references details that better support the early Christian narrative about Yeshua found in the Christian gospels.

If this still leaves you with doubts or questions, I encourage you to read and pray about what Yeshua taught and did, as recorded in the gospels, asking יהוה to guide you to the truth about what he wants for you.

I wish you well in your journey to know the will of יהוה in your life. I openly confess that I am hoping you will experience the impact of Yeshua on your life that I have experienced, due to no merit on my part, but due solely to the grace of יהוה who made me and loves me, just as he made you and loves you.

שָׁלוֹם עֲלֵיכֶם

Shalom Aleichem

10.2 TO MY BROTHERS AND SISTERS IN CHRIST

Greetings from a fellow follower of Jesus Christ.

You recognise Jesus as the Messiah prophesied in Jewish scriptures. With the possible exceptions of the final chapter of each of the gospels, the synoptic gospels appear to be reasonably reliable records of his life and teachings. You therefore have good accounts in these gospels of what Jesus did and taught whilst he was on earth. These teachings make it clear what he wants you to do.

Based on these records alone, this Jesus that the first apostles referred to as God's servant, was sent by God (whom Jesus called his heavenly father and *"the only true God"*) to point the way for us to reach the father. This is by loving the father with a complete love, loving other people as you love yourself, denying yourself every day in order to follow this path, and being prepared to endure suffering for this path, as Jesus endured suffering for us. The challenge he gives us is whether we are prepared to endure any suffering required to follow him until our death.

The records in John's gospel and Paul's epistles introduce additional doctrines that are not recorded in the synoptic gospels. The fact that they are absent from these gospels is concerning, because if they were important, surely the authors of Matthew, Mark and Luke would have included them. So, they should be taken with some suspicion. However, they are not necessarily in conflict with the doctrinal implications of the synoptic gospels; if you find them credible, they just provide additional doctrines that can be layered on top of what the synoptic gospels teach. Some of these additional doctrines have profound implications for our understanding of God and of what is required to enter the kingdom of heaven.

The two most significant additional doctrines supported by John's gospel and Paul's letters are:

- That to enter the kingdom of heaven you must be born again with an internal spiritual birth, the result of which transforms your mind and causes God to live within you.

- That Jesus existed with God before the creation of the earth and may have been involved in this creation, even though he is a different being from the father.

Debates regarding Jesus' precise identity existed for centuries following Jesus' death and resurrection, deflecting Christians from focusing on doing what he taught us to do. Then, the council of Nicaea in AD 325, under pressure from the Roman emperor Constantine, produced a statement of belief that formally excommunicated from the state-sanctioned Christendom, any followers of Jesus who did not believe everything this statement of belief said. Subsequent statements of belief produced by church authorities were also heavily influenced by political powers and were hotly debated by scholars within Christendom at the time. The fact that there was such obvious variation in the beliefs of different bishops, tells me that the truth had not been revealed by God. Perhaps the faith he wants from us does not require the knowledge of the truth regarding such points of contention? This variation in beliefs amongst bishops, as well as an open conflict of interest between political power and genuine religious faith, tells me we should view such creeds as unreliable at best and corrupted at worst.

Within this set of unreliable creeds is the traditional doctrine of the Trinity. As I have shown, some of the scriptures on which this doctrine is based have been revealed by modern archaeological finds to be unreliable. As spiritual evidence, the 'fruit' of this doctrine on Christendom are all negative: The birth of Islam, schisms that have characterised the evolution of Christendom, and the consequent barrier to faith of potential followers of Jesus. Furthermore, if one accepts the possibility of a multi-personality godhead and believes the Christian scriptures in their entirety, then according to scripture one should also accept that we can become God or God-like in the same way that Jesus is (Revelation 3:20-21; 2 Timothy 2:10-12; Matthew 19:28-29).

Therefore, based on available evidence, taking the varying levels of evidential credibility into account, the concept of the Trinity as it is traditionally understood in Christendom is inadequately supported by the evidence. Other, more credible options include:

- Jesus was not God as the father is but came from God and pointed the way to God – a belief that is supported by the gospels, the prophets and the epistles, or

- God is bigger than our concept of the Trinity – he can integrate with us to live in us, transform us and rule in heaven with us. The precise boundary of God, if there is one, has not been revealed, and perhaps we are not expected to know. We may be eternal beings living temporarily on earth with blinkers on to enable us to achieve purposes here that would not be possible with the full capacity of our eternal state which Jesus referred to as being glorified. In Jesus' prayer recorded in John 17, he speaks of restoring the glory he had before the world existed. I.e. before he took on human form. Perhaps human form limits one's glory/magnificence. If this could be true for Jesus, perhaps it could be true for other humans. In that same prayer, Jesus talks of his followers as being "not of the world", yet you Christians struggle to move beyond your mere human identity.

You do not have to believe in the Trinity (as Trinitarians advocate) to do what Jesus commanded; neither do you have to believe that the Trinity is false (as Unitarians advocate). You don't have to believe there was a time before Christ (as Arius advocated) or that Christ existed before time (as Athanasius advocated). You don't have to believe that the relationship between Jesus' human and divine natures is a prosopic union (as Nestorius advocated) or a hypostatic union (as Cyril advocated). You don't have to believe that God preselected who would enter the kingdom of God (as Calvinists advocate) or that anyone can enter the kingdom of God by exercising their free will (as Arminians advocate). Are you detecting a theme here? I think of this theme as being the defining characteristic of Christendom. If you are inside it, it can be hard to see the wood for the trees.

To follow what Jesus taught us to do, you don't even have to believe he is God. It is OK to not know the answers to such deep and controversial questions. Rather, why don't you instead approach Jesus in a much simpler way, as a child (Matthew 18:3)? Please don't cause others to stumble and miss out on the kingdom of heaven because, when they don't believe everything that you believe, you reject them as the church has done throughout its history. If this is you, then I say shame on you who put the yokes of your doctrines and rituals on people. You are risking the punishment Jesus warned of in Matthew 18:6 where he said, *"But whoever causes one of these little ones who believe in me to stumble and sin, it would be better for him to have a heavy millstone hung around his neck and to be drowned in the depth of the sea."*

In Jesus' time on earth, he sought to alleviate the burden of the yoke of religious laws and ritual practices that religious leaders imposed on people. However, throughout history, you have allowed Christendom's leadership to impose alternate rules, rituals and practices on you, even fundamentally changing the meaning of baptism from what John the Baptist practised and Jesus endorsed. For many, these ritual obligations have become the core way in which they practise their faith, departing from the way taught by Jesus.

Whether or not you choose to incorporate Johannine and/or Pauline doctrines into your belief system is up to you. After all, this is Religion, rather than Science or Philosophy, so you get to choose what you will believe. I have merely provided insight into the credibility of the evidence for some options regarding what you might believe.

That said, I do think the traditional concept of the Trinity is problematic. I have shown that some of the strongest claimed scriptural bases for this doctrine are flawed and the political context that forced its formal adoption was not as clean and innocent as you might have supposed. Also, the historical consequence of this doctrine for the church has been problematic, giving grounds for schisms within Christendom and rejection by Jews, Muslims and others outside Christendom.

I appreciate that Christian conditioning, such as I received myself, so strongly supports the doctrine of the Trinity, that it is very difficult to modify. I hope my efforts have helped make this a little easier. In particular, you may find it helpful to work through the following points:

- Many branches exist within Christendom, and the church has a history of making decisions about doctrines under political pressure, excommunicating those who find some doctrines hard to believe. It would therefore be naïve and arrogant of us to think that only our denomination at this specific point in history has it right and all others are wrong.

- It shouldn't worry us that we don't have all the answers. Jesus simplified things for us, telling us that the whole of scripture is summed up in God's commands to love him with all your heart, all your soul, all your mind and all your strength, and to love your neighbour as yourself (Mark 12:30-31). He also said that unless we become like children, we cannot enter the kingdom of heaven (Matthew 18:2-5). A defining characteristic of children is that they know less than adults. Don't let what you think you know prevent your entry to heaven – or worse – inhibit someone else from entry to heaven. Realistically, would Jesus expect a child to understand such a complex and problematic concept as the Trinity, or would he instead teach that God is a loving heavenly father? Which did Jesus do?

- Various writings in the new testament only make the notion of the Trinity more complicated – Does Christ live in us (Romans 8:10; Galatians 2:20; Ephesians 3:17; Colossians 1:27) or does the Holy Spirit live in us (1 Corinthians 3:16; 1 Corinthians 6:19; Ezekiel 36:27; 2 Timothy 1:14)? Why does the father not live in us?

- As limited humans, our ability to understand the full nature of God is likely limited. What if God is much bigger than we understand? Our partitioning God into different forms – a heavenly father who we cannot see but whom we can pray to, a son who takes on physical form and points the way to the heavenly father, and a spirit who gives us power and advice – is a natural human way we might try to understand this big god who is beyond our understanding.

- Revelation 3:20-21 tells us that if we overcome the sinful world, Jesus will share his throne with us, just as the father shares his throne with Jesus. In other words, we will be glorified in heaven just as Jesus has been. Pause for a moment to digest the profound implication of this: Could Jesus be removing the distinction between God and man when we, like him, enter Glory?

The gospels and Paul's letters frequently reveal Jesus as saying and doing things that some people may have believed that only God can say or do. Christianity uses this logic to claim this indicates Jesus is God. However, perhaps it was the traditional beliefs that were wrong. Jews in Jesus' time hadn't envisaged a scenario like Jesus and they failed to recognise him as the 'son of man' prophesied in Daniel 7:13-14. At Jesus' trial, the high priest would have been very familiar with this prophesy. He tore his robe when Jesus claimed to be this 'son of man' (not God) who would come in the clouds of heaven as Daniel had prophesied. In Hebrews 1:2-9, Paul confirms this event, describing again this scene in heaven. We read that Jesus becomes better than his fellow heavenly beings (v4) due to his willingness to endure what he did to cleanse us from sins (v3), so God anoints Jesus above his fellows (v9).

That said, if this idea is too challenging, we don't need to replace our concept of God as a Trinity with another concept of God. It is OK to accept that such details may not have been revealed. Jesus gave us all we need to know to do

God's will. The scriptures repeatedly tell of God showing up in ways people don't expect, demonstrating he is bigger than we can imagine. I encourage you not to put God in a box, even if you put that box on a pedestal and worship it. Throughout scripture, God shows us that is not what he wants. He wants us to be so near to him that he lives in us, and we live in him.

So, instead of continuing to stumble over the challenge of having to know the precise relationship of Jesus to the father, I encourage you to simply follow Jesus' teaching about what he wants us to do. Acknowledge God the father and approach him with a simple faith as a child would its loving parent. The child doesn't understand all the thinking going on in the parent's mind to protect and guide the child, it doesn't need to and couldn't understand it if it were told. Scripture makes it clear that we do not get into God's kingdom by performing the correct rituals and having the correct complete knowledge (i.e. being 'believers' of the correct version of the truth). Rather, we get into God's kingdom by repenting of our sin, determining to live a righteous life and turning our back on living by the flesh; instead, being born spiritually and 'living in the spirit' in communion with God. We should persevere through our life until we die, daily sacrificing our own self-interests to follow the leading of God who lives within us.

Throughout the history of Christendom, church authorities have frequently engendered a spirit of fear that we will be damned or excommunicated if we don't follow their decrees. However, in writing to Timothy, Paul says "*For God gave us a spirit not of fear, but of power and love and self-control*" (2 Timothy 1:7). The scriptures teach that submitting to man-made laws and ritual practices will not get us into heaven; Jesus came to free us from such burdens. Peter and Paul encourage us to throw off such yokes of slavery "*It was for freedom that Christ set us free; therefore keep standing firm and do not be subject again to a yoke of slavery*" (Galatians 5:1); "*Act as free people, and do not use your freedom as a covering for evil, but use it as bond-servants of God*"(1 Peter 2:16).

May the peace of God which **surpasses all understanding**, guard your hearts and your minds in Christ Jesus. (Philippians 4:7)

10.3 TO MY MUSLIM BROTHERS AND SISTERS

Peace be upon you.

I see your devotion and willingness to submit to God. I also see your efforts to live a life free from sexual immorality. You believe in one god and oppose polytheism and idolatry in all their forms, seeing them as fallacies.

Your Qur'an states that the Torah, the Gospel and the Qur'an are all revelations from God; that they contain God's words which cannot be corrupted. I am aware that your imams teach that the Torah and the Gospel have been corrupted. However, Muhammad confirmed the Torah and the Gospel available in his day, and we have manuscripts pre-dating that time and whatever corruptions may have encroached later. Even so, in my analysis, I have found things in the Jewish and Christian scriptures that are likely to have been modified since they were originally written, so your imams might have a point to some extent, even though the Qur'an disagrees. That said, I have found no corruption in the bulk of the Torah or in the bulk of the Gospel. They both appear to be mostly authentic and credible. Accordingly, your Qur'an tells the people of the book that they should read and follow the Torah and the Gospel that has been revealed to them. So, you should have no problem with Jews and Christians doing this rather than following the Qur'an, which was not revealed to them, but unwitnessed to one person living in Medina and Mecca during the 7th century CE.

I have found numerous failings in the Qur'an and in the life of Muhammad. This is understandable; Muhammad was not God; just a fallible human like us all. During his life, he would have observed schisms amongst the People of the Book, resulting from conflicting beliefs. He saw how this was inhibiting unity amongst them. So, he dedicated his life to driving out disunity. Unfortunately, this approach caused much violence and oppression of both Muslims and non-Muslims throughout history. Today it is still driving terrorism more than any other belief system in the world. As a human, this should concern you.

Although I cannot claim to know all that is true, I have been able to work out some things that are evidently not. From my analysis of the Qur'an and what Muhammad would have experienced in the time and place he lived, I can confidently conclude that (a) the Qur'an is not credible as the word of God, and (b) it is easy to see from the factors surrounding Muhammad and his life, why he would have come up with the statements we find in the Qur'an; this is completely explainable sociologically and historically. Faith in Muhammad's Qur'an is therefore misplaced. However, we can learn from what drove him to produce it: Disputes in Christendom about what we should believe about things that God simply has not revealed; also, the consequent schisms and excommunication of people for what they believed, even when such beliefs did not affect how one should live or treat other people.

Although Muhammad (which means Praiseworthy) may not have been your prophet's original name, there are some things he did that are praiseworthy. From what we know, it seems like he was a faithful husband to his first wife and employer, Khadija bint Khuwaylid. He also recognised the errors of polytheism and idolatry present in the tribe into which he was born. Unfortunately, the words he claims that Gabriel 'revealed' to him are so flawed that they lack credibility. His quest to carve out a new truth about God saw him fabricating a new narrative about God that borrowed from the Quraysh religion, Judaism and Christianity, making factual errors in the process.

When his arguments were rejected, Muhammad turned to violence, transforming from a caravan merchant into a caravan thief and killer. Unlike in most religions, Muhammad even encouraged his followers to be dishonest in some circumstances; particularly if this would further the cause of Islam (e.g. Surah 3:28; Taqiyya; Kitman).

Apart from the 'oil barons', have you ever wondered why the vast majority of people in the Islamic world tend to experience far lower wealth and standards of living than in the West and Israel? If Islam was the true path God desires, surely the Islamic world would be doing better. However, in the Islamic world, most of its citizens are poorer than those in Israel or the West. The nation of Israel, situated in land that was poor during the Islamic Ottoman reign, is now prosperous and powerful. It has defeated Islamic enemies many times since this land came under Jewish rule less than one century ago. It would therefore seem that God has blessed Israel and the West more than the Islamic world. Understandably, many Muslims are trying to escape to the West or are losing their Islamic beliefs. I have heard hundreds of testimonies of ex-Muslim converts to Christianity, and I am aware many others are becoming atheist. Most apostates living in Islamic states dare not make their beliefs public because Muhammad's Islamic strategy was to kill anyone who concludes Islam is false

(4:89; Bukhari 2794). Many covert apostate citizens of Islamic countries are therefore naturally living in fear. They may outwardly be pretending to still be Muslim, but inwardly they are not; they are *'defecting in place'*.

I appreciate that, for someone brought up in the Muslim faith, these facts will be hard to hear or accept, but all is not lost. This does not mean there is no God, creator of the universe; this does not mean God is not great and merciful. As you will have read by now, I also found weaknesses in the Jewish and Christian belief systems. If we put these weaknesses aside, we can see through those faiths that God is even greater than any of us imagined – greater than just a god only for the Jews, greater than the Trinity of the Christians and greater than the intolerant god of Islam who needs his followers to carry out holy wars for him because he is incapable of achieving his aims himself.

I encourage you to see God your creator as someone who loves his creation, just as you would love your own children; not as a powerful being who might reward his best slaves with the sort of carnal pleasures in heaven that Muhammad sought on earth, but as a creator who desires you to know him intimately and to connect with him. I encourage you to re-evaluate the Qur'an's Isa as the Messiah prophesied in the Book: The one sent by God to show us the way; the one whom God blessed with miraculous powers he did not bless Muhammad with; the one who ascended to heaven rather than the grave, where Muhammad lies. Isa described the God he came to show us as love and one who desires for us to live in that love and share it with others.

I encourage you to read the Gospel to learn what this Messiah taught about how we should live. When you do decide to seek the truth for yourself, I hope you find my analysis helps you to step beyond Islam, so you are able do this freely. I believe a better future awaits you than your life to date.

Ma' al-salāmah

May you go in peace

GLOSSARY

Allah

Originally, one of the Quraysh gods, represented by the Moon. Later adopted by Muhammad as the name of the only true god.

Amplified

Amplified Bible – a bible translation with extended paraphrasing

Arianism

A belief rejected by the Council of Nicaea in 325 CE as heresy that Jesus is a created being, rather than one who has existed since before time.

Arminianism

A set of beliefs (typically contrasted with Calvinism) within parts of Protestantism that holds:

- Jesus' sacrifice on the cross was for all humanity, not just a specific group preordained by God,

- Humans have free will to accept God's grace and salvation made possible by Jesus' substitutionary atonement for their sins, and

- A person who has accepted God's grace and salvation may, through their own choices, fall away from faith and lose their salvation.

Calvinism

A set of beliefs (typically contrasted with Arminianism) within parts of Protestantism that holds:

- Mankind is totally depraved, due to 'the fall' (derived from Augustine's doctrine of 'original sin'), and

- God has preordained who will enter the Kingdom of God, from which a number of corollaries follow:

    o Jesus' substitutionary atonement only applies to this group of people,

    o All these people and only these people will enter the Kingdom of God, and

    o Once someone is 'saved' they cannot become 'unsaved'.

Canon

A regulation, scripture, or dogma approved by the religious authority as unquestionable, and divinely endorsed or inspired

Cessationism

A belief within parts of Christianity that the age of miracles ended with the death of Jesus' first apostles.

CSB

Christian Standard Bible – a bible translation

Dispensationalism

A belief, particularly within parts of Christianity, that God's relationship with humanity is divided into distinct periods of history, each of which is governed by different principles and covenants.

ESV

English Standard Version – a bible translation

Gospel

Literally 'Good news'. The first four books of the Christian New Testament which document the life of Jesus are referred to as gospels.

Islam uses the word gospel to mean the revelation given to Jesus by God.

Hadith

A collection of traditions or sayings of Muhammad.

Halakha

Jewish religious law, derived from the Written and Oral Torah.

Hypostatic union

The notion that Jesus is simultaneously human and divine

Idolatry

The worship of idols or the use of idols as a physical representation of a deity to direct worship towards

Ketuvim

Literally 'Writings'. The books in the Tanakh other than the Torah and Nevi'im.

KJV

King James Version – a bible translation

Messiah

The saviour or deliverer of the people, prophesied in the Tanakh.

Midrash

Literally 'Exposition'. Used to refer to a form of discussion about biblical interpretation prominent in the Talmud.

Monotheism

The belief that there is only one true god.

NASB

New American Standard Bible – a bible translation

Nestorianism

A Christian belief system rejected as heresy by the Council of Ephesus in 431 CE, in which Jesus is believed to have distinct human and divine natures, known as a 'prosopic union'; also, that Mary should be referred to as 'Christ-bearer' rather than 'God-bearer'.

NIO

'Novum Instrumentum omne'. Erasmus' Greek bible published initially in 1516 CE

NET

New English Translation – a bible translation

Nevi'im

Literally 'Prophets'. The prophetic books in the Tanakh.

Polytheism

The belief that there are many gods, typically each with responsibility for/dominion over different things.

Prosopic union

The notion that Jesus had two distinct natures: human and divine

Qur'an

The Islamic sacred book, containing 114 Surahs (or revelations) believed by Muslims to have been revealed to Islam's prophet and founder Muhammad over the last 23 years of his life.

Sacrament

A Christian ritual Christendom holds that Jesus commanded to be performed on an ongoing basis.

Schism

A split between strongly opposed sections of an organisation or movement, caused by differences in opinion or belief.

Talmud

Literally 'Learning'. A central text of Rabbinic Judaism, centred on the Mishna and Gemara, surrounded by Rabbinic discussion points in the margins.

Tanakh

The Jewish bible, containing the same books as the Christian Old Testament, but ordered differently into the Torah (law), Nevi'im (Prophets) and Ketuvim (Writings).

Torah

The first five books of the Tanakh (Judaism) or Old Testament (Christianity), meaning 'instruction' in Hebrew and referred to as the Pentateuch within Christianity.

Sometimes the term is used to refer to the concept of Jewish religious law, so can include 'oral tradition'.

Islam uses the word Torah to mean the revelation given to Moses by God.

Trinitarian

A Christian or Christian denomination that believes in the Trinity.

Trinity

A Christian belief that God consists of three distinct co-equal persons, known as the father, the son and the holy spirit.

Unitarian

A Christian or Christian denomination that holds god the father is God, and that Jesus and the holy spirit exist but not as distinct co-equal persons in the godhead. Differences exist in beliefs about the Jesus and the holy spirit. For example, some Unitarian Christians believe the holy spirit is simply a reference to God's spirit, and that Jesus is a heavenly being who was sent by God to save the people (i.e. the Messiah).

ABOUT THE AUTHOR

With an academic background in Criminology and Criminal Justice, Dr Mark Jackson spent much of his career working with law enforcement agencies and now works as a licensed private investigator.

This book is his first publication intended for a general audience outside academia or law enforcement. In it, he documents his investigation into evidence behind some of the main doctrines of Judaism, Christianity and Islam – in particular the doctrines where these three religions conflict.

His investigation unearthed some profound insights that he hopes will be of interest to any follower of Judaism, Christianity or Islam who may have questions about either their own faith or the beliefs of any of these related religions.